INTERVIEW RESEARCH IN POLITICAL SCIENCE

D0555156

WITHDRAWN
UTSA LIBRARIES

INTERVIEW RESEARCH IN POLITICAL SCIENCE

Edited by Layna Mosley

CORNELL UNIVERSITY PRESS   ITHACA AND LONDON

Copyright © 2013 by Cornell University

First published 2013 by Cornell University Press

First printing, Cornell Paperbacks, 2013

Printed in the United States of America

Library of Congress Cataloging-in-Publication Data

Interview research in political science / edited by Layna Mosley.
    p. cm.
  Includes bibliographical references and index.
  ISBN 978-0-8014-5194-2 (cloth : alk. paper)
  ISBN 978-0-8014-7863-5 (pbk. : alk. paper)
  1. Interviewing—Congresses.   2. Political science—Methodology—
Congresses.   I. Mosley, Layna.
  H61.28.I58 2013
  320.072'3—dc23
                                       2012035673

Cornell University Press strives to use environmentally responsible suppliers and materials to the fullest extent possible in the publishing of its books. Such materials include vegetable-based, low-VOC inks and acid-free papers that are recycled, totally chlorine-free, or partly composed of nonwood fibers. For further information, visit our website at www.cornellpress.cornell.edu.

Cloth printing	10	9	8	7	6	5	4	3	2	1
Paperback printing	10	9	8	7	6	5	4	3	2	1

Contents

Preface

This volume seeks to provide guidance for political science scholars who use interviews as part of their research efforts. Although graduate programs in the discipline often provide rigorous training in econometric and formal methodologies, as well as instruction in general considerations related to research design and hypothesis testing, interview-based research receives little focused attention. Rather, interview methods are one of many topics covered in political science courses on qualitative research; or those interested in using interviews take courses in anthropology, geography, sociology, or other disciplines outside political science.

The lack of attention to interviews is particularly striking in light of the long tradition, especially in the comparative politics subfield, of field-intensive research. Although long periods at a single field site have increasingly been replaced with multi-site projects or with mixed-methods research designs, a significant proportion of graduate students and faculty in political science continues to use interviews as a means of gathering empirical evidence. The recent availability of "big data," the rising prominence of laboratory and field experiments, and the availability of archival materials in digitized form do not eliminate the need to speak directly with individual actors (whether elites or "ordinary" citizens). Indeed, for many questions, interviews remain the only means of identifying or confirming the causal mechanisms that generate the outcomes we observe.

We therefore aim to fill a gap in the methodological literature by addressing various components of interview-based research. This volume results from a conference on the use of interview research in political science, held in January 2010 at Duke University. The meeting aimed to bring together political scientists with a variety of substantive interests, from across subfields and from somewhat different epistemological orientations. This diversity allowed for a rich conversation; while it means that the authors are not always in agreement with one another, it also means that we collectively represent a range of views in contemporary political science.

The conference was funded by the Duke University Center for International Studies (DUCIS), as well as by the Christopher H. Browne Center for International Studies at the University of Pennsylvania. Indeed, it was Edward Mansfield, the director of the Browne Center, who first encouraged me to bring together political scientists working with interview data: as I complained over dinner that we did not do a very good job in training graduate students to use interviews, Ed challenged me to do something about it. Even better, he offered to supply a significant portion of the funds to support such a project. I am very thankful for the financial support that he, via the Browne Center, provided, and for his repeated encouragement for this project.

The leadership and staff of DUCIS were similarly enthusiastic and helpful: their director, Rob Sikorski, was keen to support work on qualitative methods within political science. DUCIS provided not only significant financial support, but also organizational assistance, ranging from the conference website to arranging meals and lodging. Dan Smith deserves special thanks for his work on this, especially as it ultimately involved, on the first evening of the conference, six inches of snow—an amount that, in central North Carolina, was more than sufficient to close the university and most local businesses. To that end, the conference participants also had to endure a bit of discomfort, as well as a long walk in the snow for dinner. Their good humor on that occasion, and throughout the process of revising the book, has made this volume an easy one to edit.

The book also has been improved by comments at various stages of the process—from the other chapter authors, from conference discussants, and from anonymous reviewers. Our discussants include Sarah Bermeo, Julia Lynch (whose discussant comments evolved into a stand-alone chapter), Cecilia Martinez-Gallardo, and Jason Roberts. Roger Haydon, at Cornell University Press, was particularly helpful as I revised the introductory chapter; Tim Büthe also offered many helpful comments. More generally, Roger Haydon was very supportive of this endeavor, and I appreciate his efforts throughout the publication process.

Finally, I appreciate the interest of my own graduate advisers (Bob Keohane, Peter Lange, and Beth Simmons) in the use of multiple research methods. They never questioned the value of interviewing financial market participants regarding how they made asset allocation decisions; rather, they convinced me that such work was essential to identifying the causal mechanisms that stood at the heart of financial market-government relations.

Contributors

Frank R. Baumgartner is Richard J. Richardson Distinguished Professor of Political Science at the University of North Carolina at Chapel Hill. E-mail: Frankb@unc.edu.

Matthew N. Beckmann is associate professor of political science at the University of California, Irvine. E-mail: Beckmann@uci.edu.

Jeffrey M. Berry is John Richard Skuse Professor of Political Science at Tufts University. E-mail: Jeffrey.Berry@tufts.edu.

Erik Bleich is associate professor of political science at Middlebury College. E-mail: ebleich@middlebury.edu.

Sarah M. Brooks is associate professor of political science at Ohio State University. E-mail: brooks.317@osu.edu.

Melani Cammett is associate professor in the Department of Political Science at Brown University. E-mail: melani_cammett@brown.edu.

Lee Ann Fujii is assistant professor in the Department of Political Science at the University of Toronto. E-mail: lafujii@chass.utoronto.ca.

Mary Gallagher is associate professor in the Department of Political Science at the University of Michigan. E-mail: metg@umich.edu.

Richard L. Hall is professor in the Gerald R. Ford School of Public Policy at the University of Michigan. E-mail: rlhall@umich.edu.

Marie Hojnacki is associate professor in the Department of Political Science at Pennsylvania State University. E-mail: marieh@psu.edu.

David C. Kimball is associate professor in the Department of Political Science at the University of Missouri, St. Louis. E-mail: dkimball@umsl.edu.

Beth L. Leech is associate professor in the Department of Political Science at Rutgers University. E-mail: leech@polisci.rutgers.edu.

Julia F. Lynch is associate professor in the Department of Political Science at the University of Pennsylvania. E-mail: jflynch@sas.upenn.edu.

Lauren M. MacLean is associate professor of political science at Indiana University. E-mail: macleanl@indiana.edu.

Cathie Jo Martin is professor of political science at Boston University. E-mail: cjmartin@bu.edu.

Layna Mosley is professor of political science at the University of North Carolina at Chapel Hill. E-mail mosley@unc.edu.

Robert Pekkanen is chair of the Japan Studies Program and associate professor at the Henry M. Jackson School of International Studies at the University of Washington. E-mail: pekkanen@u.washington.edu.

William Reno is associate professor in the Department of Political Science at Northwestern University. E-mail reno@northwestern.org; also see www.will reno.org.

Reuel R. Rogers is associate professor in the Department of Political Science at Northwestern University. E-mail: r-rogers@northwestern.edu.

"JUST TALK TO PEOPLE"? INTERVIEWS IN CONTEMPORARY POLITICAL SCIENCE

Layna Mosley

In December 1996, I was preparing to begin my dissertation research in earnest. I had received a fellowship to conduct research abroad, and I was excited to finally "do" political science. My proposed project involved identifying the ways in which financial market participants considered government policies and political institutions as part of their investment decisions. I had fulfilled my course requirements, defended my dissertation prospectus, and arranged for housing in London. I had even set up a few initial meetings with professional investors there, so that I could use my time in the field efficiently. But beyond making those first appointments, I had little idea how to identify and select interview subjects, how to interview someone, how much interview material to gather, or what to do with my interview material once I had it. Worried that I might confess too much in terms of my ignorance, but also concerned that I use my fellowship funding wisely, I broached the subject with one of my dissertation committee members.

His advice to me? "Just talk to people." When I pressed the issue, he explained that, once I had met a few professional investors, academics, and journalists, they would be able to recommend others to me, and I could take it from there. And he suggested that, through these initial meetings, I also would figure out how to ask the right questions, as well as how to conduct a meeting, take notes, and sift through the information. To an extent, this was all good advice: my mentor had done his share of time in the field, and he was right that interviewing involves a good deal of learning by doing.

But, in another way, his advice revealed what continues to be a gaping hole in many political science graduate programs—and the hole that this volume begins to fill. Students who want to employ regression analysis are not advised to "see what variables you can find" or to "estimate a few models and see how it goes." Rather, they are required to take at least one, and usually several, graduate courses in econometrics and statistical analysis. They are encouraged to think seriously about how to operationalize variables of theoretical interest, and how to evaluate which family of models will best estimate the statistical relationships about which they hypothesize. Similarly, students who want to use formal methods of analysis find themselves in graduate courses in positive political theory, game theory, and bargaining, where the careful, *ex ante* specification of assumptions and utilities is de rigueur.

Given the lack of formal training in interview methods, some graduate students may believe that interview-based research is less important and less useful as a method. But nothing could be further from the truth: interviews are an important, and often an essential tool for making sense of political phenomena. Interviews allow scholars to interact directly with the individuals, or some of the individuals, who populate our theoretical models. For those political scientists who think about social outcomes in terms of microfoundations—in terms of the beliefs, incentives, and behaviors of individuals—interviews can directly and deeply assess the roots of individual actions and attitudes. Such interviews can provide a basis for constructing more-general theories, or they can be used for testing the accuracy of theories; in both cases, interviews reveal causal mechanisms—why do activists focus on some human rights issues but not on others, or how do legislators allocate their time and effort across policy issues?

Interviews were an essential component of my dissertation research, and of my subsequent book (Mosley 2003a): I was interested in the relationship between private investors, especially in sovereign debt (government bonds) and government policymaking. I wondered whether, as many observers claimed in the 1990s, the need to access international capital markets created a "golden straitjacket" or necessitated a "race to the bottom" for government policies. Did portfolio market (stock and bond) investors demand that governments eschew active labor-market policies or public investments in education and welfare? Did these investors treat left-leaning governments more harshly than right-leaning governments, pressuring them for Mitterrand-style policy U-turns and market-friendly structural adjustments? Or did these investors care only that governments maintained low rates of inflation and small fiscal deficits, leaving the details of how governments achieved such outcomes to political authorities?

For scholars interested in the extent to which investors affect government policies, the most frequently used empirical approach is a statistical one. In a cross-national, time series context, what sorts of government policy outcomes and government characteristics are significantly associated with the interest rates paid by sovereign borrowers? To what extent do sovereign credit ratings vary as a result of governments' fiscal, monetary, social, and tax policies? While a large-n approach to the government–financial market relationship has many merits, including the capacity to identify general patterns over time and across countries, it leaves much to be desired.

Most important, of course, is that correlation does not necessarily mean causation. If we want to know about the conditions under which government policies change investors' behavior, statistical relationships are a good starting point, but they do not rule out alternative relationships that would generate the same statistical patterns. To draw a line more directly from cause to effect, we need better evidence about how investors make asset allocation decisions: we need to ask them how they evaluate sovereign borrowers, as well as how these evaluations might change over time (in boom periods versus bust periods), and how they might vary across countries (for example, between developed and developing nations, or between Economic and Monetary Union [EMU] and non-EMU member states). Moreover, if we are ultimately interested in how these market behaviors contribute to governments' policy choices—whether they avoid certain policies for fear of capital market punishment—we need to ask government officials what motivated their policy decisions. How much attention did they pay to bond markets, versus to domestic constituents?

My interviews, of financial market participants in Frankfurt and London, and of government officials in various European capitals, gave me just these sorts of insights. They allowed me to theorize more accurately about the conditions under which financial market influence on government policymaking was weaker or stronger, as well as the circumstances under which financial markets influenced a broad, versus a narrow, set of government policy outcomes. In my case, interviews became part of a multi-method research strategy, which also included statistical analyses, surveys of professional investors, and archival research at investment banks.

But it was the interviews, coupled with previous literature, that provided the strongest foundations for my project. Moreover, where quantitative data were not of very high quality (as was true with some developing nations), and where the concepts in which I was interested were not easily transformed into a quantitative indicator (for instance, the mix of government micro-level policies that deal with infrastructure, taxation, and labor markets), interviews were the primary source of data on which I relied. And when I surveyed a broader set of professional investors, as a means of expanding the external validity of my work, interviews were invaluable: the interviews had suggested not only what factors I should ask about, but also how I should frame and phrase my questions. Indeed, when I applied for academic jobs and when I sought to publish the resulting book manuscript, it was the interviews that captured readers' attention—the fact that I had not only hypothesized about, but actually investigated, investors' and government officials' motivations was what distinguished my work. It was not only that the interviews provided many interesting vignettes to use in presentations or as epigraphs to articles and book chapters; rather, it was that the interviews were a direct window into identifying cause and effect.

Despite the contribution of interviews to research on global capital markets, I am certain that I could have used interviews more effectively. Much of what I did during my initial time in the field was learning by doing, with an expected amount of trial (and even more error). This reflected, in many ways, the attitude toward interviews that prevailed in graduate programs in political science in the 1990s. While there has been some movement to thinking more systematically about the general use of qualitative methods within political science (e.g., Gerring 2007, 2012; Mahoney 2009; Wood 2007), there are still few graduate courses focused on using interview methods. Rather, "qualitative methods" courses tend to cover a broad spectrum of methods, ranging from case studies to archival analysis to field experiments. But "qualitative methods" is a broad category, encompassing everything from interviews and process tracing to archival fieldwork and ethnography. These methods often are quite different from one another (also see Schatz 2009b). At the same time, scholars in other fields—such as anthropology, economic and social geography, and sociology—have long used interview-based research designs. While the guidance they provide certainly is useful (e.g., Gubrium and Holstein 2002; Rubin and Rubin 2005), it does not address many of the features and issues specific to political science research.[1]

The purpose of this volume, therefore, is to encourage scholars from all subfields of political science to use interviews in their research, and to provide them with a set of lessons and tools for doing so. Many research projects in political science lend themselves to interview-based methods, either as the primary empirical strategy, or as one of several empirical tools. By providing potential users of interviews with guidance related to designing interview-based research, implementing interview projects, and analyzing data generated by interviews, we hope that students of political science will increasingly embrace interview-based methods.

In the remainder of this introductory chapter, I describe the use of interviews within political science. I begin with a discussion of the qualities of interviews that are typically used within the discipline. Next, I explore how one's epistemological orientation—broadly, where one falls on the interpretivist-positivist continuum—colors one's approach to and use of interviews. I note that this book's approach reflects that of the contemporary political science profession: its orientation is largely positivist, but with some diversity across scholars, and with the recognition that not all work fits neatly into the interpretivist or the positivist camp. I then discuss four challenges faced by political science interviewers—ethics, sampling, validity, and reliability. The contributors to this volume discuss each of these challenges, and sometimes reach differing conclusions regarding how best to address them. My purpose in this introduction is to offer a sense of the trade-offs that scholars face when using interviews as a research method. The context in which one uses interviews, and the purposes for which interviews are used, will determine the exact choices that one makes regarding how best to address each challenge.

Interviews as a Distinct Research Method

This volume focuses on in-person interviews, involving both elite and non-elite informants.[2] We consider the use of interviews across the subfields of contemporary political science. Our primary focus is on one-on-one interviews, normally conducted in person (rather than via phone, Skype, e-mail, or online chat). The contributors to this book have used interviews in a wide range of field settings and with a variety of aims. For example, Mary Gallagher describes her interviews with clients of a legal aid office in Shanghai, while Beth Leech and her coauthors discuss the techniques used to interview lobbying organizations in Washington, DC. Melani Cammett's informants are potential recipients of social services in Lebanon, as well as business leaders and government officials involved with trade policy in Morocco and Tunisia. Lee Ann Fujii conducts interviews on war-related violence in Bosnia-Herzegovina and Rwanda, while Cathie Jo Martin has met with executives of firms in Britain and Denmark, in order to assess their preferences over various welfare state policies. Reuel Rogers employs interviews with new minority populations in the United States, with an eye to evaluating how well concepts used to explain political behavior among African Americans can be applied to other groups.

What unites this diverse set of scholars and research projects is a belief that interviews are an important and distinct means of understanding contemporary political actions and outcomes. Interviews can serve to identify causal mechanisms that are not evident in other forms of data: for instance, Gallagher's (chapter 9) interviews of legal aid recipients in China allowed her to understand the conditions under which interviewees used state apparatuses to resolve workplace disputes; the interviews suggested, in a way that surveys could not, that earlier political socialization was a key influence on how individuals viewed and addressed workplace disputes. Or interviews may serve as the central source of data, particularly in situations involving civil conflict or human rights violations—as both Fujii and William Reno describe. Or interviews can be used to generate data that are later employed in statistical analyses, as Matthew Beckmann and Richard Hall (chapter 10) do by querying congressional staffs about the way in which members of Congress work on specific issues. More generally, the contributors to this volume employ interviews for a variety of purposes, including theory building, survey design and interpretation, and hypothesis testing. Some contributors use interviews as the only means of testing causal claims, while others employ interviews as one component of a mixed-method research strategy (Laitin 2003).

In addition to using interviews for a variety of purposes, scholars also use a range of terms to refer to the individuals they interview. These terms include "subjects" (a term that has fallen out of scholarly usage but is still favored by many institutional review boards), "participants," "interviewees," "respondents," "interlocutors," and "informants." Some terms, such as "informants," are less widely used today than they were a generation ago. Others, including "interlocutors," are more commonly used by scholars with a more interpretivist perspective (see part 2); positivist scholars may be more inclined to "participants" or "interviewees." "Respondents" is sometimes the chosen terminology for those who also employ survey methods. Our varied usage throughout this volume reflects the diverse usage in the discipline and the varying epistemological as well as methodological orientations of the volume's contributors.

Although interviews often are used in conjunction with other forms of empirical evidence, such as surveys, they are a distinct empirical tool. Compared with surveys, interviews usually involve a (much) smaller sample of participants. But interviews also allow the researcher to gather a much deeper set of responses: she can ask questions that allow for open-ended responses; if these responses generate additional queries, the researcher can ask these as follow-ups, probing more deeply into the actions and attitudes of respondents. Such follow-up questions can be particularly enlightening when the respondent appears to hold contradictory views, or when the phenomenon of interest is multifaceted. Length and cost considerations, as well as problems of nonresponse to certain types of questions, usually make such actions impossible in the context of a survey. Along these lines, Rogers (chapter 12) uses interviews both as follow-ups to surveys and as tools for ascertaining whether concepts developed and deployed in previous survey research can be used when surveying different populations.

Relative to an individual survey response, a single interview can generate more points of inferential leverage. The interviewer may be able to use a single in-depth interview—for example, of a pivotal figure in a policy decision—to assess a range of observable implications that stem from his theoretical framework. A single interview also can provide information about actions taken or attitudes held by others—the interviewee's neighbors, colleagues, superiors, or subordinates. And perhaps most important, the interviewer usually has more metadata at her disposal than does the survey researcher (assuming that the survey researcher does not administer each survey herself). An interview researcher knows not only what a respondent says, but also how the respondent behaved during the interview, whether the respondent hesitated in answering some questions more than others, and the context in which the interview took place. This metadata facilitates more-accurate use and interpretation of interview data, in a way that often is not possible for survey responses or other quantitative indicators.[3] Indeed, Erik Bleich and Robert Pekkanen's (chapter 4) interview methods appendix serves to provide access to such metadata not only to the interviewer, but to subsequent users of interview-based information.

The individual interview also differs from focus groups, which usually involve one researcher and multiple informants. Focus groups typically progress in a semi-structured fashion, with the interviewer posing initial questions and then allowing participants some involvement in directing the discussion. Focus groups allow access to a larger set of individuals, but they also may present logistical as well as methodological difficulties (also see Hertel, Singer, and Van Cott 2009). The tone and content of the focus group exchange may be driven by the views and personalities of participants, so that one strongly opinionated individual could dominate the discussion. Moreover, if focus group participants worry about social sanctioning or peer pressure, they may be less forthcoming—and more worried about guarantees of confidentiality. Although focus groups can be useful in some research settings and for some research questions, this book concentrates on one-on-one interview methods.[4]

Political scientists who use one-on-one interviews tend to do so in a face-to-face, in-person setting, rather than via phone, e-mail, or video chat. These other modes of communication have long facilitated the fieldwork process, allowing scholars to establish contacts, arrange meetings, and share informed-consent documents prior to arrival at the research site. The rise of new, affordable communication technologies, such as voice over Internet (VoIP) and Skype, now makes it more feasible to conduct the interview itself from a different physical location. This strategy may be particularly appealing when the researcher faces cost or time constraints.

The difficulties associated with virtual interviews, however, result in a continuing bias in favor of face-to-face interactions. First, virtual interviews lack much of the contextual information that can be important to interpreting interview data. The researcher gains an understanding of how to interpret data from observing the respondent's situation, which could range from the demeanor of office staff to the social environment in a village or on a reservation. Related, virtual forms of exchange may limit the presence of interviewer effects, generated when the researcher's personal characteristics influence the type of information gathered. This could be either a help or a hindrance to the research process. Second, it is more difficult for the researcher to establish rapport with the subject from afar, and this can limit the depth and accuracy of the information offered. Third, the ethical considerations that arise during in-person interviews certainly are present for those conducted electronically. In some ways, the risk to an informant may be greater if her responses are recorded and can be forwarded (as in an e-mail exchange), or if there is a possibility that her phone or Internet connection is not secure. Given these considerations, political scientists continue to rely largely on in-person interactions; when virtual modes are employed, they can be most useful in the context of an initial interaction (a preview of an in-person interview), or a follow-up interview (for which context and rapport have been established already). This distinguishes political scientists from journalists, who routinely rely on virtual means of communication for interacting with informants. For journalists, the practical demands of much shorter time-horizons increase the appeal of new technologies. For political scientists, new technologies sometimes are useful, but they come with some important drawbacks. While we certainly recommend attention to ethical and research design issues when nontraditional modes of interviewing are employed, we retain a focus on fieldwork that generally involves travel to the research site.

Furthermore, changes in technology may reinforce the importance of interviews to answering research questions. Technology renders many other types of evidence, such as transcripts of hearings or records of campaign contributions, more easily available. Yet this increased transparency also may lead those involved in the political process to move their activities out of the limelight. For instance, in their discussion of legislative politics, Beckmann and Hall argue that interviews have been rendered *more* important as a research tool by the increase in information availability that is a hallmark of the Web 2.0 era. As records of formal legislative activity have become more readily available to journalists and the public, legislators and their aides have moved more of their efforts behind the scenes. Interviews may be the only means of gathering data on the informal behaviors that lead to political outcomes. Technological change notwithstanding, then, "talking to people" remains a central means of producing outstanding and innovative political science scholarship.

The Political Scientist as Interviewer

The unique features of interviews offer many opportunities to political scientists, but they also require that we carefully address certain issues. Interviews are used in a wide variety of fields, including public health, sociology, economic and social geography, psychology, history, and anthropology. Indeed, in the absence of research method guidance that is specific to political science, graduate students and faculty often rely on advice based in other academic disciplines. But the features of political science interviewing—both in terms of the epistemological orientation of the discipline *and* the interviewer's relationship to interviewees—combine to create specific considerations for scholars of political science. I discuss these two issues in turn.

Epistemological Considerations

One can classify scholars of political science along an epistemological continuum that ranges from positivist to interpretivist. The positivist view acknowledges that while the subjects of social science research are perhaps messier than those of natural science research, the social researcher should aim to identify patterns of cause and effect (Steinmetz 2005). Based on these patterns and on theoretical reasoning, the researcher should develop falsifiable hypotheses and test these hypotheses empirically. While admitting the possibility of some slippage between theoretical concepts and their empirical operationalization, a positivist orientation assumes that qualitative—as well as quantitative—methods can facilitate the discovery of truths.

An interpretivist viewpoint, on the other hand, treats the world as socially made; knowledge is impossible to separate from historical context and power relationships. While some interpretivist social scientists aim to make generalizations or to generate causal explanations (Wedeen 2010), many focus instead on causal understanding—on developing knowledge about how subjects understand their own actions and circumstances, and on how this understanding is conditioned by power and social relations. When interpretivist scholars employ ethnographic methods (as many do), they are sensitive to the difficulty of separating the collection and processing of interview data from the individual researcher's circumstances and knowledge. Indeed, political ethnography—while itself encompassing a diverse set of approaches and subjects—is marked by the use of participant-observation, an attempt to understand interactions from the perspective of an insider, and a desire to develop a "sensibility" about the context in which one is immersed (Schatz 2009b). Kuhn (1970, 113) also advances such a claim: "what a man sees depends upon both what he looks at (observations) and also upon what his previous visual-conceptual experience has taught him to see."[5]

Those who work from a largely positivist tradition treat interviews as a means of generating objective knowledge, either to generate or test falsifiable hypotheses. For these scholars, interviews serve to identify the causal processes that generate specific outcomes, and—when used for theory testing rather than for theory development—to allow one to differentiate between alternative hypotheses. Although positivist scholars are sensitive to the existence of "interviewer effects"—in that their individual characteristics, and how these are perceived by their interviewees, may influence the information that is provided—their focus is more on interview data as a product, often collected over a relatively short period of time.

Scholars operating from an interpretivist stance—currently more common in anthropology or social geography, but also represented by some contributions to this volume[6]—doubt the extent to which a purely objective social science is possible. Therefore, while these scholars may employ interviews in service of broad social science aims (including testing falsifiable claims), they highlight the need for attention not only to information itself, but also to how, and by whom, the information is generated and gathered. The researcher brings subjective elements to the knowledge-gathering process; these are an asset to the research process, but they make truth claims impossible to achieve. Interpretivists tend to see interviews as a process, rather than a product: they ask how interviewees themselves make sense of the world, and why the interview data take the form that they do. Seen this way, interviews are a useful way for an individual researcher to develop knowledge regarding a certain community or issue; but replication of this knowledge by others may be difficult, and interview-based knowledge may not offer definitive tests of a given set of propositions.[7]

The discipline of political science currently is centered at the positivist end of the spectrum; this is particularly true for research-oriented universities in the United States. The content of this volume, in terms of the balance between positivist-oriented and interpretivist-oriented approaches, mirrors the current state of the discipline.[8] Although there are many scholars who would place themselves in the middle of the continuum or at the interpretivist end of the spectrum, and some scholars whose placement on the continuum shifts over the course of their careers, much of the profession remains centered on positivism. Given that the main objective of this volume is to help scholars in political science use interviews systematically and well, many of the contributors approach interviews from a positivist perspective. Such a perspective also allows us to achieve another objective, which is to complement the vast array of extant work on interviews from an interpretivist or ethnographic perspective.[9] Indeed, despite the fact that mixed methodologies are encouraged in most graduate programs, there is very little formal training available for those who want to deploy mixed-method approaches. This volume fills part of this gap by illustrating how interview techniques connect to positivist political science, and how they can be used (and are being used) by political science scholars.

Often, rather than living or working among interview participants, as would an ethnographer or participant-observer, political science graduate students choose to include two or three case studies in their dissertations, spending a few months—or even just several weeks—at each research site. Or a faculty member might conduct interviews with policymakers during a semester-long research fellowship, aiming to speak with forty or fifty interview subjects during that time frame. The information gathered from such interviews could offer greater external validity than a longer-lasting, more narrowly defined ethnography. But such interview data has its limitations: it does not allow for immersion, nor for the "insider" perspective that is a hallmark of ethnographic approaches (see Schatz 2009b). This challenge to the internal validity of political science interview data renders the appropriate design of interview studies—asking the right questions of the right people—particularly important. I return to these challenges in part 3.

Two qualifications to the generally positivist perspective of this volume are in order. First, the dividing line between positivist and interpretivist approaches in political science is sometimes blurred. Researchers may be simultaneously thinking about how to address sources of bias in interviews (something more in a positivist tradition) *and* also about why interview subjects answer questions in the ways that they do. Moreover, an individual scholar's placement on the interpretivist-positivist continuum is not necessarily fixed: it may vary with the particular research project being undertaken. Within this volume, some contributors represent approaches that are self-consciously interpretivist; for instance, Lauren MacLean (chapter 3) and Lee Ann Fujii (chapter 7) are centrally concerned with positionality and power relationships. Other contributors, including Bleich and Pekkanen, Gallagher, and Martin, work in a positivist manner, but with an awareness that converting interview transcripts and answers into more discrete concepts and categories always involves some type of interpretive work. Throughout this volume, therefore, we highlight the areas of overlap between interpretivist and positivist interview research.

Second, our volume offers many lessons that are useful to *all* political scientists who use interviews. For instance, we discuss how to navigate the IRB process, whether and how to use an interpreter, or how to report a sufficient amount of information about one's interview study. Such practical matters confront all researchers who use interviews, regardless of subject matter or epistemological outlook. Our volume intends to underscore the similarities across, as well as the differences between, broad approaches to knowledge. We acknowledge that interview studies can be used to address a range of substantive questions at a variety of stages in the research process, and as the core empirical tool or as one part of a mixed-method approach. While we certainly are aware of broader debates regarding research design within the field,[10] our volume is intended to appeal to a wide audience within the discipline.

Identity and Interview Effects

Scholars from across the epistemological spectrum recognize that their individual traits can affect the interview research process. A young woman conducting interviews with (almost entirely male) investment bankers may find the gender dynamics that prevail in the financial industry more generally (McDowell 1997) also color the interview process. A scholar who is perceived as an "expert," given his university affiliation, age, or class, may receive a different set of answers from one who is viewed as naïve or uninformed. And a scholar who is assumed to hold certain political views may have difficulty gaining access to some communities: Woliver (2002) notes, for instance, that she faced greater hurdles in attempting to interview pro-life activists (as compared with pro-choice activists), because they often assumed that she did not agree with their views.

   Scholars working in the positivist tradition usually label these as "interviewer effects"; they are important to the analysis and interpretation of interview data, because they may affect the (non)response to individual interview questions, as well as the tone and amount of information given in response to questions. Within the interpretivist tradition, these considerations closely relate to the concept of "positionality," which refers to the researcher's awareness of her position in the world relative to her informants (Ortbals and Rincker 2009a).[11] Interviewees and potential interviewees use various social, physical, linguistic, and cultural markers (ranging from eating habits and dress to accent and hair type) to make sense of a given researcher. Many of these features may be obvious to informants, while others, such as religion, sexual orientation, or previous research site experiences, may not. And informants may ascribe incorrectly certain qualities to a researcher, especially at the stage of arranging interviews (assuming, for instance, that American scholars conducting research in southern Africa will be white; see Henderson 2009).

   Whether scholars think about this phenomenon as "interview effects" or as "positionality," it is quite possible that different researchers using very similar research designs will wind up with different sets of interview data. Part of this difference could stem from variation in access (which makes providing information about how the sample was conducted important; see chapter 4); another portion of this variation would be due to differences in information provided during the actual interview process. Yet another piece of the variation comes at the interpretation stage: how a scholar understands evidence from an interview may depend on her own experiences and worldview (see, for instance, chapter 3).

Scholars vary in their concerns about the extent to which interviewer effects or positionality affects the nature of the evidence gathered in interviews. For the strictest of interpretivists, positionality cannot be overcome: it should be acknowledged and studied, but it is unavoidable that interview data (and all data) are somewhat subjective and contextual. A different researcher—one who is older, male, and African American, for instance—may well receive different responses to his questions and understand the same responses in a different way. Positivist scholars often acknowledge interviewer effects (see chapters 9 and 5, for example), but they are not viewed as limiting the objective knowledge that can be gleaned from interviews; rather, positivists view interview effects more as a source of (quantifiable) bias or measurement error (also see the discussion of reliability in part 3). MacLean (chapter 3) approaches this issue from an interpretivist point of view: she traces work on the topic in other disciplines, paying particular attention to how positionality relates to the power of the interviewer vis-à-vis the interview subjects. She suggests that a more collaborative relationship between the researcher and her interlocutors not only improves the researcher's access, but also can enhance the theoretical quality of the work itself.

Related to interviewer effects and positionality are concerns about access. In some situations, a researcher's individual qualities improve his access: local politicians may be more willing to share their views with a foreigner affiliated with a major research university than with a local scholar. Or a woman may be more willing to speak with another woman, than with a male researcher, about the use of sexual violence in the context of civil wars. Conversely, in male-dominated societies, young women may have difficulty gaining access to, or gathering sufficient information from, older male political leaders. In politically closed societies, informants may worry that U.S.-based researchers are, in fact, spies (Reinhardt 2009).

In chapter 6, Cammett explores how, in conducting research in Lebanon as well as elsewhere in the Middle East, her outsider status limits her capacity to effectively carry out interview-based work. Cammett offers the strategy of "matched, proxy" interviewing to address these limitations. With this technique, the researcher relies on carefully trained local proxies to carry out interviews. The proxies are matched with the respondents according to various features (including religion, sect, age, and socioeconomic status), with the notion being that respondents will be more forthcoming when speaking with someone who appears more similar. In describing her work on the provision of social services in Lebanon,

Cammett details the recruitment, training, and supervision of hired interviewers. And she considers the tradeoff between community access (where hired interviewers should look most like the intended interview subjects) and research skills (where hired interviewers should have training in social science methodologies, but might be of a higher socioeconomic class than their interviewees). Similarly, Fujii's (chapter 7) advocacy of using an interpreter to carry out interviews is based, in large part, on considerations related to the researcher's identity compared with those of her interlocutors.

Note, however, that not all contributors to this volume view differences between the researcher and her interviewees as impediments to access. MacLean, for example, suggests that outsider status and social differences smoothed her access to village residents in Ghana and Côte d'Ivoire. Similarly, some contributors to the Ortbals and Rincker (2009b) symposium suggest that outsider status can facilitate the research process.

Challenges: Ethics, Sampling, Validity, and Reliability

This discussion of access, as it relates to identity and interviewer effects, exemplifies some of the challenges associated with conducting interview research. While this volume aims to encourage the use of interviews in a wide array of political science research, we are very aware of the challenges associated with interview evidence. These involve not only the practical elements of gaining access to interview subjects, but also the theoretical elements of sampling the right set of respondents, convincing others of the reliability and validity of interview data, and ensuring that research is conducted ethically. Addressing these challenges allows one to reap the benefits of interviews, which often are—alone or in combination with other research methods—an incredibly useful means of measuring key variables and assessing central causal connections. In this section, I discuss four challenges facing interview researchers: ethics, sampling, validity, and reliability.

Ethics

Social scientists routinely confront ethical issues in the course of designing and conducting research. General standards of ethical research dictate that scholars do not harm participants in a given study (Woliver 2002).[12] If a study provides direct benefits to participants—for instance, a medication that can stop the growth of cancerous tumors, or a more successful early intervention for children with autism—then exposing them to some degree of risk (such as side effects from medication) may be ethically acceptable. But where research provides little in the way of direct benefit to participants—as is usually the case with social scientific studies—then the risks to participants also must be minimized.

Although one could argue that many political science research projects do not expose participants to significant levels of individual risk, it would be a mistake to assume that ethical considerations are absent from the interview process. In extreme cases (for instance, comments against a repressive political regime), breaches of an interviewee's confidentiality or anonymity could lead to imprisonment or violence. In other instances, interview participants may find that the interview leads them to discuss traumatic individual or collective experiences, such as sexual violence or civil war. More routinely, the disclosure by researchers of interview data with identifying information intact could have negative professional or social consequences. One scholar's breach of professional ethics also can diminish the willingness of participants to participate in future studies, harming the broader research enterprise.

Minimal risk to participants is not only what professional ethics demands; it also is required by university IRBs, which authorize research involving human subjects. For participants in interview studies, risk often relates to concerns about confidentiality. Interviews are generally aimed at collecting information that is specific to an individual or a class of respondents: the researcher wants to know how a policymaker came to a decision about a given issue, or how a rebel fighter decided whether to join a local insurgent group, or how connected an individual of Afro-Caribbean descent feels with others who share her ethnic identity. While the interviewer certainly can use the "people like you" phrase to depersonalize the interview,[13] the fact remains that the interview subject is being asked to provide information that may be private and sensitive. These concerns are particularly acute when the behaviors in question include illicit behavior, such as the payment of bribes or the participation in insurgent movements.[14]

In chapter 2, Sarah Brooks investigates the role of ethics in the interview research process. She explores the origins of IRBs, as well as the expansion of their purviews to social science research and their concerns with minimizing risk. She offers practical suggestions for political scientists to navigate the university-level IRB process. Brooks points out that, given its origins in medical studies, the IRB process does not always easily accommodate the types of work done by political scientists. For example, Reno (chapter 8) notes that scholars who study civil conflicts may face specific difficulties with institutional review boards: their standard categories do not normally include options for "rebel fighters." More generally, the IRB process can be focused more on protecting universities and their personnel from risk (or liability) than on protecting research participants.[15]

Central to the process of IRB approval, as well as to the conduct of ethical research generally, is the granting of informed consent by the interview participant. Informed consent establishes that informants realize the purpose of the research being conducted, as well as the risks (and potentially the benefits) to them from participation. Participants also are made aware that their participation is voluntary, and that they will not suffer harm (e.g., not have access to a given service) if they decline to participate. As Brooks discusses, the exact procedures for obtaining consent vary with the research setting; for example, semiliterate informants often give oral, rather than written, consent. And where informants may worry more about the confidentiality of their comments, oral (versus written) consent can increase participation rates (Wood 2006).

Most informed-consent procedures involve guaranteeing the confidentiality of participants, both in terms of their identities and participation in the study, and in terms of what they reveal in the interview. Policymakers in democratic nations may be willing to be interviewed "on the record" and to have their responses cited in academic publications.[16] But many other types of participants may not. And as informants' actual and perceived risk increases, the researcher must think more deeply about the limits that should be placed on the research effort—who should be contacted, and how should they be interviewed?

In the short run, guaranteeing confidentiality includes keeping field notes separate from identifying information (so that one's notes refer to interviews by number, but the master list of these numbers is stored separately, in a password-protected or encrypted document).[17] In the longer run, guaranteeing confidentiality means not naming informants in publications that result from interviews. Again, one might use a list of interviewees arranged by number (and perhaps by broad location and interview date). The scholar is ethically obliged to trade the protection of subjects against the transparency of the research process. In the case of non-elite informants, this is likely sufficient to satisfy academic reviewers. If one's informants are elite policymakers in democratic nations—who are perhaps less at risk from breaches of confidentiality, and about whom revealing more information is important to the use of interview evidence—then interview citations might offer more detail. For instance, a "senior finance ministry official" or a "mid-level central banker who works on regulatory policy" might be cited.[18]

When informants are particularly exposed to risk—for instance, when they are members of an opposition movement in a politically closed society—the "interview appendix" (see chapter 4) should reveal less about the sample. In special circumstances, such as conflict and post-conflict environments, even greater considerations of confidentiality may be necessary (see chapter 8, for instance). There may be locations and situations in which the ethical pursuit of research is impossible or nearly so (also see Wood 2006). At the extreme, then, ethical considerations could include embargoing publication or circulation of a document for some period of time. This can create professional challenges for graduate students or untenured scholars, and it suggests that some research questions, or some field locations, may need to be excluded, at least for a time.

Communicating the risks of one's study, and the ways in which respondents will be protected from risks—how confidentiality of responses is assured, for instance—often requires going beyond what one's university IRB mandates. Rather, the discussion of consent needs to be put in a context that potential informants understand, one that seeks to remove coercive elements from the process. The lead scholar also needs to ensure that all additional members of the research team—graduate students, research assistants, interpreters—are aware of the informed-consent principle and of its implications for behavior.[19]

Last, while some scholars would argue that minimizing risk to participants in interview studies, as university IRBs require, is all that is needed to fulfill the political science researcher's ethical obligations, others would argue that ethical considerations go far beyond IRB approval and informed-consent procedures. In chapter 3, MacLean notes that many entities other than universities—such as American Indian tribes—have IRBs. These entities can encourage the researcher to think about his or her relationship with the subject community. While most political science scholars do not treat their interview subjects as active participants in the research process—for instance, offering them the opportunity to collaborate in the interpretation of interview findings—MacLean posits that political scientists should consider moving in a more participatory direction (also see Hertel, Singer, and Van Cott 2009). This might include sharing the results of research—giving a public talk, or sending copies of publications—with participants (Woliver 2002). Or it may include the researcher offering (to the local community, not only to those individuals who consent to participate directly) other services, such as tutoring children in English or providing information about available government health care programs.[20]

More generally, the interviewer needs to consider her ethical obligations, as well as her professional responsibilities vis-à-vis her home academic institution. These obligations often demand a careful consideration of whom to interview, how to protect the data that are gathered, and how to interact with informants before, during, and after the interview process. Finally, note that "risk" also can extend to the researcher. Many political scientists are interested in phenomena—insurgency, human trafficking, corruption—that can be dangerous to study. Other scholars find themselves in research locations that have high levels of personal crime; that do not guarantee personal liberties; or that are undergoing momentous social change. In such instances, individual researchers must weigh the benefits of conducting interviews against the risks they present (Johnson 2009).

Sampling

Another central issue that a scholar using interviews confronts is whom to interview: How should the population of potential interviewees be defined? Are groups of individuals, such as investment bankers or Lebanese citizens, the subject of interest? Leech et al. (chapter 11) note that individuals or organizations are not always the unit of analysis; their project sought to draw comparisons across issues, which were selected in a largely random fashion. But the informants on a given issue were selected in a non-random fashion; researchers made sure to sample lobbying groups on both (or all) sides of a given issue. This level of selection was purposive rather than random. Once the unit of analysis is identified, the bounds of the population must be specified; for instance, is the sample drawn from all Lebanese citizens, only those in certain geographic areas, or only those belonging to certain religious and ethnic groups?

Next, the interviewer must decide how to sample interviewees from within the population. Researchers should always think carefully about how the sample is drawn. But, as Julia Lynch (chapter 1), Martin (chapter 5), and Leech et al. (chapter 11) discuss, sampling decisions often depend on the stage and purpose of the research (theory building or hypothesis testing). If the purpose of the interviews is to test a theory, and the researcher is therefore concerned with generating a representative sample, then a random sample may be most appropriate. Random sampling facilitates better causal inferences from the sample to the population and, as such, is the "gold standard" for observational research, including survey research.[21] A random sample helps to ensure the external validity—from the sample to the population—of one's findings. Interview researchers who pursue random sampling strategies often aim to generate "data set observations" (DSOs), which can be thought of as values (qualitative or quantitative) for a set of variables on a single observation (Brady and Collier 2010). For instance, if the unit of analysis is a member of parliament, the variables might include the amount of time she spends on constituency service, the three most important issues on which she has worked in the last year, and the three most important sources of information for her. These DSOs could be analyzed qualitatively or, as in the case of Beckmann and Hall's (chapter 10) and Leech et al.'s (chapter 11) projects, statistically. Scholars who employ random sampling strategies will need to pursue various strategies to ensure access to a representative sample—for instance, following up repeatedly on requests for interviews, or making multiple visits to the same research site.

Many interview researchers, however, employ a non-random sampling strategy. They may do so for theoretical or practical reasons. On the theoretical side, when the purpose of interviews is to develop causal explanations or to generate theories, the researcher may be interested more in specific cases than in a representative sample. These specific cases may be "most likely" or "least likely" instances, and they may be chosen because of the insights they provide regarding the causal circumstances that generate particular outcomes. Deliberately choosing cases or interview subjects that are outliers or exemplars in important ways ("least likely" or "most likely" instances) can offer "smoking gun" evidence that facilitates theory development. On the basis of one's theory, for instance, one might employ purposive (quota) sampling, selecting individuals on the basis of certain characteristics (Danish firms in specific industrial sectors, Chinese workers in specific types of firms). Used in this way, interview data are likely to take the form of "causal process observations," defined as "an insight or piece of data that provides information about context, process or mechanism, and that contributes distinctive leverage in causal inference" (Brady and Collier 2010 277–278; also see Beck 2009; Seawright 2002).[22] Within this volume, both Cammett's and Fujii's projects rely on non-random samples to generate causal process observations.

Practical considerations also can lead researchers to employ a non-random sampling strategy. Resource and time constraints, an unwillingness of individuals to participate in the study, or the sensitivity of the subject matter can render random sampling impossible. For example, in describing her research in El Salvador, Wood (2006) notes that, in the context of a civil conflict with multiple insurgent groups and low levels of societal trust, constructing representative samples of local respondents was impossible. Rather, she attempted to gain access to a wide variety of individuals, but with the awareness that bias was unavoidable. Reno (chapter 8) expresses similar concerns about, and implements a similar solution, gaining access to insurgents and rebel fighters.[23] In other contexts, activists may worry about granting access to a stranger, even one with academic credentials: Woliver (2002) notes that abortion activists worry about physical harm, thereby rendering them reluctant to be interviewed. And elite interview participants, such as former or current government officials, may be reluctant to be interviewed.[24]

Non-random samples of interviewees can limit the researcher's capacity to generalize, especially in the area of theory testing. [25] But non-randomly sampled interviewees can still provide the researcher with significant inferential leverage, as Lynch discusses in the next chapter, and as Martin describes (with respect to a snowball sampling strategy) in chapter 5. Moreover, non-random samples can be very useful for purposes other than theory testing. As both Gallagher and

Rogers (chapters 9 and 12) describe, non-random samples of interviewees can be used to assess the extent to which larger-n surveys capture the concepts that scholars aim to measure. Additionally, Cammett (chapter 6) posits that, while necessarily non-random in their selection (given the research context and the sensitivity of her subject), her interviews with ordinary citizens related to social service provision by sectarian parties in Lebanon were an important part of her overall empirical strategy. In her case, this strategy included a mass survey, geographic information systems (GIS) data, elite interviews, and government documents. Each sampling strategy, from convenience sampling (talking with whoever happens to be available) to random sampling, has its benefits as well as its drawbacks; these also vary with the type of interview data collected and the purpose for which the data are used. Regardless of the strategy one ultimately employs, an awareness of these tradeoffs is central to designing and conducting an interview study.

Furthermore, the author should make her sampling choices clear—whatever they are—in reporting interview findings. Scholars who use quantitative data are now expected to make their datasets, variable descriptions, and statistical software code available once their manuscripts are published. This not only allows others to understand more completely the results presented; it also allows others to replicate the analysis (King 1995). While confidentiality constraints may prohibit the sharing of interview transcripts (Golden 1995), information about the sampling process certainly should be shared. Indeed, one could envision two different types of replication of interview studies: one in which the collected data are provided and then reanalyzed (the way that "replication" usually is practiced in statistical studies), and another in which the entire data collection process—defining a population, identifying a sample, and conducting interviews with those in the sample—is replicated.[26] The latter is facilitated by scholars' transparency regarding sampling decisions. And even if other scholars do not attempt to replicate one's research, greater transparency about the interview process will increase confidence in the researcher's conclusions. In this spirit, Bleich and Pekkanen (chapter 4) suggest that researchers provide a wide range of information about how their samples were constructed—who was chosen for interviews, how many potential interviewees declined to participate, and what "type" (in a quota sampling sense) each interviewee is.

Validity

Information about the sampling process pertains to a third issue related to interview research: the extent to which one's measuring instrument (in this case, the interview) actually gauges the properties it is supposed to measure. In the context of the interview, concerns about validity revolve around whether the researcher is asking the right questions, or asking questions in the right way, as well as whether the interview participant is offering truthful answers (and, if she is not, whether the researcher is able to detect this).

For the interview researcher, asking the right questions often requires not only substantive knowledge of the issues at hand (for instance, what extant accounts from the media or by other scholars indicate about a given policymaking episode, or what other interview subjects have reported with respect to how violence unfolded in a particular region or village), but often some experience in conducting interviews on a given subject. For example, in my interviews of investment professionals, it was important to gain a sense of how they talked about politics, so that I could assess how political events entered their decision-making calculus. "Government partisanship" meant very little to most professional investors; but "left-leaning government" or "the Labour Party" or "the Swedish Social Democrats" did.

Early interviews that allow the researcher to discover how best to ask questions—not to get the answers she wants, but to get at the right underlying phenomena—can therefore be very important. Indeed, this is the rationale for many predissertation fellowship programs, as well as for the "learning by doing" model with which this chapter begins. Additionally, in many contexts, interview questions are more useful when they ask for information about actual behavior (*what* happened in a specific instance), rather than for interlocutors' explanations of *why* things happen (see Beckmann and Hall, and Leech et al., in this volume). In other contexts, gaining a sense of how informants understand their reality (the "*why*" view) may be a central aim of the research project (see Fujii, MacLean, this volume).

The validity of the interview instrument also hinges on the accuracy of information provided by the informant. Even if the researcher asks the right questions, she may not receive answers that are accurate or truthful; she must guard against the possibility that the interviewee is—deliberately or inadvertently—"playing her." Decision makers, when asked to reflect upon past events, may strategically misremember or revise their accounts, and likely in a way that is favorable to them. For example, in chapter 8, Reno describes how, in recent years, members of rebel groups in Africa shifted from describing themselves as perpetrators of violence to focusing on their roles as victims of violence. Moreover, even if interview subjects do not intend to deceive researchers, they may not remember accurately. Decades of research in psychology, much of it focused on the accuracy of witness testimony, suggest that eyewitness accounts are often unreliable (Loftus 1979; Wells and Olson 2003). Especially when interviewed about disturbing or chronologically distant events, interlocutors may make errors without intending to do so.

The researcher can guard against this threat to validity by considering a given interview in the context of other information—something that becomes easier to do as the research project progresses. Researchers can use what they have learned in previous interviews to check the validity of future interviews. Indeed, one of the benefits of interviews is that the researcher is aware of the context in which they are conducted, and of how informants might attempt to frame their answers or evade certain questions. The interview can use this metadata to assess validity; one of the advantages of interview data is that the researcher usually has a sense of the internal consistency of the interviewees' answers, the biases revealed by the interviewee, and the points of hesitation during the interview. This is much more information than users of quantitative indicators, especially those from other sources, usually have. And this interview metadata can be useful not only for thinking about validity of the answers, but also for understanding the social context in which answers are offered (Fujii 2010). The researcher might therefore ask herself whether one former cabinet minister's account comports with another cabinet minister's account. If it does not, she might consider why their answers to specific questions would differ, or how the context in which they were interviewed could condition their responses. Note, however, that guarantees of confidentiality—and professional ethics—usually preclude making this strategy obvious to informants ("that's not what Mr. Jones told me about what your party promised!"). Of course, the fact that there are multiple accounts and views of the same issue or story may be part of what is interesting to the researcher (Fujii 2010). In such cases, ensuring that all points of view are captured in the interviews is important. In their study of a range of U.S. public policy issues, Leech and her colleagues (chapter 11) aimed to ensure that the interviews represented every side of the issue. Often, an issue had only two sides, so that interviews with three individuals provided sufficient coverage of the issue. In other cases, though, the number of interviews required to cover the case fully was greater—up to fifteen, in one instance. This reminds us that the "right number" of interviews depends on the specific task and subject (see chapters 4 and 5).

The validity of interview evidence also depends upon the scholar's use, synthesis, and interpretation of interview material: to what extent do the facts and viewpoints revealed in interviews correspond to the researcher's theoretical constructs? [27] Is the researcher operationalizing and measuring key concepts appropriately (Gerring 2012; King, Keohane, and Verba 1994)? Once the interviews are completed, what conclusions should researchers draw from them? Here, the researcher must guard against hearing what she wants to hear. A good means of doing this is to employ various triangulation strategies, all of which evaluate interview data in light of other empirical material (see Gallagher, chapter 9, for an expanded discussion). One could consider how well interview participants' accounts fit with journalistic accounts of the same episode (this also is useful for addressing concerns about deception, as above). Or the researcher might consider how well the interviews line up with scholarly studies of the same or similar phenomena. For example, the researcher could compare what lobbyists say about which groups supported gun control legislation with the campaign contributions made by gun control advocates to members of Congress. If lobbyists' reports differ from what the contributions data suggest, then one might question whether other elements of their accounts are accurate. Or one could compare the International Monetary Fund's archival materials regarding its lending decisions with IMF staff members' accounts of such decisions.[28] Such strategies are particularly important when interviews are the sole form of evidence on which a research project relies. This concern is not unique to interview-based work; those using archival sources must confront the fact that the preservation of some materials—and the destruction of others—can generate a bias in the historical record. And an individual researcher's decisions about which archival materials to use, and how to interpret these materials, also can generate debate and criticism (Lieberman 2010).[29]

Within multi-method studies, the researcher can compare interview evidence with other types of data. She might evaluate how well the interview data line up with comparative statics from a formal model, results from regression analysis, or findings from archival research. In my research on financial markets' evaluations of government policies, I found that professional investment managers pay little attention to government ideology (whether a left- or right-leaning government is in office) in wealthy democracies. I used statistical analyses to assess whether this pattern was borne out in the sovereign bond market's aggregate pricing decisions. Using cross-sectional time series regressions, I found that left-leaning governments paid borrowing costs that, all else equal, were not very different from those paid by their centrist or right-leaning counterparts (Mosley 2003a).

Of course, if differences across types of evidence exist, these do not necessarily mean that interview information is invalid. Indeed, they could indicate that interviews are capturing a process more accurately than other forms of analysis. But such disparities do suggest to the researcher that she consider whether and how her interpretations might be biased. Furthermore, in order to make a compelling case that the assessment of the interview data is a valid one, the scholar should provide sufficient information for readers to understand the ways in which interview data are interpreted, as well as the context in which interview data are cited. Bleich and Pekkanen (chapter 4) suggest providing information about the sample frame, as well as about the broader data set from which reported interview evidence is drawn. If only some interviews or portions of other interviews are employed or quoted, why were these interviews chosen? When quoting or reporting from interviews, scholars also should provide context: To what extent is a specific view that is reported from one interview consistent with the overall tone of that interview and, more important, with the overall picture that emerges from the entire sample of interviews?

The object here is to guard against the selective use of "outliers" from the interviews. Quantifying or coding interview data—not necessarily for use in statistical analysis, but often for summary statistics—can be a useful means of providing a sense of the entire interview landscape: for instance, a researcher may note that "85 percent of informants mentioned that someone they knew had been asked to pay a bribe in order to obtain a business license." The best way to address concerns about one's interpretation of interview data might be to make all data public—the analogy to sharing one's quantitative data set and codebook, so that others can reevaluate a scholar's coding and modeling decisions. But doing so, which would mean sharing full interview transcripts, often will conflict with ethical and IRB considerations, specifically with guarantees of confidentiality (but also see Bleich and Pekkanen, this volume, as well as Aldrich 2009).

Reliability

A final, and related, concern for interview researchers is reliability. Reliability is about the confidence we can place in a given instrument of measurement. To what extent is the information collected in an interview accurate, and how much confidence do we have that, were the interview to be repeated again, the same information would be generated? Just as users of statistical data would do well to ask how indicators of interstate disputes, unemployment, or legislative effort are measured, and how these measurements might vary across units of analysis, users of interview data should be vigilant for threats to reliability.

Accurately capturing the information offered by informants requires the researcher to have an effective means of recording data from the interview. Researchers vary in their practices: some record each interview, asking for permission to record after collecting informed consent and guaranteeing confidentiality. Beckmann and Hall (chapter 10) report that their requests to record were almost always answered in the affirmative, and they do not judge their informants to have been inhibited by the presence of a recording device. Leech and her coauthors (chapter 11) also recorded almost every interview. When interviews are recorded, it is advisable to transcribe the interview as soon as possible, so that any ambiguities or gaps are fresh in the researcher's mind. The recorded interview also can be consulted in the future, as a means of addressing reliability (and validity) concerns. And for those who use an interpreter to help conduct interviews, a recorded session allows one to go over the interview later, along with the interpreter, to address any vagaries in translation. (Furthermore, as Fujii argues in chapter 7, using an interpreter can enhance reliability by allowing interviewees to answer questions conversationally and in their native language, rather than slowing the pace of their responses to match the researcher's level of fluency).[30]

Many other scholars, however, choose not to record interviews. This choice often relates to concerns about power; democracy campaigners in authoritarian societies, for instance, may worry that a recording would fall into the wrong hands. Or government officials may worry that their "off the record" comments will not be kept confidential (also see Woliver 2002). Often, then, the interviewer takes notes during the interview meeting and then more fully fills in these notes after the meeting (also see Aldrich 2009; Hertel, Singer, and Van Cott 2009; Reinhardt 2009). If this strategy is employed, the potential for measurement error is reduced by writing full notes as soon as possible after the interview concludes—perhaps in the closest coffee shop or park. In practical terms, then, it is best not to schedule immediately back-to-back interviews, but rather to allow time between meetings. Bleich and Pekkanen (chapter 4) suggest that, no matter what method of recording data one uses, information about the overall tone and context of the interview—the interview metadata—also should be noted.

Concerns about reliability also relate to interviewer effects and positionality, as discussed earlier in this chapter. First, different scholars may receive different answers (as a result of the qualities of theirs that are obvious to their interviewees). Scholars debate the seriousness of this challenge to reliability; it may be impossible to eliminate entirely, but one could use a triangulation strategy to compare the answers received by some types of interviewers (political scientists versus journalists, men versus women, graduate students versus full professors) versus others. This would provide a sense of the size and direction of interviewer effects. Second, individual scholars may receive the same answers but perceive them differently. The individual researcher's familiarity with a given research site, as well as her past experiences more generally, may lead her to privilege some details over others (or, related to validity, to privilege some interviewees' perspectives over others; see Allina-Pisano 2009). Reinterviews of the same individuals by different scholars may again be a means of assessing the extent of this phenomenon. Where reinterviewing does not occur, the individual researcher should nonetheless be aware of the potential for measurement error.

A final check on reliability addresses whether interviewees are consistent over time in the data they report: Does the same individual, interviewed by the same scholar, but at different points in time, offer similar responses? If she does not, this could indicate problems of reliability; or it could indicate that exogenous changes—things that occur between the two interviews—have affected respondents' attitudes and behavior. When reinterviews happen very soon after initial interviews, the former is more likely; when more time elapses before the reinterview, the latter may explain differences. Multiple interviews of the same individual also may be useful as a practical matter: in many cases, the researcher's questions evolve during the process of fieldwork.

Returning to previous interview subjects, with an eye toward asking additional questions, also can enhance consistency (in terms of questions asked) across interview subjects. For instance, in my research on professional investors' assessments of sovereign borrowers (Mosley 2003a), I returned to the field approximately sixteen months after my initial research trip. On this second trip, I conducted follow-up interviews with professional investors.[31] These interviews allowed me both to gauge the consistency of investors' views over time and to inquire about how changes in the global financial climate had led to changes in their asset allocation decisions: in the time between my first round of interviews (January–May 1997) and my second round (October 1998), the Asian financial crisis, as well as Russia's near-default, had intervened. Gauging the contrast between the same actors' views in a period of global financial optimism and a time of global pessimism allowed me to consider the dynamic nature of financial market–government relations. In this instance, what was interesting was that professional investors' views often were not consistent over time; explaining this dynamism became a part of my work on the subject. Of course, using repeat interviews with the same informants to increase reliability presents the researcher with a tradeoff between intensely interviewing a smaller group of informants (perhaps about a narrow set of subjects) and interviewing a larger group of informants in a less extensive manner. Again, the researcher will want to strike a balance—where the right balance depends on the research project at hand—between the internal validity that is enhanced by deep and repeated interviews and the external validity that is enhanced by a wider population of potential interview subjects.

Interviews often are, and frequently should be, an important component of political science research. For many projects, interview-based evidence is a central component of a mixed-method strategy. In other instances, interviews are the only viable source of empirical information with which to evaluate a theory or set of hypotheses. In still other situations, interviews allow the researcher to evaluate whether or not her other tools—such as surveys—measure what she thinks they do.

This volume offers advice, both practical and theoretical, about how to effectively use interviews as part of the research process. The contributors come from a variety of subfields in political science, and we have worked in a range of locations and with a variety of subject populations. Part 1 of this volume addresses the issues that will first confront the interview researcher: how to choose a sampling strategy, interact with interview participants, and collect and report interview data. In part 2, the contributors investigate specific challenges faced by researchers, including linking interviews with causal claims, using proxy interviews or an interpreter to improve access, and conducting research in challenging field locations. Part 3 offers examples of the varying ways in which scholars from across political science use interview data. Throughout the volume, the contributors provide insights from their own field experiences, as well as from those of others in the profession. The appendix contains various materials related to interviews and meant to serve as examples—of consent documents, semi-structured interview questions, and interview protocols, among other things.

We hope to fill the noticeable gap in the guidance offered regarding interviewing in political science. Today's graduate students are under greater pressure to complete graduate school more quickly and yet to acquire a broader range of methodological skills. They also may have difficulty obtaining funding for long periods of field research. Furthermore, although the rise of cross-country (and, sometimes, cross-regional) comparative projects serves to increase the external validity of many research findings, it also shortens the time spent at each field location. Taken together, these trends heighten the importance of "hitting the ground running" (Hertel, Singer, and Van Cott 2009). If there is less time to "do" one's research, there also will be less time for "learning by doing." A researcher can never anticipate all issues that will arise during his or her study, but an awareness of the challenges and complications greatly increases the probability of executing the study successfully—ultimately, of returning from the field with useful data.

Although PhD programs tend to offer less training in qualitative methods to graduate students, this does not mean that qualitative methods are easy or obvious, while econometric and formal ones are difficult and sophisticated. This may be particularly true when interviewing requires knowledge of foreign languages (although Lee Ann Fujii notes that this may be overcome with use of an interpreter) and cultures.[32] In some cases, then, our advice is similar to that provided in fieldwork "how to" guides that draw from several disciplines (Barbour 2008; Barrett and Cason 2010).[33] In many others instances, however, our advice is specific to the political science profession.[34] The contributors also acknowledge that the methodology of political science is continually evolving. Graduate students and assistant professors today face a different set of challenges, and possess a different set of methodological tools, than did scholars who were trained in previous decades. Indeed, most of the contributors to this volume completed their first research projects in a different era, one in which requirements for working with human subjects were less stringent, and in which potential interviewees perhaps were contacted by letter rather than by e-mail. "Recording" interviews may have involved cassette tapes rather than a tiny hard drive or a smartphone. And preserving the confidentiality and integrity of interview notes did not necessarily involve making sure that one's laptop and USB drive were password protected. While many of the lessons offered in this book are enduring—for instance, the tradeoffs regarding various sampling strategies—others will necessarily evolve.

While this volume does not provide a specific "how to" for every element of interview research, it offers ample food for thought as one constructs one's own interview-based project. We hope that this volume will encourage political scientists from all subfields, and at all stages of their careers, to "just talk to people"— but to do so in a way that is as rigorous, transparent, and ethical as possible.

Part 1

GENERAL CONSIDERATIONS

Research Design, Ethics,
and the Role of the Researcher

ALIGNING SAMPLING STRATEGIES WITH ANALYTIC GOALS

Julia F. Lynch

In political science, information gleaned from interviews can serve a number of purposes, depending on the stage in the research process, the goals of the research, and external constraints on the amount or type of interviews we can do. Interviews can be undertaken as a preliminary to the main study, as the main source of data for a study, or as one component in a multi-method research project. Interviews may be used to generate data or metadata, to test descriptive or causal hypotheses, to enhance the validity or reliability of our measures, or as a source of illustrative material that enlivens our analyses and makes our writing more enjoyable and accessible. Each of these uses of interview research suggests a different set of requirements for selecting people to interview (and sometimes how to interview them). In turn, the choices we make about sampling have implications for the role that interview data can play in our analyses and in the larger enterprise of theory building in political science. The aim of this chapter is to develop a set of guidelines that will help researchers align sampling strategies with analytic goals in interview-based research.

How should interview researchers sample their respondents, particularly if they hope to use interviews as a part of a larger multi-method research agenda? One argument runs that because random sampling is required to generate unbiased descriptive and causal inferences about larger populations of people, organizations, or events, "real" data from interviews can only come when there is random sampling. Some authors argue that epistemological underpinnings of arguments about the value of in-depth data derived from interviews are at the very least incommensurate with the requirements of large-n research (Ahmed and Sil 2009; Beck 2009). Hence data derived from non-randomly selected interviews do nothing to enhance the validity of claims based on statistical analysis of aggregate-level data, and multi-method "triangulation" using such interview data isn't worth much more than the paper the interview transcripts are printed on.

To be sure, studies that make claims about population characteristics based on convenience samples should be approached with skepticism. And when interview data are used as window dressing, there is often a temptation to select only quotations that are supportive of the overall argument of the analysis, or to anoint non-randomly selected respondents as "typical." These practices may enliven an otherwise dry research narrative but cannot be considered multi-method research because they do not enhance the validity or reliability of claims generated using other methods.

However, even interviews with non-random samples of individuals (or of individuals associated with non-random samples of organizations and events) can add to our store of knowledge, and to multi-method research. For example, interviews conducted as a precursor to survey work can aid in the creation of more-reliable measures used in large-n studies. Case study interviews may add meat to large-n causal arguments by using causal process observations to generate Bayesian updates about what is happening and why at a given point in a causal chain or process (J. Mahoney 2009). Purposive or quota samples may be good enough in many cases to verify relationships first observed and validated using other methods. Insights drawn from in-depth research with non-randomly selected respondents may also generate relational, meta-level information about the society or organization in which they are embedded—information that is simply unobtainable any other way. For all these reasons, even non-random-sampling designs for interview research can enhance multi-method research. And interviews of randomly selected individuals can, when conducted and analyzed with rigor, contribute data that are ideal for integration with other forms of data in multi-method research.

Most political scientists who use, or plan to use, interview data in their work are familiar with at least one or two works whose findings hinge on data drawn from in-depth in-person interviews. In American politics, for example, Robert Lane's *Political Ideology* (1962), Jennifer Hochschild's *What's Fair* (1981), and Richard Fenno's *Home Style* (1978) are three classic works that place interview data at center stage. Lane's book, subtitled "Why the Common Man Believes What He Does," draws on a small number of in-depth interviews with non-elites to explore the roots of political views in the mass public. Hochschild conducted in-depth, semi-structured interviews with a larger number of non-elites—twenty-eight residents of New Haven, Connecticut—to understand how they thought about justice and fairness in a variety of domains of life (the economy, politics, and the social domain encompassing family, friends, and schooling). Fenno's interviews with eighteen members of Congress as they went about their daily routines in their home districts allowed him to understand how elected officials' views of their constituencies affect their political behavior. Interviews need not, of course, be the only or even main source of data for a research project. Interviews can be equally useful playing a supporting or costarring role. Deciding how to use interview data and figuring out whom to interview are both important decisions that need to be made with an eye to the role the interview data will play in the larger research agenda.[1]

For the purposes of this chapter, I argue from a positivist worldview: in other words, I assume that researchers will be using interview data in the service of a research agenda that ultimately aims to frame and test hypotheses about the political world. My focus on sampling and the related problems of inference derives from this epistemological position. It is worth noting, however, that many political scientists who use interview research take a different approach. Scholars working in a constructivist or interpretivist vein are more likely to view the information that comes out of an interview as discursively constructed and hence unique to the particular interaction among interviewer, interviewee, and interview context. When viewed from this perspective, the central methodological issue of interview research is not so much sampling in order to facilitate generalization, but rather interpreting the data from a given interview in light of the interactions that produced it. (Of course, positivists who look to interviews to provide "evidence" should pay at least as much attention as interpretivists do to the quality and characteristics of data produced in the interview setting. Many of the chapters in this volume treat this topic in more detail.)

The next section of this chapter explores some of the different ways that interview research can be used to contribute to a positivist political science research agenda. The subsequent section discusses alternative sampling techniques, with an eye to understanding the analytic leverage that these different techniques offer and how this leverage can be used in the pursuit of specific analytic goals. The conclusion brings us back to ground level with a discussion of practical constraints that may hinder researchers' attempts to create optimal linkages between sampling strategies and research goals. A central message of the chapter is that the sampling methods researchers employ in their interview research are critical in determining whether and how interview data can be used to enhance the validity of interview-based and multi-method research.

Interviews and the Research Process

Interviews can be used productively in the service of a variety of different research goals, and at a variety of stages in the research process. The following examples are organized chronologically around the stage of research, and within that according to the analytic goals of the research.

Using Interviews in Preliminary Research

Preliminary research is research that occurs before collection of the data on which the main descriptive or causal hypotheses of a study will be tested. Interviews can be a valuable source of information in preliminary research, whether or not the main research project will use interview data.

In case study–based research, interviews at the pre-dissertation or scoping-out-a-new-project stage can use process-tracing questions to identify fruitful (and fruitless) avenues of research. Talking to people is often quicker than archival research for figuring out what happened when, who was involved, what were the important decisions, or where documentary materials related to your research question may be found. This type of preliminary interviewing is one method for quickly generating and testing in a "rough-and-ready" way a number of alternative hypotheses about a particular case study or case studies (Gerring 2007, chap. 3). Using preliminary interviews to get the lay of the land aids the purposive selection of cases for small-n studies, since some hypotheses have already been identified as irrelevant or, alternatively, in need of further testing.

Interviews also can be used (and often should be used) in advance of conducting a survey or behavioral experiment. In-depth interviews help the researcher get a sense of the opinions, outlooks, or cognitive maps of people who are similar to the research subjects who will eventually take part in the study. Interviews can help determine what questions are relevant and the appropriate range of response options (see e.g. Gallagher, this volume, chapter 9). Even if the researcher is fairly certain of the content of the questions she would like to ask or the games she would like her subjects to play, pretesting in a setting that allows for instant feedback from the respondent can help fine-tune question wording, question ordering, or visual prompts.

We have seen so far that preliminary interviews are often particularly useful because they allow us to refine our concepts and measures before embarking on a major research project. But interviews also can be an essential precursor to larger research projects when they are used to establish the sampling frame for a random sample or to figure out which characteristics to select for in a purposive sample. We will talk more about these types of sampling in the next section. What is important for the moment is that preliminary research is very often necessary before we can draw a sample, particularly if the aim is eventually to make inferences beyond the elements in your sample.

In some research contexts, a preexisting sampling frame may be easy to come by. For example, one could easily sample elected officials in Italian regions (Putnam 1993), or issues on which registered lobbyists have been active in the United States (Baumgartner et al. 2009). In other research contexts, however, official lists may be biased in ways that preclude representative sampling. For example, identifying the population of small-business owners in Lima, Peru, or Calcutta, India, based on the official tax rolls would exclude large numbers of informal entrepreneurs. Conducting interviews with both formal and informal entrepreneurs to identify all the business owners active in a particular area of the city or sector of the local economy could be necessary in order to establish a complete sampling frame and allow for truly random sampling of the population of interest. In still other research contexts—for example, for a study of squatter settlements, undocumented migrants, or victims of ethnic cleansing—there may be no written lists available at all, and preliminary research might be needed to establish the boundaries of the population of interest.

While it is likely to be time-consuming, doing preliminary interviews in order to establish the universe of relevant cases for a research project can have positive side effects. It is for good reason that collaborative mapping and census-taking are two standard "entry" strategies for ethnographic researchers (MacLean 2010). Talking to the people who live or work in the area in which we plan to do our research not only allows us to generate a comprehensive list of potential respondents, but also to get started establishing the rapport that will facilitate data-collection efforts as we move into the main part of our research (see MacLean, this volume, chapter 3).

Using Interviews in the Main Study

Interviews are frequently used to generate data to test central descriptive and causal hypotheses in political science research. Framing interview work in this way may make it sound little different from survey research.[2] But by "generating data" I do not only mean using tightly structured questionnaires to elicit responses that can be numerically coded and later subjected to statistical analysis. Interviews can generate both overt and latent content, which can be analyzed in a variety of ways.

The overt content of an interview comprises the answers that interviewees articulate to the questions we ask them. For example, a researcher might ask a user of social services or a civic activist, "Whom did you approach about this problem?" "How many contacts did you have?" "What was the response like?"

(Note that even when the information itself is qualitative, data like type of contacts or characteristics of the response in the example above can be coded into nominal response categories.) A number of contributors to this volume (Beckmann and Hall, Cammett, Leech et al., Martin) have used semi-structured interviews to generate responses that they then coded as data and analyzed statistically.

Direct answers to direct questions may also be analyzed qualitatively, of course. For example, interviews that elicit information about how events unfolded, or who was involved in decision-making and what their goals were, are often primary sources for researchers who use process tracing, pattern matching, and other case-based methods. For example, I used qualitative data from my interviews with policymakers and current and former officials of labor unions and employer organizations in my study of why Italian and Dutch social policies developed with such different age orientations in the post–World War II period (Lynch 2006). This type of overt content—which generates data that can be characterized as "causal process observations" (Brady and Collier 2004, 227–228)—is particularly useful for research into causal mechanisms and has been used fruitfully in historical institutionalist work in comparative politics, international relations, and American politics subfields.[3]

The overt content of interviews can also be analyzed for recurrent themes, issues, and relationships that respondents raise in the course of answering our questions (see Rogers, this volume, chapter 12). Various forms of qualitative content analysis, done by hand or with the aid of software packages like NVIVO or Atlas.ti, allow us to sift through the data in our interview notes and transcripts to think systematically about the world as our respondents have recounted it to us. (For a useful guide to qualitative content analysis based in grounded theory, see Emerson, Fretz, and Shaw 1995, chap. 6).

Latent content is information we glean from an interview that is not directly articulated by the interviewee in response to our questions. As such, it constitutes a kind of metadata that exists on a plane above the overt content of the respondent's verbal answers to our questions. Examples of latent content include the length of time respondents take before answering a question, the number of causal connections they make in order to justify a particular response, the way they link ideas together, the things they don't tell us, and even our own observations about the apparent truthfulness of respondents when answering particular questions. Latent content can provide particularly valuable information when we use systematic criteria for recording and analyzing it. For example, Hochschild (1981) examines the interconnections between ideas in her interview data to create informal cognitive maps that reveal the underpinnings of Americans' beliefs about justice. Fujii's attentiveness to the metaphors her respondents use and the lies they tell allow her to elucidate the social and political context surrounding the Rwandan genocide (Fujii 2010).

Using Interviews in Multi-method Research

Interview data have particular strengths that other forms of data may lack. Well-conducted interviews give access to information about respondents' experiences and motivations that may not be available in the public or documentary record; they allow us to understand opinions and thought processes with a granularity that surveys rarely achieve; and they can add microfoundations to events or patterns observed at the macro level. At the same time, the interpersonal nature of the interview experience can raise concerns about the objectivity or reliability of data that come out of that process; and in-depth interviews require a commitment of research resources—particularly time—that often makes it infeasible to conduct enough interviews to permit generalization to a larger population. In order to take advantage of the strengths of interview data and mitigate the weaknesses, many researchers use interviews in conjunction with other forms of data to make arguments and test hypotheses.

In some multi-method research, interviews are used in order to triangulate with other methods—in other words, to bring different forms of data to bear to answer the same question. For example, in my book on the origins of divergent age-orientation of welfare states, I used interviews in conjunction with archival research to fill in blanks in the archival record and uncover the motivations of particular policy actors (Lynch 2006). Others have used interviews to identify and explore the mechanisms underlying findings based on analysis of aggregate-level data, as in Mosley's study of the influence of political and economic factors on the asset allocation decisions of professional investment managers (Mosley 2003), or Stone's analysis (2002) of the conditions under which the International Monetary Fund continues lending to governments that have failed to comply with conditionality requirements. This type of multi-method research can be quite iterative: interviews generate new questions to examine using other methods, which may then in turn generate new questions to pose to interviewees.

Interview data also are frequently used in multi-method research to enhance the internal and external validity of data gathered using other methods. For example, interviews conducted in conjunction with or as a follow-up to survey research can improve internal validity by allowing researchers to verify that survey respondents understand the questions in the way they were intended (see e.g. Gallagher and Rogers, both this volume). Alternatively, when used as an adjunct to formal modeling, interviews can enhance external validity by empirically verifying that actors hold the interests and preferences that they are stipulated to hold.

For example, David Laitin's work on language and identity among Russian speakers in Estonia, Latvia, Ukraine, and Kazakhstan relies on interviews (as well as ethnographic observation and survey data) to demonstrate that his game theoretic model of a "tipping game" "reflects practical decisions that real people face" (Laitin 1998, 27) in choosing between languages in a bilingual setting.

While interviewing can be used successfully to enhance the validity of inferential claims in multi-method research, interview data also sometimes appear alongside other types of data in a more decorative vein. Including quotations or examples from interviews can add zest and appeal to analyses that draw mainly on more impersonal forms of data like surveys or aggregate data analysis. For example, Lawless and Fox (2005, 2010) illustrate the findings from their survey of potential female candidates for public office with extensive quotations from women with whom they conducted in-depth interviews. A well-chosen quotation or piece of information gleaned from an interview might also serve as an epigraph to an article, or the focal point of a job talk or conference presentation. Of course, selecting illustrative, theory-confirming pieces of interview data does nothing to enhance the validity of inferential claims made using other forms of evidence. This is not to argue that illustrative material from interviews shouldn't be used—but interview data used in this fashion can do little more than hint at the plausibility of claims based on other data. To generate and test inferential claims using interview data, we need sampling strategies that are appropriate to the nature of our research goals.

Aligning Sampling Methods with Research Goals

Sampling involves selecting a subset of elements (e.g., individuals, households, firms, episodes of decision making) from the universe or population of all such relevant elements (e.g., all firms engaged in textile and ready-to-wear garment manufacturing in Morocco and Tunisia in the late 1990s, as in Cammett 2007b). *Defining what elements are relevant* is a critical part of most research designs, in part because making very confident generalizations to the world beyond this population is often impossible. *How to sample elements* from the population of interest is an issue that bears no less careful consideration. Survey researchers generally aim to draw large random samples of individuals that are representative of the population of interest. But because of the time and expense involved in conducting in-depth interviews, sufficiently large random samples to allow for inference to the target population may not be feasible. Furthermore, we interview people, but people are not always the elements that we are interested in sampling. For both these reasons, interview researchers need to be attentive to the issues involved in sampling in order to make the most of our interview data, given the specific requirements of our research. In the paragraphs below, I identify some of the main ways that interview researchers may select their respondents, and when such sampling strategies are indicated. Martin's chapter in this volume highlights additional considerations.

Random Sampling

Selecting elements for study at random from the population of interest is the gold standard for making generalizations, or inferences, from the sample to the population. In interview research, however, individual interviewees are not always sampled at random, because the target population might be composed of aggregates or events, rather than individuals. For example, Martin (chapter 5) wished to generalize from a sample of firms to the population of British and Danish firms, and so she selected firms at random. But she interviewed individuals who were chosen not at random, but because they were most likely to know the answers to her questions. Baumgartner et al. (2009) studied instances of lobbying (see Leech et al., this volume), so they selected interviewees after first identifying a weighted random sample of issues about which lobbyists had lobbied. Researchers engaged in process-tracing ideally would like to be able to make the argument that they have interviewed individuals who can inform them about the full range of relevant events that happened in the world. Random sampling of elements from a population—regardless of whether the interviewees are randomly sampled (and regardless of whether interview data are coded and analyzed quantitatively or qualitatively)—is both necessary and sufficient to guarantee valid generalizations to the population of interest, as long as the elements are sampled in sufficient numbers.[4]

Stratified random sampling is a special case of random sampling that is used to generate samples that contain sufficient numbers of cases of "rare types" (of people, organizations, events) to allow for quantitative analysis that is truly generalizable to the entire population. Stratified random sampling also can be used to ensure responses from individuals who are likely to know particular facets of a story, or who represent different parts of larger aggregates that are the randomly sampled elements. For example, one might select randomly from civil servants at particular pay grades within a ministry in order to evaluate the position or behavior of the ministry as a whole.[5]

Random sampling is often difficult, though, particularly when the sampling frame is unclear or when access to respondents is limited. Although preliminary research can often be used to identify all of the elements in a population, and although, as Martin (chapter 5) exhorts, "lists are everywhere," in some cases it may never be feasible to generate a comprehensive list (e.g., of clandestine actors or events). More typically, random sampling in interview research is hindered by budget constraints and lack of time or emotional energy, or else by the difficulty of accessing randomly selected respondents.

Failure to interview all or nearly all the interviewees you have chosen to represent randomly selected elements can lead to both nonresponse bias and poor inferences. Random-plus-snowball sampling, in which the researcher selects elements randomly but uses personal contacts to aid in the recruitment of other interviewees on the list may be a solution to this problem (see Martin, chapter 5, for a description of this technique).

Non-random Sampling

The good news is that not all interview research demands random sampling. Random sampling is not needed, for example, if one is using interviews to generate hypotheses that will later be tested using other data. Of course the quality of the hypotheses is likely to suffer if the initial interviews generate data that are very unrepresentative (either because the individuals or the aggregates with which they are affiliated are unrepresentative of the target population, or because the people to whom one talks cannot provide a full account of a process that you are interested in tracing). Initial hypotheses are particularly likely to be incorrect if a non-random sample is biased such that it excludes all elements representing negative examples of the phenomenon of interest (see Martin, chapter 5). Nevertheless, careful selection of preliminary interviews can mitigate many of these concerns.

Random sampling is also generally not called for in either process-tracing or interpretivist work. Interpretivist theories posit that because interview data are discursively constructed in ways that are specific to each research interaction, generalizability is a chimera in any case. Process-tracing methodologies, including interviews, are used to generate what Brady and Collier (2004) call causal process observations (CPOs). A CPO is a piece of information that, unlike more standard "data set observations" used to evaluate correlation across cases, "provides information about context, process or mechanism, and that contributes distinctive leverage in causal inference" (Brady and Collier 2004, 277). This extra information contained in CPOs means that non-random selection of the cases from which CPOs are derived is not necessarily a threat to inference (Collier, Mahoney, and Seawright 2004; Collier and Mahoney 1996). As a result, even non-random samples of interview subjects can generate causal process observations to test process- and mechanism-based arguments. Similarly, data from interviews with non-randomly selected individuals may be used in research designs involving "pattern matching" (Campbell 1975) and cognitive mapping (Axelrod 1976).

Non-randomly sampled interviews can be used for triangulation, for example, to help interpret the results of surveys or experimental studies. And non-random sampling also may be necessary in order to avoid nonresponse bias. Like in-depth case studies, in-depth interview research often allows us to better understand the cases that we have studied, sometimes—but not always—at the price of less reliable generalizations to the cases that we haven't studied.

PURPOSIVE SAMPLING, sometimes called judgment sampling, is a form of non-random sampling that involves selecting elements of a population according to specific characteristics deemed relevant to the analysis—for example, firms of various sizes, individuals of various social classes, or legislators from various parties in a political system. A purposive sampling design does not call for a complete census of every element in the population, but it does require knowing enough about the characteristics of the population to know what characteristics are likely to be relevant for the research project (either as causal variables or as potential confounds that need to be controlled for).[6] Purposive sampling can yield a sample that is loosely "representative" of the population, at least along the dimensions that are likely to be of interest for a study, without requiring a very large number of interviews. Like stratified random sampling, it can also be used to ensure that rare types or negative cases are included in the research. When nonresponse in a random sample is likely to be selective, and so high as to negate the benefits of random sampling, purposive sampling can be a partial solution because it ensures the inclusion of particular types of elements in the sample.

CONVENIENCE SAMPLING demands little of the interviewer other than identifying and making contact with individuals who are attached to elements—any elements—in your sampling frame. "Man in the street" interviews are convenience samples, as are interviews with elites with whom you happen to have a preexisting connection, or with whom you happen to be able to schedule an interview when you are in the capital city. Convenience samples can be useful during preliminary research, and may be necessary when gaining access to respondents is extremely difficult. They can also be a very effective way of generating pithy quotes or anecdotes that illustrate findings from another, more systematic, form of analysis. In general, however, convenience sampling would ideally be reserved for situations when one doesn't need or want to draw inferences to a larger population.

SNOWBALL SAMPLING, sometimes called chain referral sampling or respondent-driven sampling, is a method for gradually accumulating respondents in a sample based on recommendations from earlier interviewees. This method of constructing a sample enhances access to respondents, since no cold contacts are required, and it can be used in conjunction with other forms of sampling (purposive, convenience, or even random-plus-snowball, as described by Martin, chapter 5). For example, in preparation for survey work, I conducted a series of in-depth interviews with Boston-area residents. I used snowball sampling to recruit a convenience sample of interviewees, beginning by interviewing one of the employees at a nearby day care center. She referred me to her former mother-in-law, who in turn introduced me to a former home health care aide, who set me up with her sister's sister-in-law, who introduced me to a colleague, and so forth. The respondents in the child care provider's referral chain were racially mixed but were mainly female and of middle to lower socioeconomic status. Since I expected responses to my questions about the fairness of inequalities in access to health care and health outcomes to vary by race, gender, and socioeconomic status, I made contact with male and upper-middle-class respondents by using additional snowball seeds, including a neighbor and an administrative assistant in the department next door to mine.[7]

INTERSTITIAL CONTACTS. One final method of selecting interview respondents is worth mentioning—although in this method, it might be more accurate to say that the interviewees select the researcher, rather than the other way around. Taxi drivers, people sharing queues or waiting rooms, the domestic staff retained by our landlords, our research assistants and translators (see Fujii, this volume, chapter 7) can all be useful informants, spontaneously offering perspectives and information that we might not otherwise encounter in the process of our research. Even researchers with a well-planned sampling design can make use of information gleaned from interstitial contacts like these, so it makes sense to keep a notebook handy at all times and to record your detailed observations as soon as possible after chancing upon an accidental interview. Of course we should guard against the tendency to give heightened emphasis and credence to these informal contacts; the testimony even of "ordinary people" who choose to share their views with us is surely no more representative than the testimony of our carefully sampled respondents. Still, when we are confronted with situations in which we know little and have much to learn, all information is potentially useful.

Sometimes, despite our best intentions, it is not possible to carry out the sampling design that would best support the analytical goals of our research. We have already identified some situations in which it may not be possible to generate a reliable sampling frame. Power dynamics built into the process of interviewing elites, political constraints, and ethical considerations may all also limit sampling possibilities.

Many researchers just beginning interview-based research, particularly with elites, are concerned above all about access. Thesis writers often grow accustomed to occupying a position low on the food chain and may not feel important enough to commandeer the time and attention of high-status individuals like government ministers, elected officials, or CEOs. Gender, language, or nationality can also seem to disadvantage researchers who must supplicate for an audience. In my own experience conducting interviews with economic and policy elites in Italy, The Netherlands, and the United States, such concerns about gaining access have been surprisingly unfounded. Beckmann and Hall, and Martin (both this volume) report similar ease of access to members of Congress in the United States and employers in Britain and Denmark. Of course, there may be circumstances when it is simply not possible for a political scientist to gain access to high-ranking societal elites, and research designs should not in general be premised on such access. Identifying in advance surrogate sources of information, and sampling the organization, event, or type of official rather than individual respondents, may help lessen problems of access. If large numbers of potential respondents refuse to participate for reasons that appear to be unrelated to key hypotheses or control variables, a purposive sample may be substituted for random sampling (making appropriate corrections for the certainty of causal claims based on such interview data).

Political constraints also may limit the type of respondents researchers can access and the sampling strategies we employ. MacLean and Reno (both this volume) interviewed members of populations—American Indian tribal leaders, and members of Liberian militia organizations deemed illegal under U.S. law—who for distinct reasons might be cautious about revealing information to (non-Native) American researchers. Both Reno and MacLean were able to reassure potential interviewees that their intentions were honorable and that agreeing to be interviewed would not place the respondents or their communities at risk. Nevertheless, under some circumstances it may be politically impossible to interview certain types of respondents. Cammett (chapter 6, this volume), for example, was not able to interview people who had used social services provided by Hezbollah in Lebanon, despite the fact that this type of respondent was initially included in her sampling frame.

Ethical constraints, too, may limit whom we interview. Institutional review boards (IRBs) intensely scrutinize research that involves populations they have categorized as "vulnerable" groups, such as prisoners and children, and with people who could become victims of retribution in the event of a breach of anonymity or confidentiality (see Brooks, chapter 2, this volume). Even where IRBs approve interview subjects, however, researchers need to use their own discretion and often deeper knowledge about the contexts in which they are working to evaluate whether their interviews could endanger respondents (for example by being seen talking to an American researcher). In circumstances where ethical considerations limit whom we may interview, sampling strategies may need to be adjusted to protect human subjects.

In sum, when researchers have the ability to interview large numbers of respondents, when respondents are accessible, and when very in-depth information about a particular case is not required, the benefits to be gained from attempting to sample randomly far outweigh the costs. If we must interview a smaller number of respondents because of resource constraints or lack of access, if we are conducting process-tracing research, or if we aren't concerned about generalizing to a larger population, then an aptly chosen non-random sampling design may be the best option—as long as we remain sensitive to any inferential bias that our particular non-random sample entails.

THE ETHICAL TREATMENT OF HUMAN SUBJECTS AND THE INSTITUTIONAL REVIEW BOARD PROCESS

Sarah M. Brooks

The protection of human subjects[1] in research is an important consideration for social scientists, regardless of the methodology employed. In addition to the ethical concerns for the well-being of research subjects, the permissible bounds of interaction and intervention with humans have been defined and enforced ever more firmly in recent years. Such concern for research ethics arose in the wake of the Nuremberg Trials, which brought attention to the horrific abuses of concentration camp prisoners at the hands of the Nazis. Public outrage over subsequent abuses by scholars in the United States in the 1960s and 1970s catalyzed the U.S. government, and other governments around the world, to draw up national guidelines to regulate and enforce the ethical treatment of human subjects in social and medical research. Those guidelines called for the creation of institutional review boards (IRBs) at universities and other research institutions, and established a set of principles governing the ethical treatment of humans in the research setting. IRBs, in turn, are charged with the oversight and approval of human subjects research, and the enforcement of federal regulations. Thus it is essential to gain IRB approval (or exemption) for a research protocol prior to undertaking research with human subjects, including social science interview research.

Navigating the IRB process is far from a straightforward endeavor, however. For social science researchers employing interview methods, this task is all the

Many thanks to Lauren MacLean, Cecilia Martinez-Gallardo, Layna Mosley, and the participants in the Interview Research Conference for helpful comments on an earlier draft.

more complicated by the nature of the guidelines, and by the forms and principles governing human subjects research that were developed on the basis of procedures and concerns in the biomedical sciences. And the resulting set of rules may increasingly put interview research at odds with disciplinary pressures for greater transparency and replicability of research findings. Thus, even as the purview and structure of IRBs have broadened to include social science research, and board members have gained familiarity with ethnographic research and interview methods, the translation of human subjects review principles into workable guidelines for interview research has been difficult and controversial (Bosk and De Vries 2004; Gordon 2003; Hauck 2008; Oakes 2002; Seligson 2008; Shea 2000; Yanow and Schwartz-Shea 2008).

Even though IRBs possess a great potential to frustrate researchers, such boards can also provide crucial assistance in the process of designing research that meets important ethical standards (Anderson 1996). Thus it is worth paying close attention to the underlying principles that inform IRB regulations in the design of interview-based research. To that end, this chapter seeks to decipher the main principles and ethical considerations relating to the risks to human subjects in interview-based field research and offers some practical suggestions for scholars seeking IRB approval for such research. The chapter also highlights some unique challenges that qualitative researchers may anticipate when seeking IRB approval for interview research protocols. Although there is no certain or fail-safe path to gaining IRB approval—as IRBs vary widely both across universities and over time in the same university—efforts to design interview research that minimizes risks to human subjects in line with IRB provisions should simultaneously advance the secondary goal of avoiding delays or, worse, the forfeiting of data, as a result of deviations from guidelines for the treatment of human subjects.

Human Subjects Protections

A vital responsibility for any researcher is to protect the privacy, well-being, and dignity of the participants in her research. Accordingly, a fundamental goal of human subjects protection is to ensure that such research entails *minimal risk* to participants in the study (Tierney and Cowen 2007). Although this may seem like an obvious or elementary concern, human subjects protection has become a crucial and high-stakes ethical and legal matter for universities and government sponsors of social science research. Much of the task of enforcing the standards for human subjects protections in the design of research falls upon IRBs, which possess the authority to approve or reject research plans. They also may require revisions to proposals, interrupt ongoing research, delay or terminate research, or even prohibit the use of data that deviates from approved practices or is deemed to be harmful to the human subjects of research being carried out at the university. Gaining IRB approval at the design phase of a research project and working within the prescribed regulations once the research commences thus have become important concerns for faculty and students at universities across the country. Indeed, failure to comply with IRB regulations may place human subjects—as well as researchers and universities—at risk.

The origin of this concern for protecting human subjects grew out of the horrors of Nazi abuses that were revealed at the Nuremberg Military Tribunals. The Nuremberg Code, which established a set of standards to evaluate the human experiments conducted by the Nazis, included a set of principles for the ethical conduct of human subjects research. Many of these principles were subsequently embraced by the World Medical Association in 1964 in its Declaration of Helsinki, which provided further guidance for the medical profession in the ethical treatment of humans in scientific research.[2]

In the United States, government intervention in the regulation of human subjects research was prompted by public indignation over the Tuskegee syphilis study. That experiment lasted from 1932 to 1972 and involved 399 low-income African American men in Alabama. Researchers failed to inform the subjects that they were suffering from syphilis and did not offer them a remedy, even after an effective therapy had been developed (Brunner 2010; National Commission for the Protection of Human Subjects of Biomedical and Behavioral Research 1979; Marshall 2003; Tierney and Corwin 2007). The Tuskegee study brought much-needed attention to the array of physiological risks of harm to human subjects that may be associated with participation in medical research. Subsequently, public concerns for the psychological impact of participating in research arose from prominent studies such as that of Milgram (1963), whose subjects were led to believe that they were administering increasingly painful electrical shocks to punish individuals for not working quickly enough. Even though the individuals supposedly receiving the shocks in that study were researchers who were introduced to the subjects at the end of the study, subjects were found to have suffered long-term psychological damage from the shame and guilt of their participation in the research (LeCompte and Schensul 1999).

In response to public anger associated with these and other social and medical research scandals in the 1960s and 1970s, the U.S. government convened a panel in the Department of Health, Education, and Welfare to review such practices. The result was the 1974 National Research Act, which established the National Commission for the Protection of Human Subjects of Biomedical and Behavioral Research. The product of that commission, which met from 1974 to

1978, was the Belmont Report (1978), which established three fundamental principles for research on human subjects: respect for persons, beneficence, and justice; it also devised a set of procedures for oversight and approval of research involving human subjects.

The principal institution charged with this oversight is the IRB. Although the Public Health Service began to require in 1966 that research institutions set up ethics committees to oversee human subjects research, it was only in 1981 that the Department of Health and Human Services (HHS) issued broad guidelines that delineated the scope and mandate of these panels. In the 1990s such regulations came to be enforced broadly in the discipline of political science, as well as other social sciences (Hauck 2008). Those regulations, issued by HHS, came to be known as the Common Rule, and have been adopted by most federal agencies that conduct or fund research on humans. The guidelines required that most research involving human subjects that is funded by a department agency must be evaluated by an IRB (Marshall 2003, 270). In 2001 the responsibility for overseeing IRBs was transferred to the Office for Human Research Protection (OHRP).[3]

For universities, the stakes in the enforcement of these standards are exceedingly high. In the years since OHRP took over responsibility for the oversight and enforcement of ethical standards for human subjects research, "the feds" have suspended research at several U.S. institutions that were found to be in violation of these regulations (Marshall 2003). Because universities that are found to be in violation of human subjects regulations may lose access to federal funding for research, some university IRBs have become quite zealous in their application and interpretation of federal rules (Anderson 1996). Such enforcement efforts have been countered in some cases with mobilization by scholars who resist or wish to amend them (Shea 2000; Seligson 2008; Yanow and Schwartz-Shea 2008).

Understanding these guidelines and their implications for interview research thus is a crucial part of planning for social science research. As Cammett, MacLean, and Reno (this volume) each point out, designing interview research protocols that conform to human subjects guidelines may take considerable effort and planning well before the research is undertaken, and may entail considerable revision of standard procedures through which research is performed, and informed consent obtained. The next section therefore offers some strategies for designing interview research that conforms to human subjects protection guidelines for minimizing risk to the participants in interview research. Of particular concern will be the special dilemmas involved in designing protocols for interview research in political science that satisfy criteria for human subjects protection that were devised for biomedical research.

Scope and Issues of IRB Concern

A very basic quandary for many scholars engaging in interview-based research is to discern what kinds of investigations are subject to IRB approval. Although the Common Rule initially required universities to convene IRBs only if researchers were seeking government funding, federal regulations subsequently have been extended to include *any* research, funded or not, that is conducted at any institution receiving federal funds. Accordingly, virtually all research—federally funded or not—that involves human subjects must receive approval or exemption from an IRB (Gray 1979, 204; Seiler and Murtha 1980, 148; cf. Murphy and Johannsen 1990, 131).

The next logical question then becomes, What is human subjects research? Given the increasing level of scrutiny and high stakes in federal oversight of social science research, the way in which a university defines "research" and "human subjects" becomes crucial to delineating the scope of government authority. In the first place, federal regulations of human subjects research are typically enforced where data gathered from the subjects render them *identifiable*, either directly or indirectly. Specifically, these guidelines state that a human subject is "a living individual about whom an investigator (whether professional or student) conducting research obtains data through intervention or interaction with the individual, or identifiable private information" (*Code of Federal Regulations,* title 34, sec 97.102(f)). In addition, the federal government defines research as "a systematic investigation, including research, development, testing, and evaluation designed to develop or contribute to generalizable knowledge" (*Code of Federal Regulations,* title 34, sec 97.102(d)).

These guidelines are not without problems. They have been critiqued for their ambiguity and narrowness in leaving some humanistic and testimony-based studies outside the realm of regulated research (Seligson 2008). For instance, some forms of interview research that are aimed at compiling history, oral history, or biography, along with interviews that are *not* meant to be generalizable or used to draw general conclusions, may not be regulated by the Common Rule, even if the participants are identifiable, since they do not meet the regulatory definition of research (UIC 2009). For most social scientists who plan to use interviews to generate knowledge that will be published or presented, however, if that knowledge may be generalizable or applied to a broad segment of the population, then it is likely to be considered human subjects research and subject to federal regulation. Given that most social science research aims to develop generalizable knowledge, it typically is considered to be subject to federal regulation when it involves identifiable individuals. And since interviews are by their nature interactive, research that engages in this way with individuals who could be identified would in most cases be considered subject to federal regulation.

There is some debate over whether such a definition includes pre-dissertation research that is used principally for the purpose of training in graduate education, rather than as research itself. Even though some scholars point out that activities whose primary purpose is to educate the student rather than to make original contributions to knowledge should be exempt, others contend that even pre-dissertation research is meant to be systematic and to lead to generalizable knowledge (Murphy and Johannsen 1990, 131). A common practice of IRBs thus has been to include such interview research in their purview, even where it entails "non-thesis, non-dissertation, unfunded, didactic ethnography" that was previously thought to be outside the mandate of the IRB (Murphy and Johannsen 1990). Accordingly, graduate students engaging in interviews intended for pre-dissertation research or exploratory study designed principally, or even solely, for the purpose of graduate training also should seek IRB approval for, or exemption of, this research.

What to Do. A first step for researchers planning to undertake interview-based field research is to determine whether this research is exempt from federal regulations; whether it may be approved by an expedited review; or whether it is subject to a fully convened IRB.[4] The federal regulations provide guidelines for exemptions of certain types of interview research, which should be used when considering whether research may be deemed exempt. Specifically, the second criterion of the HHS regulations §46.101(b) provides exemption for:

> (2) Research involving the use of educational tests (cognitive, diagnostic, aptitude, achievement), survey procedures, interview procedures or observation of public behavior, unless:
>
> (i) information obtained is recorded in such a manner that human subjects can be identified, directly or through identifiers linked to the subjects; and (ii) any disclosure of the human subjects' responses outside the research could reasonably place the subjects at risk of criminal or civil liability or be damaging to the subjects' financial standing, employability, or reputation. (*Code of Federal Regulations*, title 45, sec 46.101(b))

Thus, if interview research is carried out in a way that renders subjects identifiable and subject to the array of social risks listed above, then IRB approval from a U.S.-based university is likely to be necessary. Of course, the case-by-case interpretation of these criteria is left largely to the IRB itself, and thus for many researchers it makes sense to begin this process by inquiring with one's university

IRB about whether a given protocol may be exempt or amenable to expedited review. An expedited review typically involves evaluation of the protocol by the IRB chair and just one or two experienced IRB panel members, rather than the full board (see *Code of Federal Regulations,* title 45, sec 110(a)). Eligibility for expedited review is typically determined by the IRB staff on the basis of the extent of risk and the research strategies involved in the project (Anderson 1996).

Crucially, even if the research is determined to be exempt by the U.S. government, one should consider whether the approval of *other* IRBs may be necessary before undertaking the research. This point is underscored by Lauren MacLean (chapter 3), as her research with Native Americans required the approval of ten tribal IRBs as well as university and federal government review boards. Similarly, for scholars planning to carry out interview research in an international setting, preparation for the research should entail investigation into the laws governing human subjects research in different nations. In many cases, governments have legislated strict requirements for IRB approval of human subjects research in their countries. Such laws should be consulted, and provisions for their compliance should be described in research protocols.[5] Documentation that international research conforms to the human subjects requirements of other governments may even become a condition for approval of social science research by IRBs at U.S. universities.

Where an IRB determines that the proposed interview research is not exempt from human subjects regulation, then an initial review through an expedited process or by a convened IRB is necessary before undertaking the research. The next section describes the main principles of concern in the protection of human subjects and offers suggestions for how to design interview research in a way that conforms to these rules for the ethical treatment of human subjects.

Concepts and their Practical Meaning for Interview Research

The Belmont Report, published in 1978, provided guidelines for ethical practice based on three fundamental principles that have now become the central requirements for ethical conduct of research with human subjects: respect for persons, beneficence, and justice. These principles translate roughly into a central concern for gaining informed consent, minimizing risk, and being fair in the selection of subjects of the research. Nevertheless, turning these three concepts into practice, and designing a research protocol that adequately conforms to these criteria, is far from a clear-cut task. This may be especially troublesome for researchers using interview methodologies and conducting interviews in international settings, where the rigid and legalistic frameworks applied by IRBs may complicate the ability both to gain approval for interview research and to effectively employ such methods in social science research. This section lays out these basic principles and their application, and suggests ways to satisfy them when designing interview research to protect human subjects and gain IRB approval.

Respect for Persons

This principle obliges researchers to respect the personal dignity, self-determination, and autonomy of individuals, especially of vulnerable populations and those with diminished autonomy, such as children. In practical terms, satisfying the concern for respect for persons has focused on the task of gaining voluntary and informed consent of participants in the research. Indeed, the need to obtain informed consent of the participants in scholarly research is now viewed as a universal imperative, regardless of method used in the research. The emphasis on this principle stems directly from the Nuremberg Code, which concluded that "the voluntary consent of the human subject is absolutely essential." Thus, interviewees must be informed that they are being involved in research, and they must be aware of the purpose of the research. Research subjects also must be free to decline participation in the study without penalty.

Informed-consent rules apply whenever a researcher interacts with a subject for the purpose of research. They do not pertain to research that involves solely the observation of individuals in public behavior. Sitting on a park bench and observing people in their normal activities thus would not require that a researcher obtain or document informed consent. Nevertheless, once a researcher engages with individuals, such as by approaching them with questions, or acquiring information about them that is not publicly available, human subjects regulations apply. Consider for instance a researcher who plans to enter a café to meet locals and interview them about politics. If the intention of that research is to use the conversations in the café to generate insights about political values and beliefs, and thus the researcher would plan to take notes (during or after the meetings) and use them to inform her research, then the requirement for informed consent would apply. Even if the subjects remain anonymous, such a protocol thus would run afoul of the ethics regulations unless the researcher (1) identifies herself as a researcher; (2) states clearly that the conversation is part of a research study and describes what she will do with the information, including publish it in a dissertation; and (3) gives the interviewees a chance to decline to participate in the study. The requirements of informed consent thus extend broadly to include participant observation as well as informal methods of interview research. Interview research conducted over the Internet, such as in chat rooms or social networking sites, raises new and vexing questions for the application of consent rules, as the boundaries of public versus private space and expectations of privacy in electronic communications are unclear. I return to this issue below.

A crucial part of satisfying the "informed" part of consent, moreover, has meant in practice that researchers must notify participants of the "reasonably foreseeable" risks that they confront as a result of being part of the research, and of the potential benefits that might accrue to them as a result of participating (Labott and Johnson 2004, 11). It is typically up to the IRB panel to judge whether these conditions have been satisfied, and whether a person's voluntary agreement to participate in a study is based on adequate knowledge and understanding of the relevant information provided by the researcher. Unfortunately, the language that may be required by an IRB to fully satisfy these criteria may be less than clear or comprehensible to many subjects. Scholars should thus pay special attention to the clarity of the language used to communicate risks so that these can be understood fully by research subjects (see MacLean, chapter 3, this volume).

It is here that social scientists have faced challenges to satisfying procedural criteria that were developed around the biomedical sciences. In order to fulfill the requirement of informed consent, researchers are obliged to disclose to their subjects the nature of the risks associated with the study. However, two basic issues may arise here. First, IRBs tend to prefer consent scripts that include language describing a set of risks and benefits whose nature is typically less clear and whose incidence is less easily quantifiable in the case of social science interviews than it is in medical sciences. In the case of clinical trials for a new drug, for instance, the potential benefits of the research to the individual are direct. Second, the foreseeable risks involved in biomedical research and their magnitude are often more quantifiable than is typically the case for interview methods in the social sciences. This is not to say that political science research is necessarily less risky than medical research. Rather, as William Reno makes clear in chapter 8, interview research in conflict zones may entail considerable risk to informants and scholars alike (see also Wood 2006). Understanding that the process of elaborating risks to satisfy the requirement of informed consent is closely associated with the basic task of the IRB to weigh risks and benefits may be helpful to scholars seeking approval for a research protocol.

Another dilemma for scholars engaged in interview-based research is the tendency for IRBs to favor the more rigid form of written consent scripts. Whether this is on account of the bias in favor of the biomedical research models, or due to the Western value placed on the written over the oral word, is not clear (Gordon

2003, 305). The guidelines for informed consent in the Common Rule are very specific and highly legalistic; they may not recognize the local meaning of informed consent or may be confusing for the research subjects (Marshall 2003).[6] Written consent scripts tend to establish the most unambiguous form of protection for the university; this is not necessarily true for the subject. Indeed, a common critique of IRBs is that they often seem to protect the researchers and universities more than, or even instead of, the participants in or subjects of research (Gordon 2003, 300).

Written informed consent may not be required for every human subjects research project, however, and this may be particularly the case for types of interview-based research. Exemptions from the requirement of written consent may be requested for cases in which such procedures would undermine the quality of research or the ability of a scholar to carry it out. For instance, in cases where illiteracy is pervasive, written consent may be inappropriate, if not obstructive, for the research. This is also likely to be the case for vulnerable populations that have been exploited in the past, or who may be engaged in illegal activities, such as undocumented workers. In addition, scholars have argued that the rapport between the researcher and subjects in ethnographic research—if not the flow of the research itself—may be impeded by the requirements of obtaining a subject's written consent, if not by the language required on such consent scripts. To the extent that IRBs insist on the use of written consent scripts, therefore, a researcher's ability to carry out interview research among such populations may be impeded. In such cases, it is appropriate to request a modification of the informed-consent process to utilize oral, rather than written, consent procedures.

Such a request should be made in the initial review protocol and may be most persuasive where information is provided about the social and cultural contexts that make written consent problematic for the research, as well as the logistical complications that might arise from the requirement of written consent. The former may be more relevant for research among vulnerable or illiterate populations in international settings, while the latter may apply to Internet research or ethnographic research for which written consent forms may introduce a hierarchy or rigidity that alters the rapport between researchers and subjects (Gordon 2003). In one case where such a modification was granted, a graduate student working among tribal populations in Pakistan pointed to the high rates of illiteracy, and subjects' strong reluctance to putting a thumbprint on any document, even one that was read to them, given the history of local people having been cheated out of land after having been tricked into signing a document they couldn't read. In that case, the requirement of written consent would have undermined greatly the ability of the researcher to carry out her study among this population, therein justifying her request for modification of the informed-consent procedure. Similarly, Wood (2006) describes the ethical justification, if not imperative, of relying on oral consent when conducting interviews with vulnerable populations in war zones.

Finally, in satisfying the requirement of informed consent, it is important to make clear to interviewees that they can refuse participation in the study without fear of penalty. Of particular concern to IRBs is the assurance that interviewees are free from coercion and undue influence on the decision to participate. IRBs may be especially sensitive to these factors when scholars are working in a developing country or with vulnerable populations such as children, refugees, or pregnant women (Seligson 2008). IRBs also pay special attention to the use of inducements or gifts made as compensation for participation in a research study. Gifts that are especially valuable thus may be seen as coercive if the inducement renders low-income or vulnerable populations less free to decline participation in a study. In contrast to biomedical researchers engaging with subjects suffering from illnesses, social scientists engaged in interview research may be in a better position to make the case of minimal risk and lack of coercion, because the physical and emotional health of their subjects is intact, and their well-being is usually not at stake in the decision to participate in the study (Gordon 2003, 311). Nevertheless, special attention to the question of the value of any gift for participation—especially for vulnerable populations—may be warranted, along with attention to documentation of informed consent as a way to ensure that risks to interviewees are minimized.

What to Do. A consent script should accompany any request for IRB approval of interview research. This script should clearly describe for prospective interviewees what the research is about; it should also state that research subjects can refuse to participate without penalty and that they can likewise refuse to answer any question. (A sample consent script is included in the appendix). Where a gift or compensation for participation is offered, it should be made clear that refusal to complete the interview will not jeopardize receipt of the gift. Such compensation should be justified and should be reasonable enough not to be viewed as coercive. And in the event that written consent would impede or undermine the quality of the research or the ability to carry out interviews, researchers should request modification of the written consent protocol. Such a request will be more persuasive to the extent that the researcher can justify exactly why and how written consent would impede the ability to effectively carry out the research, and to the extent that a verbal script and a protocol for documenting the receipt of verbal consent can be provided.

It may be helpful to consult the IRB for guidance and to work with the IRB to develop acceptable ways to protect both the interviewees and the reliability of one's research process. Care also should be used in the design and implementation of consent scripts, to ensure that risks are communicated in clear language that is understandable to subjects, with ample time allocated for subjects to weigh such risks before proceeding with the interview. In many cases, IRB staff can offer guidance on the language for informed-consent scripts that are typically approved by that board. Where written consent is obtained, it is also advisable to produce two copies of the consent documents so that one may be kept by the participant and one by the researcher (Padgett 1998).

Beneficence

This concept revolves around the objective of minimizing risk to human subjects and maximizing the anticipated benefits of the research. The Belmont Report requires IRBs to consider in their judgment of a research proposal both the probability and severity of risk, and the justifiability of that risk given the anticipated benefits of the project. The IRB task thus essentially becomes one of making a cost-benefit analysis. The risks involved in interview-based research, however, differ considerably from those in biomedical research, and thus the heavy reliance on conceptual and procedural guidelines designed for the biomedical fields may complicate the task of gaining IRB approval for interview-based research.

IRBs also may consider whether there are other possible ways to obtain the stated benefits of this research, and thus their efforts may go beyond simply judgment of a project, and may become prescriptive as well (Labott and Johnson 2004, 11). Given that the risks associated with social science interview research may be difficult to elucidate, much less to quantify, it is essential for researchers to assist IRBs in this cost-benefit analysis by providing as much context and information as possible to justify a given research strategy. With this end in mind, some clarification of the concepts and strategies for minimizing risk may be helpful.

Minimal risk to a human subject is said to exist "where the probability and magnitude of harm or discomfort anticipated in the proposed research are not greater, in and of themselves, than those originally encountered in daily life" (Oakes 2002, 456; cf. Tierney and Corwin 2007, 393). What constitutes an everyday risk, however, varies markedly across contexts and countries. Indeed, the concept of risk itself is culturally bound, making it particularly difficult for IRBs to evaluate the risks associated with research in foreign countries (Gordon 2003, 311). An IRB evaluating an interview research protocol will typically be highly vigilant of a subset of standard risks associated with research, including violation of confidentiality and the possibility that solicitation of and use of sensitive information may jeopardize the social, political, or economic well-being of the subjects. For social science research in particular, the principal risks that researchers will be expected to minimize include invasion of privacy, loss of confidentiality, psychological trauma, indirect physical harm, embarrassment, stigma, and group stereotyping (Oakes 2002, 449). This may mean in practice that subjects may be embarrassed or harmed in their professional or social standing by the publication of their answers to your questions if confidentiality is violated. IRBs also may be concerned that being asked about sensitive subjects such as violence, abuse, or traumatic events may involve psychological stress for research subjects.

Many of the risks to subjects involved in social science interview research are difficult to anticipate, much less to quantify. Different types of interviews, moreover, may imply different degrees of risk to subjects, depending on the researcher's degree of control over the process and content of the interview. Whereas unstructured or open-ended interviews allow the subject to control much more of the content of the interview, semi-structured and structured (closed-ended) interviews allocate more power to the researcher to determine the types of information that are gathered, with subjects controlling only the amount of information shared or whether to respond at all (Corbin and Morse 2003).

Just the same, defining and elaborating the potential benefits to those interviewees may be equally nebulous and difficult. In many cases, there is little if any direct benefit to research subjects for their participation in social science research. Thus researchers engaged in interview research in these disciplines may be at somewhat of a disadvantage compared to biomedical researchers whose studies are aimed at the alleviation of a symptom or cure of an illness. Since the task of the IRB essentially reduces to a weighing of risk and benefit, it becomes vital to provide as much information as possible for the IRB about the subjects, their contexts, and the potential risks and benefits associated with the research. Fortunately, one advantage of social scientific interview research compared to biomedical research is that the risk of injury or death as a direct result of participation in the research is quite remote.

What to Do. Put the concept of risk as it relates to the research project into the clearest terms possible. Because IRBs may have a hard time gauging the risks associated with ethnographic or interview research, protocols should clearly state why and how they entail "minimal risk" to the research subjects. Describe in as much detail as possible the context in which the research is to be carried out, the nature of the risks and their magnitude (which should be minimal), and the potential benefits to be gained from your study. Critically, IRB approval may not depend on there being substantial or direct benefits to interviewees for participation in the project. Panels of academic researchers may be quite aware that the benefits of a study often accrue only indirectly to society as a whole through the advance of knowledge. Nevertheless, researchers should be able to state exactly how knowledge drawn from their study would be beneficial to the society they are studying, and how their study would contribute to knowledge in the scholarly community. It may be sufficient, in other words, to state that society stands to benefit even if individuals have less to gain personally. This is simply the nature of social science research, which contrasts with the biomedical fields around which the practice of making such a risk-benefit calculus was developed (Gordon 2003, 313–314). Where interviews involve sensitive or potentially distressing subjects such as violence or abuse, moreover, plans should be made to provide interviewees with referral services in the event that interviews cause emotional distress.

Justice

The third guiding principle established by the Belmont Report turns attention to the ways in which research subjects are selected for inclusion in the study. Fundamentally, the selection and recruitment of interviewees should be fair, meaning that an IRB will be vigilant to ensure that the most vulnerable members of society do not bear the greater burden of research, whether the study is domestic or international. Here again the biomedical foundations of human subjects review criteria are evident, as these concerns drew from the egregious violations of social justice for vulnerable populations as in the case of the Tuskegee syphilis study or drug trials in developing countries. IRB judgments of a research protocol thus will seek to ensure the "justness of the selection process should consider fairness to your interviewees as persons, and as members of a social, racial, sexual or ethnic group" (OHRP 1993, 12). The IRB also may pay special attention to the selection of subjects to be sure that they are not chosen for being "easy to manipulate as a result of their illness or socioeconomic condition" (OHRP 1993, 12). The incorporation of new technologies into the research process has complicated this task, however. Not only do electronic media make it difficult for researchers to verify a subject's age, gender, and other characteristics, but they also may replicate social inequalities in sample selection to the extent that a "digital divide" limits the scope of the population that is reached through the Internet.

What to Do. For researchers whose study centers on questions associated with vulnerable populations or those in developing countries, special attention in the protocol should be paid to justifying the selection and recruitment of subjects for the research. The principal concern for the IRB will be to assure that your interviewees will not be selected either because they are favored or because they are held in disdain, nor simply because they are readily available. The recruitment of subjects in the protocol should be described in a way that ensures that the researcher will avoid replicating the injustices that "arise from social, racial, sexual, and cultural biases institutionalized in society" (OHRP 1993, 12). Even though this criterion assumes that recruitment involves some form of experimentation or burden imposed on the subjects, the condition may be satisfied most clearly if the selection of your subjects is done in a way that is based on objective social science criteria. Here, a careful consideration of the purpose of interviews and the appropriate sampling strategy (see Lynch, and Bleich and Pekkanen, this volume) is helpful. Describing and justifying these case selection procedures in the research protocol thus should effectively dispel concerns about violation of the principle of justice.

Special Dilemmas for Interview Research in Political Science

Paying attention to the three ethical principles described above constitutes only the beginning of efforts that researchers should take to ensure the protection of human participants in interview research. To be sure, the strategies suggested above are far from certain to secure IRB approval of an interview-based protocol, as different IRBs within universities over time and across different institutions tend to vary in the rigor with which they interpret and enforce federal regulations for human subjects research. Despite recent improvements, researchers engaged in interview research, and in particular in research in international locations, have often found the task of designing a research strategy that will best protect subjects and gain IRB approval to be fraught with difficulty (Yanow and Schwartz-Shea 2008). This section addresses some of the concerns relating to IRB approval of interview research in political science, and offers additional guidance on strategies for protecting research participants from the most relevant risks associated with this type of research.

For some scholars, one of the most important challenges of navigating the array of federal regulations of human subjects stems from "the complete lack of anthropological or sociological input into the formulation of those regulations" (Murphy and Johannsen 1990, 128). Not only are the forms and criteria for assuring protection of human subjects oriented heavily around the biomedical sciences, but also many of the ethical problems of ethnographic research remain unaddressed by IRB regulations (Tierney and Corwin 2007, 395). Political scientists engaged in interview research, moreover, may find themselves caught between an IRB's demands for confidentiality on the one hand, and their discipline's increasing emphasis on transparency and replicability on the other, which may involve pressure to disclose the names of sources in order to publish their research. Given these tensions, it makes sense for researchers engaged in interview research to communicate directly with the IRB when formulating a research protocol. Trying to anticipate the broadest range of questions about the research contexts and the methods employed may help to ease the passage of a protocol through the IRB while at the same time making it easier for the researcher to design a protocol that adequately minimizes risks and highlights the benefits of the proposed research.

Interview researchers bear a particular burden of accounting for differences in the concept of risk across international contexts. This is because the regulatory definition of "minimal risk" entails a situation in which "the probability and magnitude of harm or discomfort anticipated in the research are not greater in and of themselves than those ordinarily encountered in daily life or during the performance of routine physical or psychological examinations or tests" (*Code of Federal Regulations,* title 45, sec 46.102). Yet, a critical problem in satisfying this criterion revolves around the definition of "daily life." Or as Labott and Johnson (2004, 11) observe, the question becomes, "Whose daily life? That of an investigator or of a potential subject who is currently homeless?" For scholars working in developing countries, IRBs at home universities may be inclined to perceive risks associated with research to be more likely to impose significant harm than those of everyday life, which will be unknown to them. They also may perceive the incidence of standard risks such as breaches of confidentiality—such as due to theft of a laptop—to be greater than is true for that country or context. Accordingly, it is worthwhile to build extra safeguards against these risks into the design of interview research protocols, while also including as much contextual information as possible in the initial review application to allow IRB members to understand how such risks are minimized in the research. The more information that can be provided to help reviewers understand the context, the better able they will be to evaluate the research.

IRBs also tend to focus on the individual as the source of informed consent for adults. In some contexts, however, it may be appropriate to seek consent from members of the family, tribe, or group who serve as "gatekeepers" for a potential interview respondent (Gordon 2003; Padgett 1998). It may be important therefore for a researcher to obtain the consent of both the research subject and his or her gatekeeper, as the latter may hold the authority to grant permission to participate. In certain instances, this means that researchers should anticipate approaching a person in authority, such as an agency director or a village chief, when seeking the consent of a participant in the research. As Cammett (chapter 6) reveals, this process obliges researchers to consider the "positionality" of the researcher in relation to her subjects, and may require a modification of the targets and strategies for gaining informed consent, particularly in plural societies and with non-elite subjects. Here again it is vital to document and justify the context and procedures through which such consent is obtained at every stage of the research project.

Gaining IRB approval for interview research in the social sciences thus may be difficult for some international settings, particularly given the ambiguous nature of risks and benefits and given the nonstandard hierarchies of access to research subjects. Researchers should pay special attention to the nature of these risks and the social context in which the project is situated when describing and justifying informed-consent procedures to IRBs. It is advisable of course to put in place a set of safeguards to protect research subjects to minimize risks in any setting; international research and projects undertaken in conflict zones or plural societies, however, require extra assurances to minimize risk to interview subjects. As Reno describes (chapter 8), in certain cases interview notes taken in pencil that may be erased by the informants may provide extra assurance that risks will be minimized.

In every case, research protocols should specify that field notes, transcripts, and recordings will not contain personal identifiers such as the names of interviewees or other personally identifiable facts that could betray the identity of research subjects. Instead, researchers should give subjects a code name or number and separate the transcript from any record that links this code to the individual's identity (Fritz 2008). Interview data and transcripts also should be stored on a password-protected and encoded laptop and jump drive—or uploaded electronically to a remote location. Doing so should ensure complete separation of the hardware on which interview notes or transcripts are stored, and the identity of the informants, in order to minimize the risk of a breach of confidentiality. Moreover, researchers should avoid sharing data or interview transcripts with anyone who has not received research ethics training or is not included as a participant engaged in the research on the IRB protocol. For researchers planning to employ one or more research assistants to help carry out interviews or focus groups, it is typically required that everyone be certified by an ethics training course. In such cases, IRBs may request that a chain of command is created for gathering and storing data, along with procedures to ensure that research data are protected from loss or theft (Fritz 2008).

Even though it is difficult to estimate the severity, likelihood, and duration of specific risks, it is always important to provide the IRB with information on the probability, magnitude, and harm associated with each risk to subjects, regardless of the medium of interaction (UIC 2009). Again, in most cases the principal risk to subjects of interview research will be the breach of confidentiality. Accordingly, it is essential to incorporate safeguards such as encryption and secure passwords to store and protect any identifiable information about research subjects as a way to minimize this risk. It also may be useful to anticipate that the IRBs will not hesitate to evaluate the validity of any claim made within the request for approval, and will consider whether some alternative measures could be taken that imply less risk to the research subjects (Labott and Johnson 2004, 13). In order to reduce the likelihood that a research protocol is delayed or revised substantially by the IRB, try to anticipate as many risks as possible that may accrue to research subjects, and establish safeguards within the research plan to minimize them. In other words, it is rarely worthwhile to fail to mention a risk and provide for it, as IRBs may anticipate such risks and forestall the implementation of the research until revisions in the protocol are made.

The Internet is also changing the relationship between interviewers and subjects in social science research, and in doing so has generated new ethical concerns and practical challenges for research conducted electronically. Not least of these challenges is the fact that the regulations governing IRBs (based on the Belmont Report) were written well before the Internet age and thus do not easily accommodate the scope and nature of risks attendant upon the electronic media through which interviewers and subjects interact. Not only has the Internet created ever-greater challenges to protecting the confidentiality of subjects, but it also raises important conceptual questions about what constitutes public versus private behavior. Even though the Collaborative Institutional Training Initiative (CITI), a prominent human subjects training course, includes a section on the ethics of Internet research, it lacks firm guidelines as to the scope and application of human subjects regulations to this research.

Among the fundamental issues to consider in the ethical design of Internet-based research is the question of what constitutes public behavior (Nissenbaum 1998). What, for instance, is the expectation of privacy for electronic posts to chat rooms or social networking sites? The question is of crucial importance, given that informed consent is not required of research that involves solely the observation of individuals in public behavior. Recording posts made in Internet chat rooms without interacting with people may not be considered to be human subjects research to some researchers; however, to the extent that data can be traced back to the individual, the privacy of research subjects is put at risk (Parry 2011). Indeed, breach of confidentiality is typically considered to be the biggest risk associated with social and behavioral research. In the case of Internet-based research, such risks are amplified by the fact that Internet connections often are not secure. E-mail communications also may not be private, as in the case where a person uses a work e-mail account that employers have the right to monitor.

Some IRBs also request a list of the specific questions to be used in interviews in order to dispel uncertainty about the sensitivity of the information that is being solicited in the research. However, it is common in ethnographic and interview-based research to conduct semi-structured, if not fully open-ended interviews, which leave subjects with considerable control over the content of the interview. Indeed, a prominent technique of interview research is to begin with a set of "grand tour" questions (Spradley 1979), which give interviewees a chance to answer in a way and with content that is important to the subject, and which may not have been anticipated by the researcher (Schwartzman 1993, 58). Depending upon the answers to these very open ("what") questions, researchers may be disposed to ask questions different from the ones listed on the protocol. Such interview methods are complicated to the extent that IRBs demand to approve all interview questions *ex ante*, in which case an amendment of the IRB protocol may be needed before research continues. Similarly, some IRBs may require a list of specific individuals to be interviewed, while others may approve a general category of subjects that will be interviewed. In both cases, the requirement of a detailed list of questions, or research subjects, may introduce delays, if not out-right obstacles, to interview-based research.

To avoid the possibility of delays in the progress of research, or even the find-ing of violations of federal regulations, interview researchers may wish to first discern whether their IRB upholds such a "strict constructionist stance," in which it grants approval to ask only a specific set of questions to a specific set of subjects (Tierney and Corwin 2007, 395). Because IRBs vary considerably in their inter-pretation and enforcement of these parameters, it is important to communicate early and continuously with the IRB chair and staff members. In many cases, IRBs may permit researchers to attend the board meeting in which their protocol will be discussed in order to answer questions and provide additional informa-tion for the panel. Viewing the process of obtaining IRB approval as an interactive one thus may offer the greatest opportunity to assure that all the requirements for human subjects protections are met; it may also help to avoid delays or, worse, suspension of your research until the conditions are met to satisfy the IRB.

Of course, the commitment to act ethically extends throughout the life of a project, of which the IRB process represents only an initial step. IRBs can estab-lish standards for research and enforce them in the design phase of the research, but their influence is quite limited in terms of enforcement of these standards throughout the implementation and publication of the research. Once a protocol has gained IRB approval, the Common Rule dictates that it has to be reviewed again no later than one year from its initial review. Any significant changes that affect the research subjects—such as revisions to the consent process or the types of data collected—must be approved by the IRB. Although every IRB varies in its precise standards for ongoing communication, most require that researchers report any "significant events" or unexpected problems affecting the rights, safety, or welfare of subjects that emerge during the implementation of research. These may include breaches of confidentiality or any social or psychological harm that occurs to the subjects. Again, however, IRBs differ considerably in terms of requirements for what should be reported, so the best course of action for a researcher is to communicate openly with IRB staff in order to determine the specific requirements of his or her institution.

Internet-based research has posed important challenges for scholars seeking IRB approval for their research. For one thing, it is often unclear whether the use of such data constitutes "human subjects" research. At issue is whether one's Internet behavior—including social network posts, chat room interactions, search engine and browsing history—is public or private; in other words, whether it may be likened to behavior in a public square, or in your living room, a town hall meeting, or a letter to the editor of a newspaper (Hudson and Bruckman 2004). The choice of metaphor matters because human subjects protection, including the requirement of informed consent, is required to record private behavior, such as in one's living room, but not the observation of public behavior—in the town square. According to the *Chronicle of Higher Education*, a rule of thumb is that if a password is required to access an online community (such as Facebook), then IRB approval is needed to study its members (Parry 2011). However, other, more open forums such as chat rooms, blogs, and Twitter may also require IRB approval to record individuals' behavior. Although there is no clear consensus on this issue, some scholars have argued that research that involves recording chat room interactions is subject to human subjects regulation because participants in those chat rooms objected to being recorded when the scholars identified themselves as researchers (Hudson and Bruckman 2004). Others view Internet posts as public behavior subject to copyright protection and proper citation, as is the case for newspaper letters columns (Bassett and O'Riordan 2002). The safest course of action for ambiguous cases such as these is surely to treat individuals as human subjects and, where appropriate, to seek a waiver of consent if the process of obtaining such consent would be prohibitive of the research.

Even though Internet research is often considered to impose less risk of social or psychological harm on subjects, it may in fact pose an even greater risk of identity exposure than conventional interviewing. Not only can an individual's activities in the electronic sphere be recorded directly into cyber databases, but his or her Internet activity also can be traced to a specific IP address, therein providing ways for an individual's identity to be exposed. This problem was laid bare in 2006 when AOL released a list of twenty million web search queries that were assumed to be anonymous, but which investigators were able to easily track to individual users whose private Internet searches were publicly exposed (Barbaro and Zeller 2006). Academics already have run afoul of confidentiality requirements in their use and publication of Internet-based data. Such was the case for a team of sociologists from Harvard University who conducted network analysis of Facebook profiles that were downloaded without students' knowledge (Parry 2011). Even though the scholars thought that the identities of the students were protected by the removal of names, the release of the data used in the study—a requirement of the National Science Foundation as a condition for funding the study—was followed quickly by exposure of the identities of the subjects, therein violating their privacy.

Internet-based research also requires careful attention to the risk of breaching confidentiality given the difficulty of anonymizing online data and communications. In part, this is a practical issue; e-mail is not secure and in some cases is simply not private, as where an individual uses a work e-mail account to respond to interview questions. And the fact that Internet communications may be captured and documented and traced to an individual IP address makes it very difficult to fully anonymize such data, or to keep confidential the identities of research subjects once identifiable data have been collected. In the absence of clear guidelines for the protection of human subjects in Internet research, scholars should take every precaution to de-identify data as soon as they are collected, and to store them in secure and encrypted databases. Communicating with the IRB prior to initial review also may help to ease approval of Internet-based protocols, as researchers can ask for guidelines from the IRB staff in putting in place protections for research subjects.

The protection of human subjects and the ethical conduct of research are crucial obligations for all researchers, regardless of the methodology employed. Among the central concerns for the ethical treatment of human subjects are the requirements for gaining informed consent of research participants, minimizing risk to research subjects, and ensuring fairness in the selection of the subjects. For researchers preparing to undertake field research using interview methods, therefore, a vital step in this process is to obtain approval for this research plan by a university-sponsored IRB—and in some cases, by additional IRBs as well. Despite the IRB's tremendous potential to exasperate or delay researchers seeking to undertake interview-based research, it is worth bearing in mind that researchers and IRBs have shared goals in protecting the human participants in research. Thus the tasks of gaining IRB approval and carrying out research in an ethical manner are closely aligned. And the fundamental concern for designing research in such a way that protects informants and interviewees should be conducive to the development of research protocols that likewise conform to federal regulations for the protection of human subjects.

Still, the process of securing IRB approval of an interview-based research protocol, and navigating the array of forms and concepts involved in that effort, may be fraught with difficulty, delay, and frustration. The fact that many of the regulations associated with human subjects research found their origin in the biomedical sciences and before the advent of Internet-based communication has made the task of securing approval for research employing ethnographic methods such as in-depth interviews, focus groups, or participant observation, whether in person or online, especially challenging. And researchers using interview-based methods may be caught between powerful pressures at once to conform to the more scientific expectations of transparency and replicability, which may demand publication of sources and interview subjects' identities, and the competing demands for privacy and confidentiality of interviewees.

There are no easy solutions to these dilemmas. Fortunately, the rules governing social science research are subject to ongoing revision, which brings hope for streamlining and rationalization of the IRB process. Even as the specific regulations evolve, their underlying principles have remained constant. This chapter has sought to describe and clarify those guiding principles, and to offer advice for scholars designing interview research in a way that conforms to the ethical treatment of human subjects with the goal of securing approval for such research by a university IRB. Although the extension of IRB regulations to include ethnographic and interview research in the social sciences has not been uncomplicated, it has brought much-needed attention to concerns for the ethical conduct of research that entails the recruitment of and interaction with people for the purpose of creating generalizable knowledge. Indeed, such concerns may often be overlooked in graduate training that increasingly focuses on the scientific design and rigor of research methodologies at the expense of ethical concerns. The task of obtaining IRB approval for field research, albeit arduous at times, thus may usefully serve as a vital component of graduate training in the social sciences. Indeed, with all our concern for acquiring ever more sophisticated research methodologies, it remains vital to the quality of academic research to not lose sight of the importance of training scholars in the *ethical* conduct of research as well.

3

THE POWER OF THE INTERVIEWER

Lauren M. MacLean

Power shapes the process of interview research from beginning to end, from the initial formulation of the research question to the final dissemination of results. Even when a scholar carefully navigates the ethical dilemmas posed when working with human subjects, as discussed in the last chapter, the interviewer still wields significant power at every stage of research. While most of this book focuses on the interview encounter, this chapter broadens the lens to examine earlier and later phases of the research process that can involve the explicit use (or sometimes abuse) of power. Since these stages serve to facilitate the interview and to deploy interview findings, it is important to give attention to them as well.

This chapter's emphasis on the everyday power of the interviewer contrasts markedly with two conventional viewpoints. One encourages political scientists to strive for a godlike perspective throughout their research, to look down from on high as objective and neutral observers of whatever political phenomenon is being investigated. The second rejects the above strategy of detachment and instead suggests that power can and should be eliminated through an erasure of all distance, where the interviewer endeavors to become socially, culturally, economically, or politically embedded with his or her research subjects.

But while political scientists are not God, they are also not "native." Just as it is not possible for political scientists to be purely objective,[1] it is equally not a politically neutral stance if they attempt to be "native" or choose which "natives" can speak for how long on which questions.[2] Furthermore, to adopt either stance obfuscates the way that power shapes the process of interview research.[3] While both of these strategies represent relatively extreme and polar opposite viewpoints, their limitations reveal the need to focus here on more earthly, ordinary, and yet persistent power dynamics in the process of interview research.

In this chapter, I propose a "rigorous subjectivity" and advocate a more reflexive and consultative approach to all types of political science interview research. To be clear from the outset, this is not a polemic against a particular methodological approach to interview research. My critique is relevant for quantitative, qualitative, and interpretive methods of conducting interviews. The chapter *does* challenge explicitly some of the assumptions of a wholly positivist *epistemological* orientation, however. Specifically, I argue that giving up the assumption that a "pure" objectivity is achievable will facilitate a more nuanced and thorough subjectivity. Indeed, by *illuminating* the power dynamics and biases involved in the process of conducting interview research, rather than assuming they do not exist, or trying to somehow eliminate them, political science scholarship can become more rigorous, not less.

In this chapter, I highlight the existence of power as experienced in interpersonal relationships in interview research. This builds on Dahl's (1957) conceptualization of power as a relation between people. Indeed, my objective is to reveal how an interviewer's individual-level interactions with the study participants are embedded in much broader structures of power, for example, of families, communities, organizations, states, international organizations, and transnational networks. On another level, the interviewer is also influenced by the disciplining power of political science, other social sciences, and long-established academic institutions in the United States. Last, the individual experience of these power relationships within academics may be uneven and particularly acute for graduate students and junior faculty without tenure.

This chapter is organized in four sections to consider how power affects the questions asked, the process of informed consent, the validity and reliability of the primary data collected (either by the principal investigator or another institution), as well as the way in which the data is represented in the analysis and write-up of the study. While the above four issues of participatory research, informed consent, positionality, and authorship have been debated for years in a diversity of other disciplines and by a minority of scholars within political science, they are often treated separately in published work as distinct issues. In contrast, this chapter employs a holistic approach that critically examines the role of power throughout every stage of the interview process. The chapter thus attempts to draw from rich theoretical discussions in anthropology, geography, history, sociology, and our own subfield of political theory to bring valuable methodological insights into the mainstream of political science. Empirically, the chapter draws heavily from my own quantitative and qualitative field research in Ghana, Côte d'Ivoire, Kenya, and in American Indian tribal communities in the United States.

How Power Shapes the Formulation of Research Questions and Designs

Until World War II, the power relationship between investigators and human subjects in research was largely unregulated by any nation-state or international organization. Then, from the late 1940s until the early 1990s, most of the national regulation of research in the United States was based on an understanding of medical or psychological experiments; it did not consider research in other social sciences, such as political science.[4]

Only in the early 1990s did political science research become subject to the 1991 "Common Rule" definition of "behavioral research." Because of the decentralization of institutional review board (IRB) powers, the implementation of IRB procedures for political scientists has varied considerably across different campus and institutional settings, with sometimes polarizing results (Seligson 2008; also see Brooks in this volume). On the one hand, some political scientists are either unaware of or disregard completely their campus IRB policies and requirements (Yanow and Schwartz-Shea 2008, 485). On the other hand, other political scientists are keenly aware of American IRB policy changes and have mobilized to critique them and call for reform (Gunsalus et al. 2007; Lederman 2006; Yanow and Schwartz-Shea 2008).

I argue that an in-depth consideration of power and ethics in interview research requires a great deal more than the satisfaction of the bureaucratic requirements of a campus IRB. The politics of the IRB process and the process of obtaining informed consent is certainly important and is covered by Brooks (chapter 2), as well as in the second section of this chapter. Still, the analysis of how power shapes interview research begins at an even earlier stage of the study.

The first and most fundamental way that power shapes interview research is in the identification of research questions and formulation of research designs. The relative power and position of the researcher affect both *what* we study and *how* we set out to study it. Traditionally, in political science, researchers develop their questions and research designs alone or in collaboration with a small number of other academics. At times, a discussion or an encounter in the field may reveal a puzzle that becomes the subject of a later investigation, but it is rare that individual subjects or communities are integrally involved in the development of the core research question. Cases are usually carefully selected according to a long list of theoretical criteria. The subject individuals and communities are frequently consulted and invited to participate only later when it comes time to implement the study. Often for a combination of some very legitimate reasons (to be discussed in detail below), in the common political science model the researcher makes decisions unilaterally, based on theories and values that may or may not be shared with the subject communities.

In contrast to the above model, a number of scholars from a variety of other disciplines call for a more participatory approach to research (Brydon-Miller 1997; Chataway 2001; Davis and Reid 1999; Dreze 2002; Fals-Borda 1997; B. Hall 1981; Kelly 2005; Kidd and Kral 2005; Park 1992; Reason and Bradbury 2001). These scholars conceptualize research as a partnership between the investigators and the subjects studied. Researchers need the local knowledge and information possessed by individuals and communities, and communities may benefit from the knowledge and insight provided by the researcher (Fals-Borda et al. 2002). Together, researchers and study participants collaborate to identify the most salient research puzzles and the most appropriate and efficient way of investigating them. This approach emphasizes action, because both the researcher and the subjects are actively involved and learning from each other throughout the process (Kidd and Kral 2005). And, through this process of learning and self-reflection, any of the participants may develop new ways of thinking and take new forms of action (Freire 1970, 1982). The above scholars argue that, ultimately, this more participatory *process* of conducting research produces an improved *outcome* for all involved (Kelly 2005; Kidd and Kral 2005; Reason and Bradbury 2001).

This appeal for a more participatory approach to research is quite revolutionary, as it demands a major shift in power relationships between the researcher and subjects of research. When collaboration is involved, power is much more equalized than in traditional research models. Advocates of this approach have acknowledged this greater power-sharing and unequivocally called for a commitment to the "full democratization of both content and method" in research.[5]

Political scientists like very much to study democracy, but it becomes more challenging to practice it in our own everyday lives at work. Democracy is valued both in the abstract, as well in the "real world" out there, but within our academic projects, political scientists tend to limit the participation of subjects in any intellectual competition regarding the research question and study design. Indeed, despite the increasing attention given to the value of participatory action research in other disciplines, many of those scholars also choose to act in a less radical role and to serve as a more authoritative principal investigator. Below I highlight several rationales that might justify the decision to *limit* the participatory nature of research, and then present a more moderate alternative to consider under certain conditions.

A very fundamental reason that many scholars might restrain the degree of collaboration with subjects in a project is that this fits their personality and management style. Indeed, many scholars were attracted to academics precisely because they value the individual control and autonomy over their research agenda and projects.[6] Even if the scholar's personal preference is to work more collaboratively, the decision to develop a participatory project might be particularly difficult for graduate students, junior faculty, and adjunct faculty for two reasons. First, graduate students and junior faculty are encouraged to demonstrate the originality and uniqueness of their intellectual contribution to the discipline foremost as individual, independent scholars, not as collaborators with their research subjects, or even as coauthors with other academics. Second, graduate students and junior faculty are driven to produce rapid results by the unyielding deadlines represented by their normative or tenure clocks. Meanwhile, adjunct faculty may not be provided the professional incentives or adequate free time from teaching obligations to develop a deeply collaborative research project. A truly participatory research project requires both an enormous investment of time and a tremendous degree of flexibility (Cornwall and Jewkes 1995), which graduate students and junior and adjunct faculty may not yet enjoy at this stage in their academic careers or in their particular academic institution. Furthermore, all these scholars may not have sufficient financial resources to support a more time-consuming and labor-intensive participatory approach to data collection.

The need to relinquish some control and the demanding time requirements for participatory research are not the only criticisms worth highlighting here, however. The push to include the active participation of subjects and local communities can obscure the power and hierarchy *among and within* those subjects and communities (Cornwall and Jewkes 1995). Much of the recent criticism of government decentralization has in fact emphasized how scholars and practitioners must be attuned to the dynamics of power and exclusion at the local level.[7] Since individual subjects and local communities do not themselves necessarily operate in a highly participatory or democratic fashion, researchers should continue to problematize the parameters of cooperation and participation. And, finally, while subject or community voices bring critical knowledge to a study, these perspectives are of course shaped by their own individual positions and political values. Subjects may have political motivations for focusing on certain questions or research designs and excluding attention to others. For example, if consulted, Michelle Bachman and a student activist for the College Democrats at a large, public university in New York might formulate very different research designs for analyzing the politics of the Tea Party movement.[8]

Even if not completely objective or neutral, the researcher's theoretical and often comparative perspective as an outsider is also quite valuable. This should not be forgotten in the rush to incorporate and validate subject and community participation. For example, local people on both sides of the Ghana–Côte d'Ivoire border repeatedly warned me that my research design was flawed because both regions were dominated by the same precolonial Akan ethnic culture. According to this logic, the people in these neighboring regions both belonged to "the same family," so there was no point in conducting interviews in both countries. Fortunately, my theoretical hunch was validated when I found puzzling empirical differences in the nature of local reciprocity and citizenship in the two country cases that surprised village residents, local scholars, and national policymakers.

In this chapter, I suggest that while fully participatory research is not feasible for most scholars, political scientists could consider the potential utility of a more moderate consultative approach.[9] In the very beginning stages of developing a new study, political scientists could allow for time to consult with interested or affected individuals or communities on the specific questions that are considered to be most worth studying. In the later sections of the chapter, I will highlight strategies for how this collaboration might continue throughout the life of the research project.

For graduate students, this could begin with pre-dissertation visits to talk with and listen to individuals and communities who are knowledgeable about the proposed topic. While funding is difficult to obtain at any stage of a graduate student's career, pre-dissertation grants can be particularly scarce and competitive. Still, support for graduate students to engage in this initial discovery and consultation with potential subjects arguably has the greatest payoff in terms of the quality and significance of dissertations that were completed in a reasonable period of time. When I visited potential village fieldwork sites in Ghana and Côte d'Ivoire during a pre-dissertation trip, informal focus group discussions revealed what were experienced as the most important social welfare challenges at the local level. The local importance of these issues later helped ensure extraordinarily high participation rates in a rather lengthy survey interview that was at times physically and emotionally taxing for individual interview subjects.

Researchers at all stages of their careers also could include preliminary scoping of future research projects with small summer research grants. Even if qualitative methods are not to be included later in the study design, small focus groups and in-depth interviews using open-ended questions can reveal research questions that are meaningful, even urgent, to the relevant individuals and communities. Much like consulting the relevant published literature and initiating discussions with the academic scholars working on the particular research topic, political scientists should consider consulting relevant nonacademic individuals or communities to generate a list of hypotheses and rival explanations for the questions that seem most pressing. In addition to poring over the relevant academic scholarship to help identify the research question for my second book project, I observed meetings where American Indian tribal leaders and staff discussed their top priority problems among themselves. The addition of this informal input from the communities did not singularly determine the precise question or study design but did help me avoid an already over-researched topic, which would have made it exceedingly difficult to obtain formal research clearance for the project.

Hence, these initial consultations can not only expand our thinking and improve our research designs; they can also be the first step toward building the trust and rapport necessary to obtaining valid data from these same individuals and communities at a later stage in the study. While this participatory approach has not become popular in the mainstream of social science, it appears to have had an impact on funders. Many grant applications, including the National Science Foundation and Fulbright program, now require statements about who will benefit from the research and ask for partnerships with those who may benefit or can disseminate the knowledge gained.

The Power of Informed Consent

While participatory research approaches may be relatively unfamiliar territory for most political scientists, the power relationships involved in the process of obtaining informed consent are better known. Building on the previous section, however, I suggest a major rethinking of how power is involved. Informed consent is not just managing to persuade what are seen as obstructionist bureaucrats on the human subjects committees on our campuses to approve a form, or a one-shot interaction in the field where a less-skilled enumerator bullies a prospective respondent into answering the questions in a survey. Instead, political scientists must think much earlier and more broadly about how to create and communicate real benefits from our work for the affected individuals and communities.

Before beginning, it is critical to emphasize that universities are not the only ones with institutional review boards. Many organizations, communities, and nations have their own institutions that review and approve research studies. For instance, my study on the politics of American Indian health policy has to date required IRB approval from two universities, one federal agency, two regional areas of the same federal agency, and ten tribal nations (MacLean n.d.). Each of these IRBs has its own rules and procedures. The first step obviously is to make sure that the study is being reviewed by all the necessary IRBs in the most appropriate order.

Researchers also need to allow ample time for the IRB process. This is particularly true for projects involving multiple nonacademic IRBs (as above), as well as with collaborative projects where multiple investigators are working at several different academic institutions. Although university IRBs are often notorious on campuses for raising unnecessary hurdles, sometimes surmounting these obstacles requires a degree of advanced thinking and planning that is actually quite beneficial in the end. For example, it is useful for any researcher to think systematically about the subjects in her study population and in what ways they may or may not be vulnerable in the context of the study and in the wider community. Becker-Blease and Freyd (2006) make an essential point when they argue that the cost of *not* talking to vulnerable populations about sensitive issues such as poverty, violence, or abuse must be incorporated into the analysis of potentials risks and benefits too.

Much of the recent writing on informed consent focuses on whether subjects truly understand the information given to them about the research project. While many IRBs stress the need to convey information at a relatively low and thus more universally accessible grade level, Hochhauser (2005) emphasizes the sheer quantity of information given to subjects. He finds that most informed consent forms give too much detailed information, creating memory overload and the impossibility of truly informed consent. Cumming, Sahni, and McClelland (2006) emphasize how the power relationship must be shifted to a two-way flow of information to ensure participant understanding rather than a top-down delivery of information. This expands the power of the individual involved in the study from being a passive and subservient "subject" to an active participant in the process. Gold (2002) similarly emphasizes how study participants may not understand how their data may be used or become public, especially if it is part of a larger cross-national comparative project.

All of the above suggests that individuals might need more time than is typically granted to read and digest the information provided in the informed consent form. Rather than informed consent being seen as a perfunctory signature or nod of the head prior to beginning the "real work," researchers might give potential participants the form ahead of time, either delivering and discussing it in person, or, where possible, sending it earlier by mail, e-mail, or fax. Scholars also might incorporate active learning strategies from teaching, and use active questioning to inquire whether and how the participants have processed the information. Many researchers tend to rush through the actual process of informed consent because they fear the consequences of participant refusal or rejection. But rather than jeopardizing the study, allowing time for discussion and questions can actually strengthen the rigor of the data-collection process by building trust early.

For example, before starting an interview with a tribal staff person, I asked a question intending to probe whether the respondent understood the informed consent form. Instead, my query provoked several comments that exposed a deeper suspicion that my research design might be systematically biased toward a certain type of Indian tribe. The discussion that ensued was indispensable on two counts. First, I was able to explain more effectively the balance built into the study, which enhanced my credibility with the subject and the value of what the subject subsequently revealed in the interview. Second, although originally initiated as a *preamble* to the *real* interview, the preliminary discussion contained important substantive information about politics within Indian country that might not have been shared in response to my semi-structured list of questions.

Another strategy that can help individuals understand the process of informed consent more meaningfully is if the project has been introduced publicly to the salient broader community. In many developing countries, no individual-level interactions can proceed until a village or neighborhood-wide public meeting has been held where the researcher openly introduces the research team and the study objectives. Even after such a public meeting was followed by the village gong-gong beater passing "the news" at 5 a.m. in Ghana, my research team and I still had to dispel many myths and misunderstandings as we went door to door greeting and introducing ourselves (and mapping the village to do a sample). While this kind of face-to-face meeting may not always be logistically feasible in larger-scale or advanced industrialized contexts, there are often large public meetings organized for other purposes where a researcher may request the opportunity to make a brief introduction. For example, I have been invited to give formal PowerPoint presentations on my research at large intertribal meetings, as well as more informal updates at smaller tribal council and committee meetings. These introductions have stimulated deeper approval of the study from existing study participants as well as generated additional contacts with potential new participants.

Since discussions of informed consent often focus on the risks of participation in a study, scholars tend to talk less about the benefits. In the previous section, I argued that a more consultative approach to research would help promote research that would be of greater salience to participating individuals and communities. This is a way of fostering long-term benefits. But what about benefits to individual participants in the short term? Campus IRBs now often ask about compensation for research participants, but the topic is rarely, if ever, mentioned in the methodological literature in political science. Compensation is one of the most obvious ways that researchers have more power than their subjects and may create new inequalities through their actions. Even if researchers working in a poor, rural setting offer a small sachet of sugar or soap in return for the time spent in an interview, jealousies and tensions might be aroused between those individuals or communities selected to participate and those not chosen. Several researchers have described their success in taking photographs of participants as a gesture of appreciation or even as an object of discussion and component of the research (Chacko 2004; Deutsch 2004; Price 2001). In their more autobiographical work, Gottlieb and Graham (1994) discuss how they gave back to the village communities where Gottlieb had conducted long-term fieldwork by donating her book royalties toward a community development project.

Many researchers finesse this issue of compensation and simply do not consider it, arguing that it is financially impossible because of their limited resources. Yet there are nonmonetary means of thanking or giving back to your respondents that are important to examine. First, researchers often have expertise in their subject area and beyond that may be of value to the participants. Some researchers have tutored participants' children in English or other subjects. Others have shared information about government policies and regulations that is free and publicly available but often unknown in rural or remote areas. For example, I was able to tell many Ghanaian families about the availability of free social services for the elderly or indigent at the district hospital. Many researchers have also provided information about both the opportunities and constraints for traveling and studying abroad in the United States. In other contexts, an invitation for coffee or lunch or a handwritten thank-you note may be the most appropriate way of compensating a respondent.

Second, researchers can share personal information about themselves. This is one way of leveling the playing field with participants by allowing them to ask questions of the investigator. Again, political scientists need to be more conscious of their power in the process of conducting research. Sharing power by being open and responding, when appropriate, to personal or even sensitive questions can not only improve the human experience of research but also again improve the ultimate internal validity of the data collected. Finally, even for those studies that never bring the researcher face to face with an individual, researchers can spend time devising appropriate outreach and publicity such that the vague notions of the practical significance of the study findings become a reality.

The Power of a Researcher's Position in the Field

The interviewer's position of relative power in terms of information and expertise has already come up in the above discussion of informed consent. This section highlights how interviewers might consider their position vis-à-vis the study participants *throughout* the collection of data, and not just at the beginning, when it is time to obtain official consent for the interview, and then at the end, when it might be appropriate to give gifts in return.

Much of the seminal literature on positionality emerges from anthropology, critical theory, postcolonial studies, and feminist studies (Abu-Lughod 1993, 1991; Acker, Barry, and Esseveld 1999; Clifford and Marcus 1986; Harding 1991, 1986). Many academics in geography, history, sociology, nursing, medicine, and public health also have contributed to these theoretical debates, but political scientists have been noticeably less involved. Many of these authors were criticizing earlier work in their fields that did not recognize the social position of the author. They similarly problematize earlier claims to objectivity as "the God trick" or the "view from nowhere" (Haraway 1991). Their contention is that all knowledge production is subjective and shaped by the situational context of our personal characteristics (e.g., race, class, gender, ideology), background, and relationships with the participants being observed (Arendell 1997). The interviewer and the participants have different types and levels of power, and the way they negotiate those relationships shapes the data collected. A fair amount of the earlier work on positionality focused on how the social identity of the researcher doing fieldwork affected his or her status as an insider or outsider (Adler and Adler 1987; Horowitz 1986; Kreiger 1985; Thorne 1983). While the discussions were heated in the 1980s, they do not appear to have cooled down.

To begin, several scholars agree in recent work, that previous work on positionality was too narrowly focused on social identities of race, gender, and class; this work must be expanded and made more complex (Nagar et al. 2003). Gold (2002) advocates a broadening of position beyond the above social categories to include differences in worldview, religion, and morality. Future scholarship could examine how social identities intersect with other aspects of an interviewer's position, such as institutional affiliation, geopolitical membership, and material power. Becker, Boonzaier, and Owen (2005) and Dowling (2000) likewise stress the complexity of insider/outsider relations, since the researcher and the study participants all have multiple social identities.[10] For example, in Kenya, one study participant was simultaneously an alumnus who attended the very same American university for his doctoral degree; a Kenyan academic and teacher; and a small-business entrepreneur working in the industry under study. O'Connor (2004) and Abu-Lughod (1991) go even further when they emphasize how a researcher's identity is constantly shifting and being renegotiated during the process of research.

While the first wave of theorists writing on positionality (England 1994; Harding 1991) were calling for researchers to be reflexive about their own position in the process of conducting research, current scholars are pushing the debate further. They have argued that researchers simply need to do more than be transparently self-reflexive in a short statement of "who you are" in the write-up of the interview analysis.[11] Haney (1996) even argues in an appendix to her article that increased reflexivity is sometimes neither feasible nor desirable, precisely because her identity was always shifting.

Current scholars also criticize past suggestions to "study up" or conduct auto-ethnography of one's "own" cultural group or lived experience (Nader 1969). McCorkel and Myers (2003) find that it is impossible to erase one's positionality by studying those who are more powerful or by emphasizing what the researcher has in common with his or her own "peers." Indeed, many researchers find that they are acutely aware of the power differentials at play when they try to gain access to and then establish rapport with a high-level political elite with very little time for an academic interview. Power, privilege, and the social context cannot be so simply renounced. But if positionality cannot simply be avoided altogether, what should interview researchers do?

Several scholars suggest that a more collaborative approach would facilitate a closer and ongoing critical feedback on the researchers' position from the participants themselves (Chacko 2004; Khan 2005; McCorkel and Myers 2003; Nagar et al. 2003). This critical dialogue with the study participants can help to reveal the problems of difference and strengthen the shared explanations. Norton (2004a) emphasizes the explicit trade-offs to this narrowing of the distance between investigators and the research participants. Norton (84) writes, "Familiarity, experience and affection limit what one sees, but they also open what might remain concealed or unnoticed." Of course, it may not be feasible to establish much of a collaborative dialogue if the researcher has only twenty minutes for a onetime interview with the minister of finance of Argentina. On the other hand, even high-level elites sometimes enjoy the opportunity to talk repeatedly with a scholar about their perspective and experiences, and a certain collegial rapport can be built in small segments over a longer period of time. Regardless, by paying attention to the social context of the interview and revealing candidly in our writing the connections as well as differences in power between the interviewer and participants, scholars can establish a more rigorous subjectivity.[12]

In fact, social differences and even a status as an "outsider" can often smooth entrée into a community and enhance the quality of the interviews (Horowitz 1986; Tamale 1996). Village residents in Ghana, Côte d'Ivoire, and Kenya were often more inclined to sit down, think through and explain things that they usually took for granted because I was such an obvious outsider as a white, highly educated American woman. Through these interactions, we were essentially inverting the power differentials by acknowledging the subjects' superior expertise on the research topic. This acknowledgment of where respondents may have more expertise than the interviewer can be extended past the domain of the research study to other situations of everyday life. This happened frequently when

I accompanied men to their farms to learn how to plant cassava, or when I spent time with village women learning how to pound cassava roots into "foufou." A certain amount of cultural competence and knowledge is critical to gain a base level of trust, but often an outsider status facilitates open dialogue with multiple groups on various sides of a persistent conflict. The researcher's outsider status can even be viewed explicitly by historically hostile groups as an opportunity to share information indirectly and thus learn about each other's views with a hope of improving the relationship. This has been clearly articulated to me on numerous occasions as I interviewed officials from federal, state, and American Indian tribal governments in the United States.

Of course, it is important for political scientists to consider not only their own social position, but also the social position of all the research team members setting up or conducting interviews. The power and position of research assistants or enumerators also shape the nature of the interview data collected and the way events are interpreted in the field. Differences in social identity and power should be weighed in the selection of the research team and should be openly and extensively addressed in training. I found that my more highly educated, urban-based research assistants had difficulty according the power of informed consent (and, most importantly, refusal) to our potential respondents who were "just villagers." I also found out the hard way the complexity of insider/outsider status for my assistants. In Ghana, a young village woman accused one of my research assistants of shrinking her breasts. This was an extremely dangerous accusation to level, as genital-shrinking incidents in other towns had recently led to vigilante violence and ultimately the death of the accused. The accusation was quickly retracted, but it was clear from the events that this research assistant, although Ghanaian, was viewed as a stranger. In later rounds of fieldwork, I chose research assistants who were born in the region and were recognized as belonging to "local" ethnic groups but who had no immediate family connections in the sampled village.

Finally, this ongoing attention to power and positionality during interview research can be accomplished regardless of the particular type of interview structure chosen by the scholar—whether highly structured with an ordered list of close-ended questions, or more loosely conversational following the study participant's lead with open-ended queries. Every scholar has his or her own unique epistemological approach to studying a particular research question, meaning that every scholar will have different concepts of the objectives and most appropriate format for each interview. Even within a singular research project, one scholar may see the use for multiple interview types in order to access different sorts of evidence from a variety of participants. Nevertheless, the recognition of the existence of the power dynamics that surround any interview type can be valuable for all approaches to research. Indeed, this attention to power during any interview can help researchers identify additional questions to pose, additional people to interview, and/or new types of methods to employ in order to enrich their understanding of the complexity of the politics they study.

The Power of Authorship

While much of the writing outside of political science initially focused on the importance of power and position of researchers while conducting interviews in the field, scholars now emphasize how important it is to consider power relationships during the later stages of analysis and writing (Charmaz and Mitchell 1997; Kreiger 1985; Radcliffe 1994). As in the earlier stages, researchers are encouraged to be self-reflexive about how power might shape the interpretation of data and presentation of the findings (Denzin 1994). This might be particularly important when analyzing qualitative data, since the boundaries between the stages of data collection, interpretation, and writing are often blurred in the act of writing field notes or summaries of interviews. This nonlinear blurring of the stages of research continues for qualitative researchers when they return home to write and are rereading, reexperiencing, and reinterpreting information provided in interviews in the field (Barz 1997).

Importantly, it is not only critical theorists who insist on leveling the power relationships between the researcher and the subjects during this later analytic stage. Many American Indian / Alaska Native tribal governments assert that their communities have the power to oversee data interpretation as well as the dissemination of results. These tribal nations, often in collaboration with intertribal organizations, are setting the parameters for how future research will be conducted in Indian communities (American Indian Law Center 1999; AIATSIS 2000; Caldwell et al. 2005; Macauley et al. 1998; Mihesuah 1993).[13] Hence, researchers approved by tribal IRBs submit their draft presentations and writing for tribal approval prior to the study findings being made public. Many tribal communities also are making research clearance conditional on the agreement that the tribe—not the researcher—owns the interview data.

Again, power in the process of authorship has not been addressed systematically in the political science literature. As we have seen, political scientists have tended to adopt a more authoritative model of conducting research—from the formulation of the research design, conceptualization of informed consent, collection of interview data, and now, the interpretation and writing up of the findings. Many graduate students, new to the discipline, talk about the solitary and often lonely aspect of the write-up of their dissertation research. Others appreciate the autonomy and are delighted that "you can write up anywhere"; all you need is your data and your laptop. When it comes to the later stages of interpretation and writing, political scientists might discuss their thoughts with a small number of coauthors or academic colleagues but do not usually consider the analytic viewpoints of their interview respondents.

The literature on authorship from other disciplines is valuable in highlighting several additional strategies for political scientists to consider adopting in the future. First, political scientists could allow time to begin interpreting and writing up from their interview data in the context of their fieldwork sites. In particular, political scientists might investigate whether there are ways to share the analysis and writing, even if preliminary and imperfect, with the individuals and communities who participated in the interviews.[14] Providing interview subjects an opportunity to interpret and react to your analysis before the article or book is published can be intimidating precisely because it is sharing power with subjects in a way that has not usually been done in the past. It is important to note here that this more consultative approach and discussion of results prior to publication do not imply that the investigator has been co-opted and lost all ability to critique. Similarly, this collaboration is also not a strategic game to manipulate or coerce study participants. Schram makes this point when he advocates maintaining "a powerful critical connectedness."[15]

Furthermore, if a study participant disagrees with the researcher's interpretation, it does not necessarily mean that the project was a failure. Scholars may be able to include these other "voices" in their text by using attributive tags, or, when the interview participant wishes to remain anonymous, broad descriptions of the types of people or communities who presented these views. Again, this does not mean that the researcher relinquishes all power, and that his or her findings are entirely politicized by the subject individuals or communities. In contrast, this discussion can provide the researcher with an additional opportunity to learn about multiple perspectives on the same question—what a more positivist researcher might term triangulation, and a more interpretivist researcher would likely describe as attending to the social construction of knowledge. At last, the final product could benefit from a candid acknowledgment of how researcher and subject interpretations of the same event were in tension or conflict.

Power also must be considered when it comes time for outreach and the communication of study findings. Researchers have often been criticized for taking their data and running; the researcher may get promoted for publishing the results in what the community may view as an arcane and unreadable venue, and the community gets nothing (Mihesuah 1993). Subsequent researchers who then attempt to do more work with these communities often find that the door is shut and locked. Even in remote parts of rural Africa, some communities are protest-ing the lack of follow-through from previous generations of scholars.

I advocate a more consultative approach where participating individuals and communities are asked about appropriate outreach and follow-up. In addition to disciplinary journals and academic presses, researchers may be able to present information in a more concise and accessible format to local people, community groups, or other relevant organizations. In some cases, local communities can identify websites where findings may be posted more accessibly or may be dis-tributed via e-mail to interested subscribers.

The above proposed strategies may be particularly challenging to implement for graduate students and young faculty who frequently lack professional status, are sometimes gaining their personal confidence, and usually feel pressed for time. But the process can be navigated with ongoing dialogue between the re-searcher and subject communities about their mutual expectations and responsi-bilities. Finally, the above strategies also must be carefully implemented by all scholars in order to ensure the level of confidentiality promised to the individu-als, organizations, and communities participating in the research project. This is a particularly acute and even dangerous issue for scholars working in conflict zones (Wood 2006; see also Reno, this volume, chapter 8). Of course, extreme care should be paid to protecting subjects in preliminary and final professional publications as well as more informal and personal communications or blogs. Again, the theme of the potential value, under certain conditions, of a moder-ately consultative approach to political science research is reinforced.

On the basis of a review of the relevant literature emanating largely from other disciplines, I conclude that power plays a significant role, from beginning to end, in the process of conducting interview research. In each of the above four sec-tions, I have suggested how power shapes our overall approach to research; whether and how individuals consent to participate in an interview; the nature of the interview data we collect; and how we interpret, write up, and disseminate our findings. The concerns emphasized here have been hotly debated in other disciplines and by a minority of scholars within political science for years. This chapter's objective is to bring some of these important methodological insights into the mainstream of political science for those who are conducting interview research.

Throughout the chapter, I have identified strategies that political scientists might use in their interview research. I term these strategies, taken together, as a more "rigorous subjectivity." I argue that greater reflexivity as to the way power shapes our research will actually increase the internal validity of our data collection, interpretation, and presentation. While the issues surrounding informed consent and positionality in the field might seem most obviously useful for those qualitative and quantitative researchers who collect their own primary data, the core issues at hand should still be considered by those researchers using existing data sources. Even if the investigator does not personally have to face the above issues of power, they were unquestionably at play during the collection of the data set and merit consideration. The other issues raised regarding participatory research approaches in research design, analysis, writing, and outreach are all equally relevant whether scholars do all their own interviewing on a remote island in Indonesia, or are able to download their data with a few quick keystrokes at home.

Political scientists spend a lot of their energy theorizing about power and its consequences in every realm of life. In particular, we concentrate many of our efforts on understanding how various political systems can become more democratic. If we begin to consciously consider and reveal the power differences between ourselves and our interview subjects, we may not only improve the quality of our data collection and analysis but also invigorate our own everyday lives and research communities with a new level of democracy.

4

HOW TO REPORT INTERVIEW DATA

Erik Bleich and Robert Pekkanen

Interviews offer a potentially valuable yet often neglected or mistrusted source of evidence in the investigation of political phenomena. Readers may fear that the interviews were gathered from unrepresentative individuals and are thus biased, that the information gained through the interviews is inaccurate, or that the interviewer may distort the evidence through selective presentation undetectable by the readers. We believe that much of this mistrust can be alleviated if scholars follow the procedures we recommend below for reporting how interview evidence was gathered. We see these procedures as extremely helpful not only for researchers that rely primarily on interview data, but also for those—most likely the majority of our readers—who deploy interviews as one type of evidence in a multi-method research project. Our aim in this chapter is to create guidelines that will increase the rigor and transparency of the interviewing process and therefore enhance readers' confidence in interview data. This will encourage scholars to use interview evidence more frequently and systematically, enabling gains in knowledge by unfettering this stream of evidence.

Such a goal would be laudable at any time, but it is especially in tune with the recent burst of interest in qualitative methods.[1] Over the past several years,

For their comments and advice on earlier drafts the authors thank Layna Mosley, Andrea Arai, Ian Barrow, Rebecca Bennette, John Bowen, Henry Brady, Sara Curran, Robert Efird, John Gerring, Jennifer Hochschild, Sunila Kale, Diana Kapiszewski, Michèle Lamont, Tony Lucero, Ian Lustick, Julia Lynch, Andrew Moravcsik, Saadia Pekkanen, Michael Sheridan, David Stoll, Jessica Teets, and participants in the Middlebury College Political Science Department Faculty Research Group (FROG) and the University of Washington JSIS Writing Group.

scholars have reinvigorated the use of qualitative research, arguing that it has advantages over quantitative methods in many contexts. This renaissance is not just about redeeming qualitative methods, but also about improving them. It is perhaps inevitable that the uses of interview evidence should enter into discussion of this research program.[2] This volume itself reflects this development, as does work on qualitative data archiving spearheaded by Elman, Kapiszewski, and Vinuela (2010) and related arguments about standards for active citation (Moravcsik 2010).

After touching on the uses made of interview data in various research projects, we identify three key problems plaguing the reliability of interviews as a source of information in social science projects. We then suggest several concrete solutions to each of the problems. Finally, we detail how researchers can formulate an interview methods appendix and an interview methods table as tools that help communicate the reliability of information garnered through interviews.

The Uses of Interview Data

In establishing this connection between the new qualitative methods literature and interviews, Tansey (2007) compellingly argues that interviews make particularly good evidence for process-tracing research. However, we contend that interviews as a stream of evidence are generally compatible with most research goals. For example, Lynch (this volume, chapter 1) details the uses of interviews for preliminary research, the main focus of the research, part of multi-method research, as well as for "window dressing."[3]

All too often, interviews are utilized only in this tepid final category. There is no denying that a vivid quotation can enliven a scholarly article or memorably summarize an argument. We certainly do not advocate excising these with the effect of making scholarship *less* readable. However, we feel that scholars use interviews disproportionately as illustrations, not as evidence, because authors and readers alike are concerned that interview data may be less reliable than quantitative data or than written primary or secondary sources. The limitations of these other sources, and the problems of quantitative data reliability in particular, are widely acknowledged. Therefore, there is no reason that interviews cannot form a valuable, if also imperfect, source of systematic evidence for political scientists.[4] However, quoting from a single interview as an illustration while rigorously presenting statistical analyses does not equate to relying on both sources equally.

To highlight the parallels between different forms of evidence, it is useful to consider briefly the differences between surveys and interviews. In contrast to interviews, surveys are widely deployed as evidence not only by political scientists, but also by scholars from a variety of disciplines. Like interviews, surveys rely on information and responses gained from human informants. Gathering and assessing survey data involves many well-understood complications. Surveys respond to these challenges by reporting their methods in a manner that enables others to judge how much faith to place in the results. We believe that if similar criteria for reporting interview data were established, then interviews would join surveys as a more widely trusted source of evidence. After all, surveys can be thought of as a collection of short (and sometimes not so short) interviews. Surveys and interviews thus fall on a continuum, with trade-offs between large-n and small-n studies. Just as scholars stress the value of both types of studies depending on the goal of the researchers (Lieberman 2005), both highly structured survey research and semi- or unstructured small-n interviews, such as elite interviews, should have their place in the rigorous scholar's tool kit.[5]

Problems with Interview Data

We believe that the pervasive skittishness about the reliability of interview data stems from three fundamental challenges: representativeness of sample; type and quality of information obtained; and accuracy of reporting.

Representativeness of Sample

Authors who have conducted numerous interviews typically report some information about their interlocutors. They usually provide names and job titles, or mention the places and dates of the interviews, or both. Whenever an interviewee is quoted, this information appears as a citation, as is appropriate. At times, authors also summarize their interviews as a body. They may state that they interviewed sixteen NGO leaders, eight bureaucrats, and three local politicians. This kind of reporting serves the dual purpose of giving the reader a sense of the author's sources while also, perhaps, impressing the reader with the author's authoritativeness on the subject.

Such reporting, however, does not go far enough. This kind of reporting leaves us in the dark about nonresponse bias. Surveys always report response rates, because the higher the response rate, the more valid the survey results are generally perceived to be. Such nonresponse bias might also skew results in the interviewing process. In a set of interviews about attitudes toward the government, for example, those who decline to participate in the survey might do so because of a trait that would lead them to give a particular type of response to the interviewer's questions, either systematically positive or negative. If so, then we would be draw-ing inferences from our conducted interviews that would be inaccurate, because we would be excluding a set of interviewees that mattered a great deal to the reli-ability of our findings.

Currently, we have no way to assess response rates or possible nonresponse bias in interviews; the standard process involves reporting who was interviewed, but not whom the author failed to reach, or who declined an interview. Even more troubling, some common sampling techniques can easily exacerbate biased results. For example, the "snowball" technique refers to the process of seeking additional interview leads from one's interviewees (also see Martin, this volume). In an environment where interviews can be hard to come by (say, United States senators), the technique has an obvious attraction. Important actors approached with a referral in hand are more likely to agree to an interview request than those targeted through "cold calls." In addition, if the original interviewee was a good source, then she is likely to refer the researcher to another knowledgeable person. All in all, snowball sampling has much to commend it as a technique.

Yet, one danger with this strategy is that researchers become trapped within a network of interlinked respondents who see the world through the same lens. Snowball sampling clearly introduces the possibility of bias, because the original interviewee and subsequent contacts may share similar views on the subject of the interview.[6] This could involve deliberate manipulation by sophisticated po-litical actors, but it need not. For example, in researching a controversial policy decision, an author may be steered toward interviewees who all agree that the right decision was made, simply because those are the only people that the initial interviewee (and the source of the snowball referrals) feels are "worth" talking to—because anyone who really understands the issue would have to agree with the decision, and so anyone who disagrees obviously does not understand it and is not worth talking to. After interacting with a number of bureaucrats, politi-cians, and interest groups linked through the snowball technique, the researcher could conclude that she has reached a well-rounded consensus view on the issue at hand. In actual fieldwork, researchers can mitigate these problems by selecting initial interviewees from a wide variety of backgrounds and by being attentive to the perils of relying too heavily on information obtained from one person's re-ferrals. An important point for us is that when snowball sampling is used to generate some or all interviews, and the "snowballed" interviews are not indi-cated in any way, readers are left without valuable information needed to enable them to assess the reliability of the interview data.

Type and Quality of Information Obtained

The second problem is that the interviews might not have produced accurate information, regardless of how many or what variety were conducted. This could happen for a variety of reasons. Interviewees might not transmit accurate information, perhaps because they are ill informed or because they are intentionally deceiving the interviewer to bolster their reputation or for other purposes. For example, one of the authors of this article conducted an interview with a former prime minister upon referral by a senior journalist. The author opened his questions with a query about the role of factions within the prime minister's party, to which the politician replied that factions simply did not exist. It may have been the case that the senior journalist's presence in the interview inhibited this politician from speaking frankly, or perhaps he simply could not be bothered to tell the truth (it is extremely unlikely that he believed what he said). This meant that the interview data were of extremely low quality, and in fact the author chose not to incorporate the data in the results of his research.[7] In other cases, of course, interviewees say things that are quite surprising, against their own interests, and very credible. Both the authors have been told things in interviews that would, if made public, result in the firing of the speaker, or in the near certain loss of office by the politician who confided in the author.[8]

On the other side of the equation, the interviewer might not be skillful enough to ask the right questions or to understand what was being communicated, might deliberately misinterpret the information communicated and thus falsely use it as evidence, or might unintentionally misconstrue the interview data, perhaps because of subconscious biases. In one author's experience, his interpretation of a key interview differed dramatically from that of a second scholar who was also present. After lengthy discussion it became apparent that the other scholar had not fully grasped the subtleties of the statements because of imperfect fluency in the language in which the interview was conducted.[9] The point here is not to highlight linguistic competence, but rather the perils of inaccurate reporting. If the other academic had cited these interviews, suitably anonymized, in a publication, readers would have no way of knowing that this account was based on a complete misunderstanding of the interview.

These types of challenges give rise to well-founded concerns. Readers may harbor serious doubts about the quality and reliability of data gleaned from interviews. Just as with the problems associated with quantitative studies, these misgivings can never be totally overcome. Yet, just as in quantitative studies, we can think of them as the "measurement error" of the process of collecting information or data through interviews. Viewed in this light, they are not insurmountable problems, but rather garden-variety challenges to which scholars must develop the most compelling solutions possible.

Accuracy of Reporting

The third problem arises when authors selectively report interview data in a way that generates or reflects a particular bias. Anyone who has ever read a full movie review, then seen a few glowing words quoted out of context on an advertisement for that movie, is aware of this phenomenon. The interviewer could choose the few quotations that illustrate her points, using the evidence to support her argument. Processes of cognition also influence researchers to weigh interpretations provided at the beginning of the interview process more heavily as compared to those provided at the end, and to seek out and convey evidence in support of their argument over disconfirming evidence.

Along with the problems of gauging the quality of data obtained, there are thus parallel problems with assessing what data (out of all data gathered) is reported. Without access to the complete set of interview data, we cannot tell if the spicy quote from the Italian Foreign Ministry official represents the consensus opinion in the government, or is the ranting of a lone crackpot which happens to be well suited to illustrate the author's arguments. Because of the tendency to credit quotes that agree with our own understandings of the situation, this kind of selective reporting is likely to creep into the research even of conscientious scholars. Because there is typically no way for the reader to know the full content of the interviews, it is virtually impossible to judge the accuracy or representativeness of the statements conveyed by the researcher.

These three problems shortchange us all, because they limit the potential contribution to our understanding of political phenomena that may be derived from interview data. When we lack important information about the evidence, we cannot have adequate faith in interview data.

Solutions

Qualitative social scientists can benefit from a common set of standards for reporting the reliability of their data so that readers and reviewers can judge the value of their evidence. As with quantitative work, it is impossible for qualitative researchers to achieve complete reliability. But producers and consumers of qualitative scholarship profit from being more conscious about the methodology of interviewing and from being explicit about reporting uncertainty. This increases the value of interviews in social scientific research, elevating them from the status of supplementary information or simple adornments to that of widely accepted evidence that can contribute to developing and testing causal theories.

Representativeness of Sample

For any research that relies on interview data as a significant component of theory development or testing, it is important to move toward systematic sampling (Lynch, chapter 1). For some projects, especially those that attempt to gauge the general views of a broad population, systematic sampling will entail random samples of business leaders, bureaucrats, or politicians (Aberbach, Putnam, and Rockman 1981; Martin and Swank 2004). In the types of interviews we focus on, generally related to particular policy or political decisions, there is typically a narrower population of relevant actors, and random sampling is not likely to be the most appropriate or efficient methodology.[10]

Yet it is often possible for the researcher to identify a theoretically motivated set of target interviewees prior to going into the field. Doing this in advance of the interviews, and then reporting interviews successfully obtained, those refused, and those where the interviewee never responded, has many benefits. For one, this kind of self-conscious attention to the sample frame allows researchers to hone their research design before they enter the field. After identifying the relevant population of actors involved in a process, researchers can focus on the different classes of actors within the general population—such as politicians, their aides, civil servants from all relevant bureaucracies, NGOs, knowledgeable scholars and journalists, and different types within the classes—progressive and conservative politicians, umbrella and activist NGOs, for instance. Drawing on all classes and types of actors relevant to the research project helps ensure that researchers receive balanced information from a wide variety of perspectives. When researchers populate a sample frame from a list created by others, the source should be reported—whether that list is of sitting parliamentarians or business leaders (perhaps drawn from a professional association membership, as Martin describes in chapter 5).

Reporting the sample frame is a vital first step, but it is equally important to report the number of interviews sought within the sample frame, the number obtained, and the number declined or unavailable. This process allows readers to better assess the evidence the author has gathered. Knowing that the author set out to interview ten people, including three politicians, three bureaucrats, and four NGO leaders, but only succeeded in talking to three NGO leaders and one bureaucrat will suggest that a certain type of information may be systematically absent from the analysis. It also gives readers more confidence in the evidence that is presented. Reporting the nonresponse rate encourages researchers to think carefully about bias and to devise strategies to compensate for potential biases. It also allows readers to assess the researchers' strategies.

Of course, any experienced field researcher knows that the ideal list of interviewees can change dramatically in the field. For example, a rival political party can be discerned working actively behind the scenes, and the field researcher from the example above now needs to add two more politician interviews. Or, one of the bureaucrats interviewed advises that the key person within the bureaucracy is not on the interviewees list. Researchers should always ask interviewees for recommendations for additional interview subjects. This snowball sampling technique can effectively reveal networks or key actors previously unknown to the researcher, thereby expanding the sample frame. We do not advocate eschewing these interviews because they were not on the original list. But we do argue that the researcher should report these developments to readers and expand the sample frame accordingly.

What is most useful, however, is not simply reporting that the researcher engaged in snowball sampling. Rather, the crucial element is reaching the point of saturation in the interview process. At saturation, each new interview within and across networks reveals no new information about a political or policymaking process (Guest, Bunce, and Johnson 2006).[11] If respondents are restating the same causal process as previous interviewees, if there is agreement across networks (or predictable disagreement), and if recommendations for further interviewees mirror the list of people the researcher has already interviewed, then researchers have reached the point of saturation. Researchers must report that they reached saturation to convey to readers that they have exhausted the relevant information to be gained from interviews. Over time, reporting sample frames and interview results will allow scholars to learn from each other's methods (and not just from each other's findings) and arrive at superior interview and qualitative methodology.

Type and Quality of Information Obtained

In our experience, the type and quality of information obtained in interviews can vary dramatically. Some "interviews" consist of two minutes of an influential politician's walking time between meetings, which reveals little or no useful information. Other interviews may consist of multiple conversations with key bureaucrats during which they take the interviewer through the intricacies of complex policy decisions and disclose previously unpublished details that cast the decision-making process in an entirely new light. Some interviews are on the record, others are off the record, and still others are on background. Sometimes interviewers use recording devices or take notes while the interview is in progress; other times they run to the nearest park bench after the event to empty the contents of their memories into their notebooks.

Researchers also deploy a plethora of strategies for obtaining information from their subjects. They may conduct structured, semi-structured, or unstructured interviews, which range from asking each interviewee a predetermined and consistent set of questions, to simply letting the conversation go where the interviewee takes it.[12] They may obtain interviews through the equivalent of academic cold calls or by ingratiating themselves with the interviewees' colleagues or even family members. They may ask key questions out of the blue to get an honest and unguarded reaction, or they may prime the respondent by giving the context for the question and perhaps even some other key players' previous responses.

How a researcher obtains the interview, how long that interview lasts, the quality and methodology behind the questions asked, whether the interview is on or off the record, whether it is recorded or not, and a host of other factors can deeply influence the quality of the information obtained from interviewees. There are excellent resources that point researchers toward best practices for conducting interviews (Berry 2002; also see this volume). For us, the most important thing a scholar can do is report about the nature of the interviews he or she conducted. Of course, a full description of all these elements for each interview would be time and space consuming. But it helps a great deal if researchers are explicit about key interviewing techniques, such as how the researcher created a record of the interview—through live recording, simultaneous note-taking, or post-event note-taking (and the delay between the interview and the note-taking)—whether interviews were structured, semi-structured, or unstructured; and the length of interviews, especially when the researcher relies on them for critical observations or elements of the analysis.

Absent a video recording (which may be possible in some limited circumstances) or complete transcript of each interview, there is no way for outsiders to assess the quality of the interaction. To that extent, observers must have a degree of trust in the integrity and skills of the interviewer, just as they must trust the capacity of quantitative researchers to accurately code variables and faithfully report results without engaging in data mining. But just as with quantitative projects, observers can be more confident of the process and of the reliability of the results if researchers share as much information about the interview process as possible.

Accuracy of Reporting

Once researchers have conveyed to readers that they have drawn a valid sample and have conducted the interviews in a serious and thoughtful way, they face the task of convincing observers that their reports based on the material reflect the reality of the situation. One simple solution to this dilemma is to post full interview transcripts on a website, so that the curious and the intrepid can verify the data themselves. This ideal standard of qualitative data archiving should be the discipline's goal, and we are not alone in arguing that it should move in this direction (Elman, Kapiszewski, and Vinuela 2010; Moravcsik 2010).

At the same time, however, we fully recognize that it is impractical and even impossible in many cases. It would take significant time and money to transcribe every word of every recorded interview—these are resources most researchers simply do not have. Even if such resources were available, interviews are often granted based on assurances of confidentiality, or are subject to constraints imposed by human subjects research, raising not only practical but also legal and ethical issues (Parry and Mauthner 2004). And, of course, the vast majority of interviews are not recorded at all.[13] These facts inherently constrain the reliability of interview data, but the limitations are not necessarily more severe than analogous problems that plague survey research or data set coding.

Even without providing transcripts, it is possible to communicate the accuracy of reported interview data in a rigorous manner. In many scenarios, the researcher aims to convey that the vast majority of interviewees agree on a particular point. Environmental lobbyists may judge a conservative government unsympathetic to their aims, or actors from across the political spectrum may agree on the importance of civil society groups in contributing to neighborhood policing. Rather than simply reporting this general and vague sentiment, in most instances it is possible to summarize the number of lobbyists expressing this position as a percentage of the total lobbyists interviewed and as a percentage of the lobbyists specifically asked or who spontaneously volunteered their opinion on the government's policy. Similarly, how many policymakers and politicians were interviewed, and what percentage expressed their enthusiasm for civil society groups? This is easiest to convey if the researcher has gone through the process of coding interviews, which is common in some subfields of political science.[14] It is more difficult to present this information if scholars have not systematically coded their interviews; but in these circumstances, it is all the more important to convey a sense of the representativeness of the information cited or quoted.

When quoting an interviewee, researchers are particularly open to the charge that they have simply cherry-picked the most eye-catching statement without regard to its representativeness. To convince readers that such lines are more than a mere adornment to the text, it is vital to communicate whether the quotation represents the average intensity and direction of the response, or whether it distills the most extreme form of reproach or approval. If it is the latter, how many interviewees expressed equivalent intensity in their sentiments? Was that intensity particularly important as a motivating factor for explaining the actions of key players in the policy debate, even if those players were a numerical minority? In other words, researchers can explicitly convey the meaning of a quotation by addressing its representativeness and the salience of the underlying sentiment for particular actors.

If a researcher's sample frame is sound, if saturation is reached, and if all respondents answer in same way, we can be relatively certain that the responses have yielded accurate information. But the confluence of these happy circumstances is rare. More often, the sample is incomplete in one or more ways: some people cannot recall key points, others' memories may be inaccurate, or interested parties may misstate facts for private gain. In cases where the interview process is imperfect (in other words, in virtually all real-world cases), it is imperative to report the resulting uncertainty. What percentage of core interviewees were unavailable? How many were unable to answer key questions? What is the range of dissonance among actors over a key point?

These issues are particularly pressing if the goal is to uncover a historical turning point through a process-tracing methodology, such as if a researcher is exploring the genesis of the Iran-contra affair. But they are also central to interview research about less clandestine or event-specific topics, such as if a scholar is focused on the comparative role of doctors in health care reform in advanced democracies. If statements by doctors, policymakers, and other knowledgeable observers suggest disagreement over the relative influence of physicians' associations on policy reform, it is crucial for the researcher to convey this uncertainty.

Once the divergence in opinion is clear, researchers can be explicit about their rationale for trusting some interviews over others and for drawing overall conclusions. There are several common tools and techniques for doing this.[15] In general, evidence drawn from multiple segments of the sample frame is likely to be more reliable than evidence from one part of the sample frame, particularly if a narrow group is arguing for its own significance in the process. For example, if most leaders of doctors' associations assert their groups' importance in the policy process, but if some concur with the vast majority of interviewees from the insurance industry, the pharmaceutical industry, hospitals, and policymakers that physicians' associations were relatively powerless in the process, the latter interpretation is clearly the more credible. In a related manner, information reported against one's interest is almost always more reliable than reports that serve to puff up a particular individual or group.[16] Politicians typically seek credit for good outcomes and try to avoid blame for bad ones. If sitting politicians grant credit for important measures to others—particularly to members of an opposing party—or accept blame when there is nothing to be gained, their statements gain a great deal of credibility.

Beyond reporting the basis for trusting some interviews over others, it is useful to remember that very few studies rely exclusively on interview data for their conclusions. While other types of sources have their own weaknesses, when interview evidence is ambiguous or not dispositive, scholars can fruitfully triangulate with other sources to resolve ambiguities in the record. Perhaps no method of reporting will fully convince skeptics about the accuracy of information gathered through interviews. But strategies such as those suggested here will make evenhanded readers more certain about the reliability of the interview data when judging the rigor of the scholarship and the persuasiveness of the argument.

Forming an Interview Methods Appendix

Keeping in mind these general principles for overcoming some of the most serious challenges to interview reliability, how can researchers quickly and efficiently communicate that they have done their utmost to engage in methodologically rigorous interviewing techniques? We propose the inclusion of an "Interview Methods Appendix" that can be included in any book that relies heavily on interviews. The Interview Methods Appendix can contain a brief discussion of key methodological issues and large amounts of relevant data summarized in an Interview Methods Table. Elements of the Appendix can also be incorporated into articles where space constraints are typically more severe. This is possible in an abbreviated version that follows the main text; or some central elements may be woven into the methodology section of the article itself or—in order to avoid space constraints—as a web link to a full version of the appendix (Moravcsik 2010).

The easiest way to report interview methodology is to break it down into several distinct sections. To illustrate the usefulness of the Interview Methods Appendix and the Interview Methods Table, we use the hypothetical example of a study that explores an attempted ban of the far-right-wing National Democratic Party (NPD) in Germany.

Sample Frame

Report the universe of actors relevant to the study, broken down by subsets to demonstrate a sample frame that draws on a variety of networks and perspectives based on theoretically motivated considerations. In most cases, the author will choose to discuss the construction of the sample frame in the text, especially if interview data are central to her arguments. Even if discussed at length in the text, a short summary of her rationale should appear in the Appendix, perhaps a paragraph or so long. If the sample frame construction is discussed only in the Appendix, the discussion should be more extensive.

We believe that explicit reporting of the interview sample frame will improve readers' confidence in the results, by displaying the interviewer's sources openly. An additional benefit may be through encouraging the interviewer to pay more attention to sampling strategies.

> Example: Interviewees were divided into categories based on their occupations, with particular attention to political divergence within categories of politicians, since they were central to the decision to launch the ban attempt. We sought a diversity of actors from across different levels of the state—politicians, courts, and bureaucrats—and nonstate observers of and participants in the process. See the Interview Methods Table for the breakdown of the categories.

Response Rate and Type

Report the number of interviews sought, obtained, and declined, across each relevant subset from the original sample frame. This kind of information is so often lacking, even in scholarship that relies extensively on interviews, yet it needs to be reported in order for readers to judge the reliability of the interview data. The author should provide full information about her attempts to gain interview access. This means distinguishing reports of requests that were refused, merely ignored, or agreed to but then later canceled or refused or simply not scheduled. It is best to err on the side of providing more information in reporting these results. It is also important to note whether the interviews were conducted in person, by phone, by e-mail, or by some other method. See the Interview Methods Table for examples.

Additional and "Snowball" Interviews

Researchers may add interviews without using snowball sampling if they are unable to get information from respondents from a particular category of the sample frame. For example, if a researcher were unable to obtain an interview with her first choice Constitutional Court judge, she may seek an interview with a second judge as a substitute.

The author should distinguish interviews obtained from "snowball" techniques in two ways. First, the interviewer should report an introduction even if the "snowballed" interview falls within the sample frame. From our example, assume that after her first interview with a party politician, a researcher receives an introduction to a second mainstream party politician that was already in our researcher's initial sample frame. The second mainstream party politician interview should be listed as part of the sample, but the researcher should also report the connection between the first interviewee and the second interviewee. That way, readers can assess any potential for bias.

It is also possible, however, that snowball sampling may lead the researcher to add interviews beyond the originally specified target group, typically because saturation has not been reached, or because one of the original interviews was very poor quality, or perhaps because the author realized that a player previously perceived as minor was in fact central to decision-making and merited an interview. It could also be that the author felt obliged to conduct an additional interview because one of her sample frame interviews insisted she talk to someone else. No matter the reason, these "snowball" interviews should be reported as such. The appropriate manner to report this would be in the "Source" column in the Interview Methods Table (see tables 4.1 and 4.2).

Saturation

Report that saturation has been reached within and across categories, and any residual uncertainty. Researchers may or may not pursue saturation strategies depending on the goals of the research. Even if they do not, it is valuable to know whether saturation has been achieved. If it has, then we are more confident that additional interviews would not have altered the researcher's conclusions.

> Example: Saturation reached among and across all categories, with the exception of Far Right party politicians and lawyers, and Constitutional Court judges.

Format and Length of Interviews

Report the type and length of interviews. Because the broad terms "semi-structured" or "structured" include wide variation in practice, a footnote at the bottom of the table should clarify what they mean for the research project at hand. Many researchers prepare a list of questions and sub-questions to ask in advance of the interviews. These sometimes are altered or updated throughout the course of the field research. Unless some other considerations preclude it, the author should provide a set of the interview questions for "semi-structured" or "structured" interviews.

> Example: Semi-structured interviews in all cases but one, with three core questions: (1) What were the motives in trying to ban the NPD?

(2) Why did the attempted ban fail? (3) What were the consequences of the failed attempt to ban the NPD? There was also allowance for the interviewees to raise additional issues or comments. The exception was a structured e-mail interview in which the above three questions were posed, with an open-ended fourth question asking for further reflections on the topic.

Recording Method[17]

Report whether the interviews were video- or tape-recorded, whether the interviewer took notes during the interview, or whether the interviewer summarized the interview afterward.

> Example: Most interviews involved written notes during the interview and were supplemented by extensions on those notes immediately following the end of the interview. In those cases, quotations are the best recollection of the precise phrases used rather than guaranteed verbatim reproductions.

Although for the purposes of clarity and illustration we have summarized some information in points 1 through 6 above, much of this can be easily contained in an interview methods table. In some cases, the interview methods table will have to include additional explication in notes at the bottom of the table or in footnotes. See Table 4.1 for an example of an extended interview methods table.

In addition to the evidence presented in the interview methods table, at least two other kinds of information are needed for observers to gauge the reliability of findings based on interviews.

Response Rates and Consistency of Reported Opinions or Quotations

Report the response rates to any key questions or issues flagged in the text of the book or article. Report the representativeness of the opinions or quotations provided.

> Example: All respondents answered the three core questions listed under Format and Length. Eighty-five percent of interviewees concurred that the motives for the attempted ban were political, representing at least one person from each subset. Of the 15 percent who thought they

TABLE 4.1 Interview methods table

INTERVIEWEE	STATUS	SOURCE	SATURATION	FORMAT	LENGTH	RECORDING	TRANSCRIPT
Category 1			Yes				
CDU politician	Conducted in person 4/22/2004	Sample frame		Semi-structured	45 mins	Concurrent notes & supplementary notes w/i 1 hr	Confidentiality requested
SPD politician Hart	Conducted in person 4/22/2004	Sample frame and referred by CDU politician		Semi-structured	1 hr	Audio recording	Transcript posted
Green politician	Conducted in person 4/23/2004	Sample frame		Semi-structured	45 mins	Concurrent notes and supplementary notes w/i 1 hr	Confidentiality requested
FDP politician Weiss	Refused 2/18/2004	Sample frame					
Die Linke politician	No response	Sample frame					
SPD politician's aide	Conducted in person 4/26/2004	Referred by SPD politician Hart		Semi-structured	1 hr 15 mins	Audio recording	Confidentiality required
Category 2			No				
REP politician	No response	Sample frame					
DVU politician	No response	Sample frame					
NPD politician	Accepted 3/16/2004; then declined 4/20/2004	Sample frame					
NPD lawyer	Declined 4/20/2004	Sample frame					

(continued)

TABLE 4.1 (continued)

INTERVIEWEE	STATUS	SOURCE	SATURATION	FORMAT	LENGTH	RECORDING	TRANSCRIPT
Category 3			No				
Constitutional Court judge 1	No response	Sample frame					
Constitutional Court judge 2	No response	Substitute in sample frame					
Category 4			Yes				
Interior Ministry bureaucrat 1	Conducted in person 4/24/2004	Sample frame		Semi-structured	45 mins	Concurrent notes and supplementary notes w/i 1 hr	Confidentiality required
Interior Ministry bureaucrat 2	Conducted in person 4/24/2004	Sample frame		Semi-structured	45 mins	Concurrent notes & supplementary notes w/i 1 hr	Confidentiality required
Justice Ministry bureaucrat	Conducted via e-mail 4/30/2004	Referred by Interior Ministry bureaucrat 2		Structured	N/A	E-mail transcript	Confidentiality required
Category 5			Yes				
Constitutional law scholar Schwarz	Conducted by phone 4/18/2004	Sample frame		Semi-structured	45 mins	Concurrent notes and supplementary notes w/i 1 hr	Transcript posted
Constitutional law scholar Berg	Conducted in person 4/20/2004	Sample frame		Semi-structured	1 hr	Concurrent notes and supplementary notes w/i 1 hr	Transcript posted
Category 6			Yes				
Far Right scholar Hacker	Conducted in person 4/23/2004	Sample frame		Semi-structured	1 hr 10 mins	Concurrent notes and supplementary notes w/i 1 hr	Transcript posted

Interviewee	Contact	Sampling	Consent	Interview type	Duration	Recording	Transcript
Far Right scholar Meyer	Conducted in person 4/19/2004	Sample frame		Semi-structured	1 hr 30 mins	Concurrent notes and supplementary notes w/i 1 hr	Transcript posted
Far Right scholar 3	Not sought	Referred by Far Right scholar Hacker					
Category 7			Partial				
Expert journalist 1	Conducted by phone 4/17/2004	Sample frame		Semi-structured	55 mins	Concurrent notes and supplementary notes w/i 1 hr	Confidentiality requested
Expert journalist 2	No response	Sample frame					
Category 8			Yes				
Antifascist NGO leader Korn	Conducted in person 4/22/2004	Sample frame		Semi-structured	1 hr 10 mins	Audio recording	Redacted transcript posted
Antifascist NGO leader Knoblauch	Conducted in person 4/25/2004	Sample frame		Semi-structured	30 mins	Audio recording	Redacted transcript posted
Antifascist NGO leader 3	Not sought	Referred by Antifascist NGO leader Korn					
Anti-discrimination NGO leader Spitz	Conducted in person 4/29/2004	Referred by Antifascist NGO leader Korn and by Far Right scholar Meyer		Semi-structured	1 hr 30 mins	Audio recording	Transcript posted
Overall			High				See www.bleichpekkanen.transcripts

were problem-driven (i.e., a response to the objective rise of racism in German society), all came from the NGO sector, with one coming from the scholarly sector. The quotation from the SPD politician in the text is representative of the average response to this question among the 85 percent of interviewees who viewed the motives as political.

Confidence Levels and Compensation Strategies

Report concerns about uncertainty over particular points, explicit attempts made to reduce uncertainty, and any residual uncertainty.

> Example: Absent interviews with Far Right politicians, we devoted a portion of our interviews with scholars of Far Right political parties and with the expert journalist to ask their opinions of Far Right party perspectives on the attempted ban. Their direct contact with Far Right leaders allowed them to speak with moderate confidence about those views, increasing our certainty about the positions of the NPD in particular. Similarly, lacking interviews with Constitutional Court judges, we tracked down scholarly articles and previous court opinions about Far Right parties by key judges. In both these cases, our certainty about their perspectives cannot be complete, but we are confident that the missing information does not inordinately bias our findings given the convergence of information and saturation obtained from other sources.

The discussion we have provided above applies most directly to researchers who use interviews as an integral part of their information gathering. Yet most scholars use interviews as only one source of information among many, and some use interviews quite sparingly as a way to supplement information gathered from written material. In these cases, the interview methods appendix and interview methods table can easily be adapted. For example, it may be that a researcher conducting a similar study had access to previous work that included internal political party documents revealing strategies and approaches to the attempted ban of the NPD, credible investigative journalism that uncovered the attitudes of Constitutional Court judges, book-length assessments of the topic from expert journalists, constitutional scholars, and Far Right, scholars and multiple policy statements of NGOs that participated in the process.

Supplementing this extensive record with additional interviews from categories 1–3 and 5–8 may be extremely useful. But it may not be necessary. Here, the scholar can discuss her sample frame and note that saturation has been achieved

TABLE 4.2 Interview methods table

INTERVIEWEE	STATUS	SOURCE	SATURATION	FORMAT	LENGTH	RECORDING	TRANSCRIPT
Category 4			Yes				
Interior Ministry bureaucrat 1	Conducted in person 4/24/2004	Sample frame		Semi-structured	45 mins	Concurrent notes and supplementary notes w/i 1 hr	Confidentiality required
Interior Ministry bureaucrat 2		Sample frame		Semi-structured	45 mins	Concurrent notes and supplementary notes w/i 1 hr	Confidentiality required
Justice Ministry bureaucrat	Conducted via e-mail 4/30/2004	Referred by Interior Ministry bureaucrat 2		Structured	N/A	E-mail transcript	Confidentiality required
Overall			High				See www .bleichpekkanen .transcripts

from written sources across all but one category. The interview methods table would then serve to demonstrate the type, character, and extensiveness of the limited set of interviews that were conducted, as well as to highlight the rigor of the scholar's approach to using interviews as part of a well-planned research strategy. In this case, the table would look like Table 4.2.

We do not argue that interviews are the only or the best source of information. However, in line with the contentions of this volume, we think there are cases when interview data can contribute greatly—and perhaps uniquely—to research. This motivates our attempt to bolster the trustworthiness of interviews as a valued source of data. We certainly expect that most scholars will use other streams of evidence besides interviews—be it secondary sources or data analysis—to construct their arguments. In such mixed-methods approaches, the researcher can and should signal when sources besides interviews are used to gain information needed to round out the sample frame.

We recognize that legitimate concerns may force researchers to keep some details of the interview confidential and anonymous. We all must respect constraints imposed by institutional review boards, by informants themselves, or by professional ethics. In certain cases, the interview methods appendix may contain "confidentiality requested" and "confidentiality required" for every single interview. We do not seek to change prevailing practices that serve to protect interview subjects. However, we believe that even in such circumstances, the interviewer can safely report many elements in an interview methods appendix and interview methods table—to the benefit of researcher and reader alike. Whether or not scholars are at liberty to provide video recordings of every interview in an online "appendix" or through a qualitative data archive, they should still report elements such as their sample frame, nonresponse rates, format of interviews, use of snowball sampling, and confidence levels. A consistent set of expectations for reporting these will give readers more confidence in research based on interview data, which in turn will liberate researchers to employ this methodology more often and with greater rigor.

To the extent that researchers are able to provide transcripts of their interviews in online appendixes or qualitative data archives—perhaps following an initial embargo period standard among quantitative researchers for newly developed data sets, or for archivists protecting sensitive personal information[18]—there are potentially exponential gains to be made to the research community as a whole (Elman, Kapiszewski, and Vinuela 2010). Not only will this practice assure readers that information sought, obtained, and reported accurately conveys the reality of the political or policymaking process in question; it will also allow researchers in years to come access to essential interviews with key practitioners that would otherwise be lost to history. Imagine if in forty years a scholar could reexamine a pressing question not only in light of the written historical record, but also with your unique interview transcripts at hand. Carefully documenting interviewing processes and evidence will enhance our confidence that we truly understand political events in the present day and for decades to come.

Part 2

ADDRESSING THE CHALLENGES OF INTERVIEW RESEARCH

CRAFTING INTERVIEWS TO CAPTURE CAUSE AND EFFECT

Cathie Jo Martin

You don't have to eat the whole ox to know that the meat is tough.

Attributed to Samuel Johnson by Boswell

Research is the process of going up alleys to see if they are blind.

Marston Bates

The above quotations suggest very different methods of researching cause and effect. In the first, which is consistent with much of the positivist tradition, a phenomenon can be captured by the sum of its parts, and causal relations are likely to be fairly straightforward—tasting a morsel enables us to make judgments about the essence of the whole. In the second, and consistent with the interpretivist tradition, experience is more multifaceted, causal relations are less easily revealed, and investigators may go up blind alleys before grasping a map of the terrain. Good research often tries to incorporate both approaches, attempting to gather samples that reflect on characteristics of broader populations, even while struggling to ensure that the findings accurately interpret the complex meanings of actions or relationships between independent and dependent variables.

This chapter considers how an interview tool may be constructed to achieve multiple research goals—to help us simultaneously to make causal claims about broader populations or relationships among factors *and* to be sure that these claims reveal the underlying motivations of actors or experiential processes. Choices in research design are vitally important to the satisfactory attainment of research goals: drawing a sample, maximizing validity with well-chosen research questions, and interpreting interview responses all matter to our abilities

The author wishes to thank for their many helpful suggestions Layna Mosley, Cecilia Martinez-Gallardo, Tim Büthe, and the participants of the conference on Interview Research in Political Science, sponsored by Duke University and the University of Pennsylvania.

to draw generalized conclusions and to interpret the way the world works. The practical lessons in this chapter demonstrate how a well-designed interview tool may speak both to the positivist ambition to test hypotheses and to the social constructivist goal of interpreting accurately the meaning of actions or preferences. For example, one might develop an interview tool that links structured and open-ended questions; moreover, some interview questions may be used simultaneously for qualitative process tracing (causal process observation) and quantitative data (data-set observation).

This chapter contributes to the volume's goal of offering a "how to" manual for the interview method. But it also makes a broader contribution: I show how the interview format is perhaps uniquely equipped to bridge the gap between positivist and interpretivist concerns. Scholars often draw distinctions between those quantitative methods seeking to define the characteristics of a population or to identify the causal determinants of cross-unit comparisons, and those qualitative ones relying on rich description to reveal processes in a single case and "to develop valid measures of thick concepts" (Coppedge 1999, 468; also Gerring 2007; King, Keohane, and Verba 1994; J. Mahoney 2009). It is widely accepted that the interview method is terrific for theory building in exposing new avenues for future analysis, but the research presented here suggests that interviews also play an important role in theory testing, and in illustrating and bolstering the validity of findings derived from other sorts of analyses (see also, in this volume, Bleich and Pekkanen, Gallagher, Leech et al., and Lynch). The trick is to retain sufficient indeterminacy in the interview to allow for unanticipated insights, even while using interview data to test for findings obtained through quantitative statistical tests. In an ideal research world, one balances one's need for specific information with space for the stories, surprises, and synchronicity that an interview has to offer. I use my research choices to illustrate this balancing act.

A Mixed-Methods Research Design

The chapter draws from my research with Duane Swank, which resulted in many articles as well as *The Political Construction of Business Interests: Coordination, Growth and Equality* (Cambridge University Press, 2012). The central research goal of this project was to understand why employers sometimes support or even participate in the provision of social policies, and why these patterns of participation vary across nations. Although conventional wisdom suggests that employers would automatically reject any social spending that imposed costs on firms (through higher taxes, increased costs of production, or decreased profitability), "corporate liberals" sometimes favor social protections for workers, and calculate that the benefits of social programs contribute to the firms' bottom lines (Hall and Soskice 2001). Business support for social programs varies widely across both nations and firms; Swank and I set out to uncover the reasons for this variance.

Scholars have diverse views of employers' attitudes toward the welfare state. Some assume that employers will reject all forms of social spending; therefore, large welfare states only develop when business opposition is countered by strong countervailing forces such as labor unions. Others believe that employers sometimes use social programs to expand workers' skills and productivity; therefore, companies with a skilled workforce or those competing in international markets may have particular interests in training programs. Still other scholars assert that managers may accept social policies when they wish to curry favor with politicians pushing a social agenda or to impose costs on their competitors; therefore, companies with significant sales to the public sector might well endorse social spending.

Duane Swank and I hypothesized that employers' views about social protections in particular and public policy in general also should reflect how managers get their information about government programs and how they form their preferences. Employers' views about social policy are largely shaped by their peers; therefore, their sources of information and membership in professional organizations matter as much or more than the economic characteristics of their companies. Paradoxically, positive business views toward social policies are more likely to be found in countries with highly organized business associations than in countries where employers are weakly organized. This is because well-organized and fragmented business associations have very different modes of teaching members about public policy and engaging them politically.

The centralized, highly coordinated groups found in some European countries include most parts of industry and help their members to find common ground. In countries with these "macro-corporatist" business associations, employers are invited (together with their labor counterparts) to participate in the development of social programs, and they often believe that government programs can work to the advantage of industry. The groups also provide a vehicle for the dissemination of information from government about the benefits of social spending, and these groups tend to speak about business concerns in the legislative process more than do individual firms. In sharp contrast, the United States and Britain have many competing, encompassing employers' associations— such as the National Association of Manufacturers and the United States Chamber of Commerce. These groups all claim to be the most important representative of business, but they compete for members, fail to aggregate business priorities, and make it difficult for employers to express collective preferences. Thus employers' positions depend on the way they are brought into political debates through organizations and party competition, and these political processes are particularly important to views about the needs of marginal workers.

We set out to evaluate the causal relationship between high levels of business organization and spending on active labor market policies with a mixed-methods research design, in which my interviews with randomly selected firms would be matched with Duane Swank's cross-national, quantitative analysis. We assumed that companies' preferences for social programs specifically should be driven by dynamics similar to national business communities' willingness to tolerate high levels of welfare state spending generally. By testing for matching causal factors at both the cross-national and firm levels, we sought to reveal the micro-level logic of the relationship between employer organization and high levels of welfare state spending (Martin and Swank 2004, 2012). At the macro level, we constructed a research design that tested for determinants of cross-national variations in active labor market spending in the core OECD countries; in particular, we investigated our core hypothesis, that the existence of highly organized, macro-corporatist employers' associations was a significant determinant of variation in social spending.

Swank and I paired national level hypotheses about the independent variables driving welfare state spending on active labor market policies (ALMP) with those shaping firms' tolerance of and engagement in active labor market programs. To offer some examples, we posited at the national level that "the greater the centralization of national employer organizations, the greater the ALMP spending," and at the micro level that "membership in an association makes firms more likely to participate in Denmark but not in Britain." We hypothesized in our national-level study that "the higher the affluence, the larger the resources committed to ALMP," and at the micro level, "Firms with higher profits as percentage of total revenues are more likely to participate." At the national level, "the greater the trade openness of the economy, the larger the share of GNP for ALMP spending," while at the micro level, "Firms with higher exports as a percentage of total sales are more likely to participate" (Martin and Swank 2004).

At the micro level, we used interview data to investigate the processes underlying macro-structural causal relationships. We posited that membership in corporatist-encompassing business associations should be a significant determinant of firms' willingness to participate in active labor market programs, but that membership in a pluralist association would not enhance employers' participation. I used interviews to implement this research agenda, and met with individuals in 107 randomly selected firms in Britain and Denmark, to evaluate the causal determinants of companies' participation in active labor market programs. The interviews generally lasted for one to three hours; I conducted most of the Denmark interviews in Danish.

Using information collected in these interviews, I conducted two separate but parallel firm-level comparisons (comparing firms within a country but not between countries), using OLS regression and ordered probit analyses. These allowed me to isolate the significant causal factors driving firm behaviors in each country and compare significant variables across countries. My central hypothesis was that Danish firms belonging to a corporatist employers' association would be more likely to participate in the programs, but British firms would not, because the British pluralist associations play a very different role in the lives of their members. Moreover, I assumed that Danish firms would be more likely to participate for real skills needs, whereas British firms would participate for public relations advantages or to secure cheap labor (Martin 2004, 2005).

Drawing a Sample

Drawing a sample, of course, is one of the earliest decisions that one must make in an interview research project. As Julia Lynch's chapter notes, the research design for conducting interviews depends heavily on the intended use of the data; therefore, choices about sampling techniques and the specific content of research questions must mesh with the ambitions of the project. Random samples are not necessary for exploratory research to generate future hypotheses or to investigations tracing processes in specific case studies, yet they are mandatory in projects that seek to identify the characteristics of a population or to test causal relationships among a broader set of phenomenon. When constructing a case study to investigate causality in a particular case, one looks for the smoking gun: one cares less about getting a representative sample of the individuals who may have been affected by an event than about identifying the individuals or institutions responsible for causing the particular action. When one engages in process tracing to get information about how events unfold—how a specific bill becomes a law—one speaks with the relevant actors (in this case, lawmakers, lobbyists, or congressional aides), and sampling is less important. (But even in these cases, various actors may well have different interpretations of events.)

Taking a random sample is de rigueur, however, if research seeks to define the characteristics, attitudes, preferences, or behaviors of a population, or to establish the effect of an independent variable on a dependent one. In these cases, scholars wish to generalize and must draw a sample that allows for broader external representation. Should one wish to evaluate the sorts of companies that hire lobbyists, for example, interviewing assorted employers based on a list of lobbyists' clients may not be sufficient; one doesn't know whether one's selected respondents are representative of the larger population. In particular, selecting on the dependent variable (firms that engage in the activity) tells you nothing about the nonparticipating companies (see Lynch).

Thus, random sampling is particularly beneficial because it reveals processes at play in both the positive and negative cases, and one learns from the silences. Even when interviewing a small subset of individuals (for instance, firms in a given sector in Denmark), introducing an element of chance into sample selection may be possible because—at least in advanced industrialized countries—lists abound, and creative use is being made of them in diverse settings and toward manifold ends. The intrepid scholar might take a page from U.S. Republican Party strategists, who put together registries of potential GOP voters in swing districts in Wisconsin by compiling registries of snowmobile owners. Political philosopher Alan Wolfe drew names from phone books to compile his sample of Americans for a book on middle-class morality, in which he interviewed roughly two hundred respondents across the country about their views of sex, money, work, children, and religion. Wolfe matched these interview data to broader public opinion polls, and he was able to reflect on the processes by which individuals arrive at and act upon their views of virtue (Wolfe 2001).

In my study of employers' participation in active labor market programs, I chose a random sample to generalize the findings to a larger set of employers; moreover, the interviews were part of a multi-methods research design that sought to deliver broadly generalizable findings about the broad relationship between business organization and social spending. This design aimed to test the impact of institutional and economic variables on companies' involvement with active labor market programs. Much of the past research on employers' views toward public policy either inferred companies' preferences from structural characteristics of the firm or industry using broad cross-national quantitative analyses, or relied on in-depth interviews with a small group of firms that engaged in specific behaviors but which might not have been representative of the larger pool. To construct a random sample, I picked every fifth company from a list of the top five hundred firms in Denmark and the United Kingdom. The sample was therefore selected without regard for participation in labor market programs; including nonparticipants in the sample promised to generate insights into the processes of preference formation. If the sample had been limited only to companies that participated in the programs, I would not have been exposed to employers' reasons for not participating.

Constructing a random sample has drawbacks, however. In particular, it complicates gaining access to participants, because one cannot simply interview the people who have engaged in a behavior that interests one (and who are presumably more willing to talk). Gaining access to those who do not engage in the behavior can be exceedingly difficult. This problem is slightly mitigated by the fact that some individuals are simply more willing to be interviewed than others (regardless of program participation), and some companies known for their involvement with a program feel overwhelmed with requests for interviews. For example, I anticipated in my study of Danish and British firms that two firms in the sample with strong profiles in corporate social responsibility, Body Shop and Lego, would participate; yet both refused. Lego had suffered recent, serious financial setbacks and appeared to be in retrenchment on the social front, and the Body Shop HR manager reported feeling overwhelmed by interview requests. These cases provide a reminder that our preconceived notions about respondents do not always hold true. A helpful mechanism for coping with this problem of selection bias (from within the randomly drawn sample) is to compare the characteristics of individuals or units who agree to participate in the study with the characteristics of those who decline to grant an interview—a strategy also used to deal with nonresponse bias in survey research (Brehm 1993).

A random sample combined with a snowball technique can help to improve access, yet this also presents some problems with bias. Here, one draws the sample, shows the list to contacts in the relevant community, and asks these contacts to identify people they know. Working one's way through the list can greatly enhance participation rates. In this vein, I began my study by showing my lists to a few contacts, who then allowed me to use their name to approach subsequent respondents. Yet, while increasing access, the snowball technique also increases the potential for bias, because people reached through personal networks might be inclined to answer questions differently than would otherwise be the case. Interviewees might be more willing to share information with a perceived insider, or conversely they might be more guarded if they feared that the interviewer might share their data with other respondents. This technique increases the need for clear guarantees of confidentially of the content of interviews, and cannot be used in situations where security is a concern (that is, where confidentiality of the identity of interviewees, as well as confidentiality of the information provided, is key).

Another technique for gaining access to interview subjects is to frame letters in terms of issues that are important to the sample population but that may be less crucial to the study. For example, in asking firms about their participation in programs for the long-term unemployed, I stressed in my initial letters and phone calls my interest in workforce training. Although I genuinely wanted to collect data about training, it was something of a secondary interest for me; however, I highlighted this interest prominently in initial communications and believe that it expanded access. In using this strategy, of course, one must be attentive to research ethics (see Brooks): one can highlight one aim of the project over another, but one should not fabricate an aim that does not exist.

Follow-up phone calls are another way to enhance access. The person with the most knowledge of one's object of study may be difficult to reach; therefore, one might begin with an entry-level person who specializes in public relations and request subsequent follow-up phone calls with a more appropriate respondent. Face-to-face interviews are extremely worthwhile in helping one gain access to and information from respondents; in addition, traveling to an organization gives one a sense of place that helps to put information in context. But multiple contacts may be necessary to gain access to all the relevant players within the organization, and follow-up phone calls can be very helpful to this ambition.

Another important decision is the choice of whom, within a given firm or organization, to interview. I primarily interviewed the benefits managers or vice presidents for human resources within the company, although in a few cases I also spoke with the CEOs. I chose these individuals because I anticipated that they would either be the decision makers or would have been told why their superiors decided to participate. Moreover, I asked each participant to identify the individual or group within the firm with the greatest decision-making power about whether to participate.

These data on decision makers within the company were fascinating in helping me to grasp motives to participate. As table 5.1 demonstrates, Danish human resources and benefits managers were almost always involved in the process; but British CEOs often drove participation from the top down, as a political boon to Prime Minister Tony Blair. One respondent recalled, "The first anyone in the company heard about the CEO's interest [in participating in the New Deal (the British active labor market program)] was from reading about it in the press." Another manager blamed the government for misunderstanding corporate chains of command: "They come and talk to the chairman or the CEO, but they also need to talk to the people who will have to make it happen."

TABLE 5.1   Person responsible for deciding to participate in active labor market programs

WHO MAKES THE HIRES	DENMARK (%)	BRITAIN (%)
CEO	9	31
CEO together with HR manager	31	13
HR manager	24	35
HR together with line manager	18	6
Line manager	14	11
Don't know	4	4
Total	100	100

Using Interview Data: Research Questions

The design of interview questions is another critical decision, as the interview may include questions designated for theory testing and opportunities to follow respondents' core concerns about the dependent variable. The choices in the questionnaire reflect the aims of the interviews in the research design and the multiple ways that interviews contribute to mixed-methods approaches. Interview questions may be used to provide *both* quantitative and qualitative data: they may help to identify characteristics of the population, to test hypotheses, to reinforce the validity of the quantitative analysis, or to offer thick description about the processes by which the independent variables shape the dependent one.

First, interview data may be used to evaluate hypotheses about the general effect of independent variables. They may be coded and analyzed with quantitative analyses similar to those used to make causal inference about data that come from other empirical sources. Coding enables the interviews to produce data that can be generalized to the broader population or statistical analysis to test causal relations, and these coded interview data are virtually interchangeable with other types of data, such as those generated through surveys (see Martin and Swank 2004, 2012; Beckmann and Hall, Gallagher, and Leech et al. in this volume). As Leech and her coauthors point out in chapter 11, the semi-structured interview often permits a quantification of interview data. Although social scientists have historically had greater confidence in surveys than in interviews, interviews with randomly selected respondents, in fact, can be viewed as long surveys, and their findings may be analyzed in ways comparable to survey techniques (see also Bleich and Pekkanen in this volume). Indeed, as Mosley notes, the researcher may have more information about the metadata that accompany interview-based indicators than one has about the metadata that accompany economic statistics or quantitative measures of democracy, conflict, or government ideology.

Therefore, a semi-structured interview questionnaire format is appropriate to the goal of coding the data and using these data to evaluate causal arguments and to establish the characteristics of a population. Respondents may wish to tell us what they think we want to hear or to present themselves in the most favorable light; and we, as researchers, may be tempted to hear what we expect the interviewee to tell us. Therefore, interview questions should be designed to maximize neutrality and to minimize leading questions. Whenever possible, it is advisable to ask questions about behaviors rather than about attitudes or preferences. One might explore the conditions under which participants are likely to participate in certain types of behaviors or to take certain preferences, rather than simply ask whether these behaviors or attitudes are part of their repertoire. Finally, one does well to match interview data with other types of data, because while other types of data (such as larger-n quantitative measures) may allow one to establish relationships among variables, interview data illustrate the underlying processes that serve as a microfoundation for these relationships. Approaching the same question using different types of data also can serve to increase the researcher's confidence in the reliability and validity of her data.

In my study of companies' involvement with active labor market programs, I coded interview subjects' responses to questions about their companies' participation in the programs, their membership in encompassing employers' associations, the skill levels of their workers, their unionization rates, and various other factors. For my dependent variable, I gathered data on the actual participation of firms in the relevant programs rather than eliciting their opinion about such programs, and used these data to construct a five-point scale of participation, ranging from strongly participating to strongly against participation. For my independent variables, I gathered data on various economic and institutional characteristics of the firm; these included, for example, a firm's exports as a share of its total revenue, the level of unionization of its employees, workforce skills, sales to the public sector, membership in an encompassing employers' organization, and size of the human resources department. The coded interview data were combined with data derived from other sources, such as firms' annual reports on size, average wages, and profitability. I used this combined data set for statistical tests of hypotheses about the conditions under which firms perceived social programs to be in their interests. (See this volume's appendix for the semistructured questionnaire for the Danish firms.)

Second, interviews can be used for process tracing in mixed-methods approaches in a way that is analogous to their use in qualitative analyses that investigate causality in a single case study or small set of case studies (Hochschild 1981). At the heart of the case study method is the ambition to observe causal processes: direct evidence of the proverbial smoking gun can convince us that a given cause has had its expected effect. Adept researchers engage in a careful temporal reconstruction of the case, or "process tracing," to identify the intermediate steps between an independent cause and the dependent effect (J. Mahoney 2009). There is an obvious problem of knowing which intermediate steps are important, but a sensitivity to historical sequential processes helps to overcome this problem; in addition, the burden of proof for a causal process observation is somewhat higher than for a data set observation (J. Mahoney 2009). Researchers also may use qualitative data, including interviews, to construct analytic narratives to reveal the underlying rational choice games that structure incentives and produce action (Bates et al. 1998).

Along similar lines, interviews and case histories may be used in mixed-methods approaches to reveal micro-processes underlying observed large-n relationships. Thus causal relationships uncovered in quantitative analysis may be consistent with a range of causal processes; interviews help us to differentiate among these potential causal mechanisms. The multidimensional research design also addresses the problem that while process tracing may provide compelling evidence for a single case, its capacity for broader generalization is more limited because case studies do not easily lend themselves to generalizations.

Uncovering causal processes may best occur through open-ended interview questions that leave room for the respondents to express their own perceptions of the issues and that take the researcher into unknown territory. A great virtue of interviewing is that it enables a sensitivity to the worldviews of one's respondents—an entry into the issues, concerns, and stories that motivate, compel, and capture the lives of others. This intimacy and interpretive advantage is impossible to capture in survey or quantitative analyses, and the best-designed set of interview questions capitalizes on this great advantage. Sensitivity to the concerns of the subject helps one both to avoid the instrumental molding of narratives to fit one's theory, and to leave oneself open to the unanticipated discoveries that often constitute the most joyful moments in the process. Thus, the most interesting research projects often leave room in the interview for both types of questions: some questions should be framed to address the core concerns of the interviewees, while others (such as those described above, and used in my work for statistical analyses) cull information that sheds light on the specific research hypotheses.

In my study, I used interview data to reveal the motivations and processes underlying companies' decisions to participate in labor market programs. For example, I knew from the quantitative analysis of the coded data on worker skills that firms using workers with higher skills were more likely to participate in Denmark than in the United Kingdom. I also expected that Danish firms would be more likely to participate to improve the skills of their workforce (and to participate for economic reasons), while British firms were more likely to be motivated by lowering labor costs or by participating to win political favor with the Blair government.

The interviews confirmed that the Danish companies were more likely than their British counterparts to view the programs as a source of real skills. Thus while the programs were not generally designed to improve the employment of college-educated, white-collar workers, and the countries had exactly the same percentage of manufacturing workers (25 percent), 53 percent of British firms felt that they could not participate because their workers were too highly skilled. By contrast, only 34 percent of Danish firms expressed this view. On the flip side, while unemployment rates were exactly the same in the two countries, 20 percent of British firms reported participating to gain access to new labor sources, while 31 percent of Danish firms participated for this reason. As one British respondent put it, "The company has been recruiting at the skilled level, but government schemes are irrelevant to this labor pool" (Martin 2005). Thus, as reported in table 5.2, I asked open-ended questions about motivations for and constraints against participation, and found that, indeed, Danes are more likely to meet real economic needs, while British employers are more likely to curry political favor or seek cheap labor.

Duane Swank and I sought to use the micro-level study to bolster the validity of the macro-level findings about business organization and social spending (Martin and Swank 2004, 2012). For example, I knew from the regression analysis that firms with a high level of sales to the public sector were significantly more likely to participate in Britain but not in Denmark, and the interview data gave me greater confidence that political factors mattered to firms' calculations. A much higher proportion of British respondents (31 percent) than Danish respondents (9 percent) identified "political pressures" as a reason to participate. In 31 percent of the British firms, the decision to participate came from the CEO (indicating a high level of political commitment), while CEOs made the decision to participate in only 9 percent of the Danish firms, where the human resources departments were much more likely to make the judgment call to participate. The strong political pressures to participate in Britain were revealed in comments made by many respondents. One manager reflected: "The firm's business is heavily tied to the Ministry of Defense and to the government. So we felt obliged to support a new, and very key program for the Blair government." Another manager remembered the local employment center urging, "You don't need to take anyone, but would you just sign up?" Yet another company signed up for the New Deal as part of its application to secure permits to build an airport (Martin 2005).

I also used interview data to observe the processes underlying the quantitative finding that the stronger employers' associations in Denmark were more likely

TABLE 5.2 Motivations for and constraints against participation

MOTIVATIONS AND CONSTRAINTS	DENMARK (%)	BRITAIN (%)
Firms participated	**68**	**40**
Subsidies motivating participation	38	10
Labor needs motivating participation	31	22
Social responsibility motivating participation	51	26
Political pressures motivating participation	9	31
Need for high skills preventing participation	36	53
Firm's not hiring preventing participation	20	28

to bring employers to support welfare state spending than were the weak employers' associations in Britain. This was, in part, because the Danish associations educated their member firms about the programs and provided a channel for employers to have input into the design of the programs. To investigate these relationships, I asked firms open-ended questions about the sources of their information about the programs (see table 5.3). The interviews told me that a much larger percentage of the Danish firms (31 percent) offered their employers' associations as their *major* source of information, as compared with the British firms (14 percent). In contrast, 34 percent of British firms derived their information from the popular press, newsletters, or the Internet, compared with 15 percent of Danish firms (Martin 2005). Respondents also told me that the Danish employers' association created network groups in which employers could discuss the emerging labor market programs and were responsible for inviting local company participants to sit on municipal social coordination groups. Many respondents learned much about the programs through participation in these groups and felt that they had substantially more input into the policymaking process than their British counterparts. Representatives from the encompassing Danish employers' organization also reported taking this issue area seriously because they wished to maintain a high level of societal control over and input into the design of the active labor market and social programs. Thus, one respondent told me, "DA [the Danish Employers' Confederation] and LO [the Confederation of Danish Trade Unions] were like Siamese twins, in both needing to retain their credibility as willing participants in the political dialogue" (Martin and Swank 2012).

Third, interview data may be used to address our concerns about reliability and validity, when causal process observations either offer empirical verification for or cast doubts on quantitative findings (see Bleich and Pekkanen in this volume.) In a mixed-methods, multilevel research design, case study data are used

TABLE 5.3 Primary source of information for the firm

SOURCE OF INFORMATION	DENMARK (%)	BRITAIN (%)
Employers organization (formal)	**31**	**14**
Human resources group (formal or informal)	13	10
Advisory group formed by the state	7	16
State agency	22	8
Private consultant or experts within firm	7	14
Written trade press, newsletters, Internet	4	30
Regular newspapers	11	4
Not informed	5	4
Total	100	100

in conjunction with comprehensive quantitative analysis. A nested hypothesis approach examines the aspects of a case that can be explained by general quantitatively verifiable theories, identifies unexplained phenomena, and uses qualitative methods to investigate these unexplained empirical findings (Coppedge 2005, 292). As Mary Gallagher suggests in this volume, mixed methods are complementary, in that they allow the researcher to use one approach to make up for deficiencies in another. With triangulation, one can check the findings of the various methods against each other. Thus, interviews are a great correction for the unfortunate possibility in large-n analyses of massaging data, running multiple tests until one gets at the set of causal variables that confirms one's predispositions.

Although quantitative data may be shown to support suggested causal relationships, the thick description of interviews increases validity. Process tracing within a case study cannot definitively prove a causal relationship in a wider set of cases; the absence of a causal factor in a positive case or presence of a causal factor in a negative case would raise questions about how externally valid the case findings were. But causal process observations, by virtue of the richness of the information they provide, can be an invaluable tool in theory testing. The researcher can estimate the likelihood of finding such causal processes should an alternative theory be true. In such analyses, the Bayesian likelihood of finding an observation becomes more important than the frequency of the observation. Additionally, a causal-process observation may suggest that an apparent (from analysis based on data set observations) causal relationship is spurious (J. Mahoney 2009). Thus, a small-n study can support or refute a broader large-n, quantitative investigation (Mosley and Singer 2009).

Of course, interviews also have their own problems of bias, which also can be mitigated through a mixed-methods research design. Throughout such a research project, attention to selection bias is key. Research designs that fail to examine variation on the dependent variable, for instance, compromise one's ability to suggest causality. If we wish to understand the origins of revolution, we must also include cases in which the revolutionary outburst failed to occur (King, Keohane, and Verba 1994; Collier and Mahoney, 1996; Geddes 1990). Within the interview method specifically, the somewhat subjective quality of data can permit the instrumental molding and interpretation of the interviews to fit a theory (Carpenter 2010). Here, large-n analyses can serve as a "reality check" on interview-based findings, as can the careful reporting of material from the interview study (see Bleich and Pekkanen's chapter).

Furthermore, bias also may be introduced through the self-selection of respondents. As I discuss above, this problem transcends the various uses of interview data. Thus, a completely random sample used to study the characteristics of a population obviously addresses many potential sources of selection bias; however, even a random sample cannot eliminate issues related to the self-selection of respondents into a given category. Subjects who self-select into a category measuring an explanatory variable constitute a source of bias, and causal inferences must be treated, to some extent, as suspect if the investigator cannot control for the allocation of subjects across explanatory categories. In addition, even when interview subjects are randomly chosen, selection bias remains a concern if the subjects' decisions whether or not to participate in the study are influenced by unknown factors that complicate the causal relationships. Yet, while the issue of self-selection cannot be completely eradicated, one might explore systematically the bias of subject selection within the categories of the independent variable to ensure that this bias is not replicated in the distribution of subjects across the dependent variable's categories.

For example, in my study of American employers' preferences for comprehensive health reform and employer mandates in the 1992–1993 health reform cycle, I hypothesized that firms with a Washington, DC, government affairs office would be more likely to support national health reform than companies without such an office. Government affairs employees would be exposed to technical arguments in support of reform from meetings with experts in government and labor (Martin 1995, 2000; Dobbin 1992). I recognized that firms that had formed a Washington office might also be generally predisposed to favor social policy (so that their support for reform in the 1990s and the existence of an office were driven by a common causal factor, the firm's stance toward social policy). But, in exploring this issue empirically, I found that many Washington offices were created in the early 1970s, in order to *oppose* reformist government policies such as environmental and consumer protection acts. Thus, I could convincingly argue that the circumstances of the government affairs offices' creation were quite separate from the institutional impact of these offices, once they had been in place for some time.

Multiple research approaches may aid in the dual objectives of generating observations about a broader phenomenon from a sample and understanding the motivations and processes that produce these observations. Interviews are an important part of the tool kit in this endeavor. First, this method of investigation allows for both the careful construction of the sample and specification of questions that allow one to test hypotheses; second, interviews offer researchers the opportunity to pursue unanticipated openings in the conversation that may well reveal essential truths.

To pursue the first goal at the stage of designing the study, the researcher is best served by introducing as much randomness (in selecting respondents) as possible, so as not to systematically skew the interview data. At the stage of designing research questions, one should seek to obtain the specific information about the range of factors hypothesized to be important. To pursue the second goal, one should also invite interview subjects to tell their stories, as the sensitive researcher will benefit from listening to the respondent, and by balancing the questions on the structured-interview sheet with the story that the subject has to tell. Thus the adept interviewer is something like a psychotherapist, framing the questions to address the core concerns of the interviewee, even while gathering the information essential to making a diagnosis. Accessing a respondent's insights, experiences, and accumulated wisdom is the part of the research program that delivers the biggest bang for the buck—the unexpected gems of insight that transform research proposals (where we ask questions to which we already know the answers) into journeys into new knowledge. Interviewing is a wild ride, and the sensitive scholar will learn as much as possible from the bumps in the road, even while trying to stay on track. To quote Albert Einstein, "If we knew what it was we were doing, it would not be called research, would it?"

USING PROXY INTERVIEWING TO ADDRESS SENSITIVE TOPICS

Melani Cammett

In November 2007, I met with a high-ranking official of Mabarrat, a Shia Muslim charitable organization that runs a vast network of welfare programs and income-generating projects in Lebanon. The meeting had been difficult to arrange, given the official's busy schedule and, more important, her suspicions about the goals and assumptions underlying my research. In order to set up our initial appointment, her office asked me to prepare a short summary of my research, which focused on social service provision by sectarian and religious organizations in Lebanon, and to provide background on the funders of the project.

In our first meeting, the official questioned me extensively on the objectives of my research. The Mabarrat representative had good reason to be wary: The George W. Bush administration had recently deemed the organization's founder, Sayyid Mohammed Hussein Fadlallah, the "spiritual adviser" of Hezbollah.[1] Accordingly, the United States threatened to cut off vital Western funding sources for Mabarrat's charitable programs, despite Fadlallah's open break with Hezbollah years earlier (Egan 2007). In the aftermath of the 2006 Israeli-Lebanese war, when many Lebanese perceived U.S. policy toward the conflict as pro-Israel and biased against Shia organizations in particular, an American researcher would likely be viewed with suspicion by a representative of Mabarrat. In follow-up meetings, I established greater rapport with the interviewee, and we addressed more substantive questions related to my research.

My efforts to gain access to officials from Mabarrat indicate the challenges of conducting research on sensitive contexts and illustrate how perceptions of the researcher affect access to information. In this chapter, I address strategies for gaining access to interviewees and gathering valid information from interview-based research. Although I draw on my experiences in conducting interviews on diverse topics in the Middle East, these approaches are applicable far beyond the region and to a wide range of topics. In the first part of the chapter, I briefly review the challenges posed by "outsider" positionality, or "where [the researcher] stands in relations to the other" (Merriam et al. 2001, 412) when conducting research on sensitive topics. I also highlight the added complexity of positionality in a "plural" society,[2] in which the researcher may be received in diametrically opposed ways by different communities. In the bulk of the chapter, I describe a method that I used in my research in Lebanon—what I call "proxy" interviewing—to address some of the challenges posed by "outsider" status, particularly with non-elites.

"Positionality" and Interview-Based Research

The concept and effects of positionality in qualitative research have generated a large and growing literature, particularly outside of political science.[3] Ongoing debates detail the relative merits of "insider" versus "outsider" status in conducting social research. Decades ago, a positivist consensus held that outsiders were more "objective" than insiders, who suffer from in-built sympathies and identification with the communities they aimed to study and therefore could not draw "value-free" conclusions. On the other hand, insider status has obvious advantages, not least of which is entrée to informants and data sources that foreigners often do not share. Given the importance of access to appropriate sources for field research, this is a powerful argument in favor of the insider advantage.[4] Furthermore, outsiders can come laden with theoretical baggage and prior expectations, which prevent them from interpreting phenomena as they actually function in distinct sociopolitical contexts.

Scholars increasingly reject the dichotomous treatment of insider-outsider status in social research as overly stylized. The boundaries between insider and outsider positionality are often vague. Perceptions of an insider or in-group researcher's positionality may vary—even by members of the same community—depending on factors such as gender, race, class, age, or region of origin (O'Connor 2004). Time in the field also may modify outsider status, as researchers become more immersed in the communities they study (Labaree 2002). At a minimum, insider-outsider status should be viewed on a continuum rather than in dichotomous terms; it is subject to change and multiple interpretations within the same community. Each position has its advantages and disadvantages.[5] For example, despite its presumed advantages for access to sources and in-group events, insider status is not always superior, especially with elites (Herod 1999). When interviewing foreign elites, a researcher may benefit from outsider status both in gaining access to informants and in interpreting the data with a fresh perspective.[6]

Positionality has received minimal attention in mainstream political science. If the quality of our findings is contingent on access to data, however, then all social scientists should care about the effects of positionality on the research process. Indeed, the survey research literature implicitly recognizes the effects of positionality in its attention to "interviewer effects" (Hatchett and Schuman 1975; Kish 1962). More explicitly, the growing body of methodological research on in-depth interviews emphasizes the importance of building rapport between the participants in the dialogue—a process that implies the need for reflection on perceptions of the interviewer by the interviewee or respondent community (Berry 2002; Kvale and Brinkmann 2009; Leech 2002b; Rubin and Rubin 2005).

In any research method that entails sustained interactions between a researcher and a target population, as in ethnographic or interview-based research, the perceived positionality of the researcher automatically affects the degree to which respondents will share information. This is even true for relatively innocuous topics. For example, my research on trade liberalization and business politics in Morocco and Tunisia was not the most sensitive topic, and it occurred largely in the late 1990s and 2000—prior to the "war on terror," which has posed significant challenges to Americans conducting fieldwork in the Middle East (Cammett 2007b; Lust-Okar et al. 2007). In Morocco and Tunisia, however, I was received in varied ways by different categories of respondents. For example, as a U.S. citizen, I was assumed to favor a free-trade agenda, a position that incensed some of my informants who were tied to the import-substitution, protected economy and therefore threatened by falling trade barriers. Some even assumed that I was a representative of the U.S. government or a U.S.-based multinational corporation seeking to break into new overseas markets.

In a plural society, politicized cleavages further complicate the dynamics of positionality in interview research. Distinct groups may have radically different preconceptions about foreign researchers, depending on their nationalities; trust building may therefore require very different approaches and, with some informants, may never occur at all. During field research in Lebanon, I was received differently by representatives of diverse sectarian parties and organizations. As a U.S. citizen, it is difficult to gain access to and conduct meaningful interviews with representatives or supporters of parties such as Hezbollah, which has hostile relations with the U.S. government. Representatives and supporters of the Free Patriotic Movement, a Christian party that is currently allied with Hezbollah, were also initially suspicious of me as a U.S. citizen, in part because they feared that the U.S. government would cut off vital Western funding sources as a result of their alliance with the Shia party. At the same time, my status as a U.S. university professor opened some doors to elite interviews that might not have been available to Lebanese researchers: a meeting with me provided officials a potential opportunity to convey their viewpoints to a Western audience, which they perceived as hostile and otherwise inaccessible. Conversely, pro-American Christian parties and the predominantly Sunni Future Movement were far more open to receiving me. Thus, U.S. foreign policy sometimes hindered and sometimes facilitated my access to informants, depending on their organizational affiliations and partisanship.

The ability to access and conduct interviews with non-elites is often shaped by the same macro-political and social considerations, but interviews with non-elites present their own opportunities and challenges. On the one hand, making contact with ordinary people can be easier than with elites. Non-elites may have fewer time constraints than elites and can be approached through everyday channels, such as social networks or mundane interactions in public settings such as markets and cafés. On the other hand, ordinary citizens have little incentive to share personal information with researchers, particularly in restrictive political settings where they may justifiably fear loss of reputation, property, and physical security. By necessity, lower-income non-elites are consumed with making ends meet and therefore do not have the luxury of free time to the same extent as members of higher-income groups. Furthermore, on average, non-elites with limited education may be less familiar than elites with the goals and practices of scholarly research and therefore may not recognize the value of sharing their personal experiences for broader research purposes. Given the potentially high personal stakes and possible lack of familiarity with research processes, non-elites may not accept or comprehend researcher pledges to ensure confidentiality or anonymity. These conditions, then, can hinder efforts to arrange interviews, particularly for an outsider who may be viewed with suspicion and who lacks established social ties to possible informants.

In the next section, I describe a strategy for arranging and carrying out interviews with non-elites. The strategy, which I term "proxy interviewing," builds on approaches in the literature on positionality that leverage both insider and outsider advantages to access interviewees and interpret findings (Bartunek and Louis 1996).

Proxy Interviews as a Research Strategy

For my book on welfare and sectarianism in divided societies (Cammett, forthcoming), I conducted research on social service provision by sectarian parties in Lebanon. Focused on the political dimensions of welfare, I seek to explain the conditions under which sectarian organizations distribute social benefits such as health care, schooling, and material assistance broadly, notably to out-group members and to marginal or non-supporters. In brief, I argue that the type of political mobilization strategy prioritized by the organization, as well as the degree of control over political representation of the in-group community, shapes the propensity of sectarian parties to serve beyond their core, in-group base of supporters. When parties emphasize electoral and nonviolent approaches, and when they are the dominant representative of their respective communities, they are more apt to distribute welfare goods broadly (Cammett 2012).

The research for the book employed multiple data sources, including a mass survey on citizen access to welfare, Geographic Information Systems (GIS) data on community characteristics and the locations of welfare agencies, in-depth interviews with providers and party representatives, and the collection of relevant government, party, and charity documents in Lebanon. I realized that, to better interpret and enrich the findings, these sources needed to be supplemented by in-depth interviews with ordinary citizens who may have tried to access social assistance from the organizations in my sample. A comprehensive perspective on how sectarian groups allocate welfare goods in Lebanon would require more than the views of the providers themselves, government officials, and other elites. The closed-ended, two-thousand-household national survey provided baseline information by presenting a general picture of the extent to which Lebanese citizens sought social assistance; it showed that higher levels of political activism are associated with increased access to social assistance and suggested that different sectarian parties distribute welfare goods in distinct ways. But a mass survey could not adequately shed light on how people experience the welfare programs of sectarian organizations and interpret the treatment they receive when seeking assistance.

Conversations with neighbors in Beirut, as well as brief discussions with patients in health clinics run by various nonstate providers, suggested that in-depth interviews with ordinary citizens would yield a wealth of information. Two of my neighbors' children were enrolled in a low-cost school with an excellent academic reputation run by the Hariri Foundation, the charitable organization established by the assassinated former prime minister of Lebanon, Rafiq al-Hariri. My neighbors also were ardent supporters of Hariri's political movement, the Future Movement, which headed the governing coalition in Lebanon at the time. Other neighbors suggested that the family's partisanship and access to services were not coincidental: active supporters of the movement receive coveted spots in the school and privileged access to subsidized social services from the foundation and its affiliated programs. My neighbors made no attempt to deny these allegations and proudly proclaimed their support for the movement, demonstrating their partisanship with stickers and posters of Hariri on the outside door of their apartment.

In this situation, the ability to establish a linkage between partisanship and access to social benefits was facilitated by a preexisting social rapport with the informants and my quasi-embeddedness in neighborhood social networks. I regularly went to their home to drink coffee and discuss the day's events while our children played together. As a foreigner, I could not hope to replicate this on a larger scale, because I lacked extensive social ties. Even if I were a long-term resident of Beirut, my social networks would inevitably be limited by my social position, hindering my ability to tap into some communities or geographic areas relevant to my research. Furthermore, brief interviews with patients in clinic waiting rooms or with families enrolled in schools that I visited yielded limited information. Interviewees approached in welfare agencies were reluctant to share their experiences with an unknown foreign researcher whom they had met only five minutes earlier. These interviews also were constrained by the pressing medical or social needs that brought potential respondents to clinic waiting rooms and other institutions in the first place. Furthermore, school or clinic officials often lingered in waiting rooms and school facilities while I conducted interviews, limiting the candor of the information I received. Finally, a sample of interviewees contacted through provider institutions would be hopelessly biased because it would include only people who received or were about to receive services—not those who tried to obtain benefits and were refused or who did not try at all.

Proxy Interviewing: Addressing (Outsider) Positionality in Non-Elite Interviews

These limitations compelled me to devise a new strategy for carrying out in-depth interviews with ordinary beneficiaries (and non-beneficiaries) of the social programs of sectarian and other nonstate organizations in Lebanon. Intergroup tensions among the different communities coexisting in Lebanon at the time of my research, as well as the lessons of "interviewer effects" in the survey research literature, led me to conclude that only resident Lebanese citizens who were more embedded in the local social networks of the diverse communities I wished to reach could carry out the interviews.

Embeddedness in local communities, however, would not suffice: the interviewers also needed familiarity with the goals and principles of social science research and an understanding of the purposes of the project. Thus, I opted to recruit graduate students from top Lebanese universities in relevant disciplines

to conduct the interviews. By virtue of their education levels and social positions, the students were not true insiders in the low-income communities that
seek social welfare from sectarian and religious organizations. Trained interviewers, however, could strike an appropriate balance between community access and
requisite research skills.

Ideally, the research design would have entailed interviews conducted by multiple types of interviewers to gauge systematically the effects of the interviewer.
For example, a coreligionist and a non-coreligionist could conduct interviews with
the same respondents using the same protocol. A comparison of the data collected
from parallel interviews with individual respondents could enable an assessment
of the impact of the interviewer "treatment." For both logistical and financial
reasons, however, this approach was not possible; but wherever possible, it should
be considered in conducting in-depth interviews, particularly with non-elites in
societies with politicized cleavages relevant to the research topic. Below I describe
the nuts and bolts of proxy interviewing as carried out for my research and suggest ways in which the approach can be deployed in other settings.

Interviewer Recruitment and the Logic of Proxy Interviewing

In the summer of 2007, I flew to Lebanon to select a team of five Lebanese
graduate students, one from each of the main religious communities—Christian,
Druze, Shia Muslim, and Sunni Muslim. Prior to my arrival, I sent e-mails to a
wide range of academic and NGO contacts in Lebanon asking them to alert their
best students and researchers that I planned to recruit a team to work with me
on the project and to invite any interested candidates to send me their CVs in
advance of my arrival. Thus, by the time I landed in Beirut, I already had a pool
of almost forty students from the top universities in Lebanon who applied for
positions on the interviewer team.

Over a ten-day period, I screened and interviewed each candidate with the
help of a Lebanese postdoctoral research fellow at the American University of
Beirut Faculty of Health Sciences with which I was affiliated. In selecting candidates, I looked for a number of relevant qualities. First, personality characteristics were important because the interviewers would need to establish rapport
with individuals who likely came from lower-income groups, which were most
likely to seek social assistance from private, quasi-charitable sources. By virtue of
their educational credentials and, often, family income status, all the candidates
came from relatively high socioeconomic status groups in Lebanese society.
A key criterion for selection was therefore the ability to communicate respectfully
with people across class lines (also see Fujii, chapter 7, this volume). Second, the

candidates needed a baseline understanding of the goals of social scientific re-search, notably the importance of gathering data through a systematic process to address a research question and to test competing hypotheses. Respect for the ethical principles of research, particularly the protection of human subjects, also was of paramount importance.

Third, prospective interviewers would ideally suggest feasible and even imag-inative ways of gaining access to interviewees. Finally, none of the candidates could have close ties to any of the organizations targeted in my research, lest these relationships compromise their presentation of the findings or inhibit the interviewees from expressing themselves freely. For example, one applicant's father was a prominent member of parliament affiliated with the Future Move-ment. Lacking sufficient local knowledge, I might have missed this relationship; but thanks to thorough "detective work," the Lebanese postdoctoral fellow as-sisting me with the interviewer screening process flagged his affiliation. As a re-sult, I chose not to hire the candidate. Once I selected the team of five Lebanese graduate students, I signed contracts with each interviewer that clearly identified the scope of work, time frame, mutual obligations, and compensation associated with the research tasks.

This component of data collection for my research in Lebanon entailed a par-ticular subset of proxy interviewing, which we might call "matched" proxy in-terviewing. In selecting applicants for the interview team, I opted to match in-terviewers with respondents from the same religious background. Given the politicization of religious identities in Lebanese politics and society, this choice was logical. None of the interviewers was a hard-core supporter of a sectarian party, nor did any adopt religion as her most prominent identity. Regardless of their self-images, however, the interviewers were *perceived* to be members of a given sect by others based on a variety of factors, including direct knowledge, family reputation, family name, place of residence or family region of origin, and other sociologically relevant characteristics. In a sociopolitical context where religion is viewed as "descent-based" (Chandra 2007), or a virtually immutable characteristic inherited by blood, these apparent external markers were suffi-cient to assure potential respondents that the interviewer was from the same sectarian communal group. Although not every respondent necessarily would have preferred an in-group interviewer, on the margins, matching by sect helped to establish rapport and, in some places, vastly improved the richness of the data beyond what could otherwise be expected. In addition, matching by sect facili-tated initial access to respondents, since social networks were increasingly struc-tured along sectarian lines in the post–civil war period, particularly among families with lower socioeconomic status who were the most likely to seek social assistance from sectarian organizations (Labaki 1984; Nasr 1993).

Although the logic of matching interviewer and respondent by sect was motivated by the realities of the Lebanese sociopolitical context, this approach has broader applicability. In any research setting where ostensibly identity-based characteristics such as ethnicity, race, tribe, or region are politicized or sensitive, interviews conducted by a perceived in-group member are likely to yield more valid information and facilitate access to more respondents. Matched proxy interviewing could extend to other social categories such as gender or class and to a broad range of research settings, whether in the Global South or in industrialized countries. For example, in the United States, where a rich and long tradition of scholarship demonstrates the enduring political salience of race and ethnicity, in-group members may be the most appropriate researchers to conduct in-depth interviews with respondents on many topics related to racial and ethnic politics.

Interviewer Training

The mere selection of interviewers with research experience who were matched to corresponding sectarian communities, however, was not sufficient. It was critical to invest substantially in training in order to ensure that the interviewers had the requisite background and knowledge of interviewing techniques and were thoroughly versed in the goals of the research and interview protocol.[7] Furthermore, the training process and subsequent team meetings facilitated an atmosphere of dialogue and exchange, in which the processes of conducting the interviews and interpreting the findings could benefit from multiple insider and outsider ideas and perspectives (Easterby-Smith and Malina 1999).

Before initiating pilot tests and the interviewing process, I held a two-day intensive training session. This was designed to familiarize the team with the goals of the research, convey procedures for ensuring the confidentiality of respondents, and allow team members to help develop and practice interviewing techniques. A detailed discussion of the training procedures is beyond the scope of this chapter, but the following points summarize the main topics covered in the session:

1. *Question, hypotheses, methods*: An overview of the key research
   questions, preliminary hypotheses, rationale for case selection, and
   research methods for the project. In planning the training session,
   I initially hesitated to enumerate the working hypotheses in order to reduce
   the chances that the interviewers would bias the results by consciously
   or unconsciously steering respondents to particular responses. In the
   end, however, I chose to share the preliminary hypotheses with the team

in order to more fully convey the nature of the research goals; but I stressed the importance of refraining from discussing them with interviewees or nudging interviewees toward particular answers. The open-ended nature of the interviews (discussed next) also helped to ensure that respondents would develop their own responses to the questions.

As with many research projects, the precise research questions were reframed during data collection and analysis, so that the hypotheses discussed in the training sessions were slightly different from those assessed in the book. The initial working hypotheses focused on three sets of issues, not all of which remained germane to the final product. The first set of hypotheses posited that different types of nonstate providers—whether linked to political or religious organizations—allocate welfare goods in distinct ways. As the research progressed, I narrowed the focus of the book to compare sectarian parties only, rather than diverse types of nonstate providers, effectively eliminating the first hypothesis. The second set of hypotheses, which were specific to power-sharing systems, suggested that political parties and religious charities favor in-group members in such polities. Finally, the third set of hypotheses maintained that political parties bestow distinct types and quantities of welfare goods to core supporters versus other types of beneficiaries. The presentation of the working hypotheses also included examples of the types of findings that would invalidate these claims. The book ultimately included more disaggregated and nuanced elaborations of the second and third sets of hypotheses. As a result, the researchers were familiar with the broad focus of the project but not the precise claims that were ultimately developed and assessed in the book.

2. *The role of interviews in the project*: An introduction to distinct types of interviews, including survey interviews, highly structured interviews, and open-ended interviews, as well as a justification for the choice of in-depth interviews to complement other modes of data collection in the project.

3. *Conversational interviewing techniques*: A discussion of the data-generation process from "conversational interviewing" (Rubin and Rubin 2004) and a brief discussion of readings assigned in advance of the training session.[8] The open-ended and in-depth nature of the conversational interviewing approach used by team members ultimately provided rich material for the final product, even if the initial hypotheses shifted during the course of the research.

4. *Interview protocol*: An extensive segment devoted to a line-by-line review of the interview protocol in order to address any sources of confusion or

ambiguity in the question wording, order, or related issues. While the actual interview protocol was rather extensive, interviewers were not expected to adhere strictly to the question order and were trained to foster a relaxed exchange, as emphasized in conversational interviewing techniques.

5. *Sampling and recruitment*: A brainstorming session on strategies for recruiting interviewees, including varied techniques in light of each participant's existing ties and potential links to in-group community networks, ways to break down class barriers between the interviewer and interviewee, and methods of ensuring variation in the sample according to theoretically relevant demographic, geographic, and other characteristics.[9]

6. *Running the interview*: An extensive session devoted to the process of running the interview, covering the following subtopics:

   - Appropriate forms of self-introduction and introduction of the project to the informant;
   - Ways to ensure confidentiality and protect the interviewee's identity;
   - Techniques for opening the substantive portion of the interview, maintaining the flow of the interview, and persisting in seeking answers without offending;
   - Tips for handling flexibility in the question order and other potential deviations from the interview schedule;
   - Techniques for listening and maintaining rapport; and
   - Ways to pose sensitive or potentially uncomfortable questions.

This segment also included mock interviews and role playing to provide preliminary experience in running the interview.[10]

7. *Pilot tests and interview protocol adjustments*: Procedures for pre-testing the interview protocol, with a scheduled follow-up group meeting to revise the questionnaire based on pre-test experiences.

8. *Recording the interview*: Techniques for recording the interview, whether by digital recording devices, which I supplied to each team member, or by note-taking, contingent on the interviewee's preference. This segment underscored the importance of taking notes alongside the digital recording in order to document observations and ensure a reliable backup in case of mechanical failure of the recording device.

9. *Ethics and informed consent*: An introduction to the concept and importance of informed consent, the process of obtaining informed consent for participation in the interview, ways of assuring confidentiality and safeguarding the confidentiality of the data. This segment also

reviewed the stipulations of the Brown University Institutional Review Board (IRB), including the requirement that all team members complete the web-based Collaborative Institutional Training Initiative (CITI) examination on research ethics via the Brown portal prior to conducting any interviews.[11] Interviewers were provided with a script that was preapproved by the Brown IRB, and during the actual interviews they obtained informed consent orally.

10. *Translation and transcription*: A set of guidelines for transcribing and translating the interview after completion, with the strong recommendation that interviewers complete these processes within a day of the interview. A local freelance journalist, journalism trainer, and professional Arabic-English translator joined the group to provide useful suggestions for the transcription and translation processes.

11. *Logistics*: A final segment on logistical issues, including time management and scheduling, the mechanics of operating the recording device, and the schedule of team and individual meetings.

These components of the interviewer training session that I ran in Lebanon provide a list of basic topics to be covered in training sessions for proxy interviewing. Throughout the training and interviewing processes, it is especially critical for the lead researcher and all team members to be sensitive to the power dynamics embedded in relationships established both within the team and between interviewers and respondents. Ultimate authority over the project obviously rests with the lead researcher, but it is critical to foster a nonhierarchical working environment that promotes receptiveness to all input from and exchanges among team members. Similarly, the interviewers should convey respect for the concerns and viewpoints of interviewees, particularly where class and other social hierarchies are salient.

Interviewee Sampling and Recruitment

After a thorough training session, pilot testing of the interview protocol, and follow-up meetings, each team member interviewed between twenty and thirty respondents over a two-month period. Two factors were critical for the non-random sampling of interviewees—ensuring variation on theoretically relevant criteria and identifying viable and ethical strategies to locate potential respondents.

First, variation along criteria such as age, gender, geographic location, and partisanship was critical because each of these factors might independently affect access to social welfare in general and/or influence the respondent's ability to benefit from services offered by particular political or religious organizations.

For example, older individuals or women of childbearing age are more likely to seek medical care than other respondents, while residents of areas with multiple welfare agencies might enjoy more options for various types of social assistance. It was particularly important to identify interviewees with different partisan affiliations, given that a central hypothesis in the project centered on the relationship between partisanship and access to social services. Variation on these demographic and political characteristics mirrored the variables represented in my national survey, which aimed to capture the relationship between partisanship, sectarian identity, and access to social benefits. Given the non-random sampling procedure employed, it was not possible to generalize from the findings collected from these in-depth interviews. Nonetheless, the data greatly enriched both the design and interpretation of the mass survey and shed light on the nature of interactions between individuals and party-based or religious charitable groups.

Second, the mode of access to potential respondents potentially shapes the richness and accuracy of the information obtained from interviews, as well as the process of obtaining informed consent. In approaching possible interviewees, the interviewers worked through informal networks and referral chains, but, at the same time, they did not select family members or close friends and associates as respondents. In any case, the latter strategy would not have yielded an appropriate sample, given the class differences between most interviewers and the population of interest. But class differences raised an additional area of concern, notably the ways in which power differentials between the interviewers and interviewees could shape the responses and, hence, the interview data, as well as the comfort and terms of consent of the interviewee. Less-privileged interviewees might feel subtly pressured by requests from wealthier or more-educated individuals and therefore could agree to the interview out of fear or deference. Furthermore, the gap in social status could also compel respondents to provide answers that reflected what they expected the interviewers wanted to hear rather than those that reflected their "true" opinions or experiences. Thus, interviewers were required to strike a balance between seeking respondents in readily accessible social networks while ensuring that their relationships with respondents were not overly intimate, and that potential respondents would not feel coerced to participate. In most cases, the interviewers relied on referral chains initiated within their neighborhoods by individuals to whom they were familiar but not particularly close.

The interviewers used diverse approaches to identify and recruit potential respondents. Referral chains were particularly valuable, given that family reputation and place of origin are important sources of social trust in Lebanon. By working through networks, the interviewers were able to establish trust *ex ante* with potential respondents. Many used family and social connections to make contact with initial informants, who then referred them to additional, more distant respondents from middle- and low-income groups. Others who lived in socioeconomically mixed neighborhoods arranged meetings with neighbors with varying partisan proclivities. Referrals from individuals known through employment relationships or retail interactions also proved useful. For example, one interviewer held an especially productive meeting with an aesthetician who worked with many family members and neighbors. Another interviewer held an initial meeting with a local hairdresser who resided in a lower-income neighborhood. No interviewers relied on a single referral chain; rather, all relied on varied initial contacts in order to ensure the recruitment of respondents from diverse social networks and areas.

Proxy interviewing raises a dilemma about whether the lead researcher should be present during the interviews themselves. This choice is not clear-cut: the researcher's presence at the interview can serve as a quality-control measure, but it may deter respondents from free discussion. I opted not to take part in the interviews because I was concerned about biasing the results in the tense political climate of the research site, potentially undermining the very rationale for proxy interviewing. Time constraints and the sheer number of interviews across multiple communities also prevented me from traveling with researchers to interviews. I tried to compensate for the possible disadvantages of this choice by asking researchers to tape the interviews wherever possible and by holding weekly and biweekly individual and group team meetings to review the results and discuss strategies for improving the interviewing process. Keeping the interviewers engaged in the process and the selection of highly motivated and skilled researchers in the first place helped to ensure that the interviews were generally well executed and comprehensive.

Feasibility

At least three factors affect the feasibility (and utility) of matched, proxy interviewing: the quality of the interviewers, the ability to spend significant time in the field, and sufficient resources. First, recruiting appropriate respondents and collecting valuable and relevant data are contingent on the skills of the interviewers themselves. Thus, the screening, selection, and training of the interviewers, described above, are critical.

Second, matched, proxy interviewing requires a significant time commitment on the part of the lead researcher. This team-based interviewing method requires close supervision. Unlike omnibus and perhaps even subcontracted mass surveys, the researcher must be present in the field while the interviews are conducted. To maintain momentum, ensure that the interviewers remain on schedule, and monitor the protection of confidentiality in the research process requires regular group meetings, during which team members discuss their results and trade ideas about effective and ineffective interviewing techniques. If the lead researcher is not present at the interviews, it is particularly essential to review transcripts and notes from each of the interviews on a regular basis to ensure that individual team members continue to address the key questions, carry out productive interviews, and sufficiently diversify the respondent pool. Group and individual meetings also enable the interviewers themselves to provide feedback on the larger questions at hand—a valuable contribution, given their insights into their own societies and intimate familiarity with the research topic.

A third factor shaping the feasibility of matched, proxy interviewing is sufficient financial resources. A team-based approach to interviewing can call for a larger research budget than many faculty and graduate students may possess. But matched, proxy interviewing need not be prohibitively expensive, even for researchers with small budgets. Costs vary widely depending on the research site and scale of the project. Wages, research-related costs, and, if applicable, benefits differ markedly across research sites. In low- and middle-income countries, compensation rates can be relatively low vis-à-vis standards in industrialized countries.[12] The scale of the project also affects the budget required for matched, proxy interviewing. Not all projects entail a large team of interviewers, either because the number of ethnic, religious, or other theoretically relevant categories for the project is minimal, calling for fewer corresponding interviewers, or because in-depth interviews may not be central to the project, and therefore a small number of interviews is sufficient.

The Advantages and Disadvantages of Proxy Interviewing

Proxy interviewing can yield rich data. In my research on social service provision by sectarian groups in Lebanon, the results were striking, particularly when compared with findings from elite interviews and survey research. In-depth interviews with citizens shed light on the complex decision-making processes that compelled individuals and families to seek services from different providers, their experiences of receiving or being denied services or assistance, their perceptions of provider organizations and interpretations of how political engagement and religious identity shaped or did not shape their access to services, and other issues germane to the core questions and hypotheses. Respondents were candid in their answers to questions posed by the interviewers. For example, all spoke openly about their efforts to seek health care for themselves or family members and, where applicable, their attempts to gain coveted spots in schools or financial assistance for tuition. Most had sought services or aid or both at one time or another from sectarian parties and religious charities, and they recounted in detail their interactions with these types of providers. The contrasting accounts of those who are party loyalists and activists and those who lack party connections were noteworthy, with the former enjoying greater access to a broader and more continuous array of benefits.

Almost all of the proxy interviews conducted for this research produced at least some relevant information. In any project, not all interviews are equally valuable for the final product. Among the proxy interviews in this research, however, virtually all yielded at least one or two insights related to the central hypotheses and, in most cases, many more. Systematic content analysis of the interview data showed this clearly. Using NVivo, a software program that enables content analysis of qualitative data, I coded all of the in-depth elite and non-elite interviews carried out for this research. To conduct the content analysis, I created codes to categorize segments of the interviews by relevant topics, facilitating more systematic analyses of their implications for the working hypotheses and opposing interpretations, and left uncoded those portions of the interview that were irrelevant to the project. Even in the least informative interviews, about twelve segments of the interview were linked to coding categories. In the most useful and richest interviews, as many as fifty-six portions of the interview were coded.

In the absence of an experimental study comparing the responses of randomly assigned individuals to the same questions posed by the lead researcher versus proxy interviewers, it is impossible to make definitive claims about the value added by proxy interviewing. My experiences and common sense, however, strongly suggest that the approach produced more fine-grained and valid data than would otherwise be possible. My own efforts to gain access to interviewees were not productive, because interactions with potential respondents often occurred in welfare facilities with staff members present, which constrained people from speaking freely, and respondents were clearly reluctant to share their thoughts with a foreign researcher whose background and intentions were unfamiliar. By building on local referral chains and conducting interviews in more neutral locations, usually in respondents' homes, the interviewers largely succeeded in establishing good rapport and facilitated open and deep exchanges during the interviews.

The data gathered through the team's interviews also improved the quality of other research methods that I employed in the project. In particular, the interview data provided essential background for the construction of a mass survey, which was carried out about four months after the interviewing process concluded. Information on what services respondents sought and possible channels for access to services spurred the inclusion of specific questions and the addition of a variety of options in the closed-ended survey instrument.[13]

Like any research method, the team-based approach has its drawbacks. First and foremost, the approach is dependent on the ability of the interviewer to tap into appropriate social networks and to select interviewees that vary according to theoretically relevant demographic or other characteristics. For some interviewers, this was a nonissue. For example, in my project in Lebanon, the interviewer assigned to the Druze community had easy access to respondents in this tight-knit, minority community, in which her family was known and respected. Similarly, respondents from the Sunni and Christian communities were easily recruited and forthright in their comments, thanks to preexisting ties that the corresponding interviewers enjoyed in neighborhoods, towns, and villages with concentrations of these communities.

Our ability to penetrate the Shia community, and specifically core supporters of Hezbollah, however, was more limited. Hezbollah is relatively closed to outsiders, including Lebanese and coreligionists who do not have established track records of support for the organization. It would have been impossible to recruit an active Hezbollah supporter—or even someone with strong ties to the group's supporters—to participate in the team. Given the hostile relationship between the United States, which labels the organization an Iranian-backed "terrorist" group (U.S. Department of State 2010), and Hezbollah, which views the United States as an imperialist force in the Middle East with a biased, pro-Israel foreign policy, any research conducted by an American researcher is viewed with suspicion. The history of assassination attempts on top Hezbollah leaders and efforts to infiltrate the organization by U.S., Israeli, and other foreign intelligence services have compelled the group to assume that most foreign researchers are spies and to subject journalists and researchers to extensive formal and informal security clearances. Under these circumstances, anyone with ties to core supporters of Hezbollah would be reluctant to take part in the project. Furthermore, even if an interviewer succeeded in tapping into these social networks, word of her activities would soon spread to the organization's representatives, who would closely monitor or even put a stop to the interviews. As a result of these political restrictions, the interviewer matched to Shia respondents was not able to interview core Hezbollah activists and members but rather focused on more marginal supporters and on individuals who were refused or did not seek services from Hezbollah.

The data that the Shia community interviewer collected, however, were highly instructive, particularly in conjunction with information gathered through survey research, GIS analysis, and elite interviews. The interview data helped to construct profiles of Shia respondents who sought but did not receive assistance from Hezbollah welfare agencies or who never sought assistance in the first place, developing a contrast with hard-core supporters. By and large, these respondents were marginal or non-supporters of the party. By Hezbollah's own admission (conveyed in elite-level interviews), these categories of applicants receive fewer social benefits than core activists.

Variable access to different categories of respondents might suggest that proxy interviewing—and perhaps interviewing as commonly practiced in political science—is of little utility; it can point to a larger methodological issue, notably that non-random recruitment inevitably introduces bias into the sample of respondents. What can we possibly conclude from data gathered from interviews collected through a particular researcher's social network and associated referral chains? At best, such non-random sampling techniques limit the generalizability of the findings. At worst, they present an anomalous slice of a larger population, which has distinct central tendencies in its attitudes and behaviors.

For research on controversial topics or in politically sensitive contexts, however, sampling via social networks and referral chains is likely to yield richer data and, indeed, may be the only workable strategy (Atkinson and Flint 2001). The contrast is most obvious with respect to closed-ended survey research, in which the truthfulness of respondents poses a serious problem to the validity of the findings. Although researchers have devised methods to gauge and even compensate for misrepresentation by survey respondents (Chikwanha, Sithole, and Bratton 2004; Corstange 2009), the problem is particularly threatening in politically sensitive settings. In-depth, open-ended interviews are more likely to elicit truthful responses, particularly when the interviewee and interviewer enjoy a bond of trust and have some prior contextual knowledge of each other.

Thus, interview research based on non-random sampling presents a trade-off: on the one hand, it is vulnerable to bias and limited external validity. On the other hand, in some circumstances, it presents the most viable strategy for boosting the depth and vibrancy of the findings. To mitigate the negative aspects of interview data derived from non-random samples, researchers can incorporate respondents who represent a range of perspectives or positions on variables of interest. This approach necessarily relies on strong theory, which guides the selection of appropriate factors to vary.[14] Purposive variation in the interviewee sample at least partially compensates for the limitations of non-random sampling by ensuring that the researcher does not focus on a single category of respondents or a narrow range of perspectives. It also enables the researcher to probe competing explanations for the outcome of interest.

Obviously, this solution is not perfect. In the ideal world, then, in-depth interviews should be supplemented with data collected using alternative methods. To the degree that findings from distinct research methods converge or complement each other,[15] the researcher may have greater conviction in her findings. Comparing findings from interviews with distinct categories of respondents—

including those who are both sympathetic and hostile to a particular viewpoint or organization—is another means of bolstering confidence in data collected from interviews based on non-random samples.

In-depth, qualitative interviews constitute a valuable method for gathering valid information in political science research, but gaining access to appropriate interviewees can be difficult, particularly for outsider researchers who are not integrated in local social networks. The challenge is all the more daunting when conducting fieldwork in plural societies, where members of different communities and organizations may have distinct perceptions of the researcher. At the same time, outsider researchers may bring unique theoretical and methodological perspectives that enrich the research. Thus, insider-outsider status poses a tradeoff. Proxy interviewing offers a method for capitalizing on the unique advantages of both insider and outsider status, while recognizing the ambiguous boundaries between these categories. The approach potentially facilitates access to a broader and more appropriate sample of interviewees and, hence, richer and even more valid interview data than might otherwise be possible.

The principles behind proxy interviewing have been applied in survey research for decades. Researchers routinely train and assign enumerators to communities with populations from similar racial, ethnic, or religious backgrounds. Gender also can guide the assignment of interviewers to respondents, particularly on personal or sensitive topics (Catania et al. 1996).[16] To my knowledge, however, few scholars in political science have used a similar process for in-depth interviews.[17] Beyond the developing and plural societies mentioned in this chapter, proxy interviewing can be deployed in any research setting where ostensibly identity-based or other social characteristics shape relationships of trust with respondents, and hence is useful for most field research sites and on a broad range of questions.

7

WORKING WITH INTERPRETERS

Lee Ann Fujii

In the Sophia Coppola film *Lost in Translation*, Bill Murray plays a washed-up American actor who travels to Japan to film a whiskey commercial. In one scene, the Japanese director gives Murray extensive feedback through an interpreter. The director talks "at" Murray's character at great length using animated gestures. When the director finally finishes, the interpreter turns to Murray's character and says, "He wants you to turn, look in camera, OK?" to which Murray responds, nonplussed, "Is that all he said?" (Rich 2003).

Many international travelers have experienced the sense of utter dismay that Murray's character felt in that moment—the sense of missing out on most of what is going on despite, or perhaps because of, the presence of an interpreter. To avoid such situations, scholars generally arrive in their research site already fluent in the local language and able to conduct interviews on their own. But what if a researcher is not fluent in the local language or does not have the time or facility to become fluent? What if there are multiple local languages and the researcher is only fluent in one, or what if local dialects are unintelligible to outsiders? Should researchers simply avoid cases like these or exclude them from their projects?

This chapter argues no: language proficiency should not be the criteria for deciding whether or not to conduct interviews in a given place. In cases where language proficiency is an issue, researchers should consider working with an interpreter. Working with an interpreter is no substitute for fluency, but neither is it a completely inferior option. Working with an interpreter can bring many advantages beyond translating words from one language to another.

144

This chapter seeks to demystify both the process and practice of working with interpreters in interview research. It draws from the author's experiences working with interpreters in Rwanda and Bosnia-Herzegovina (hereinafter "Bosnia"). In both countries, I spent months talking to people living in rural areas about war-related violence that occurred in their communities. My interviewees were ordinary people who, for the most part, did not occupy positions of power. The focus is therefore on non-elite interviews, but some insights might also apply equally well to other types of interviews.

In Rwanda, I worked with French-Kinyarwanda interpreters. My interpreters were native speakers of Kinyarwanda (the language spoken by all Rwandans); they translated my questions from French into Kinyarwanda and people's answers back into French. In Bosnia, I worked with native Serbo-Croatian speakers who also spoke English. My interpreters in this country translated my questions from English into Serbo-Croatian and people's answers back into English. I knew enough Kinyarwanda and Serbo-Croatian to recognize and use key words, but not enough to articulate complex questions or follow people's responses on my own. Additional insights for this chapter came from personal communications with colleagues who have conducted fieldwork in Asia, Eastern Europe, and Latin America.

Weighing Pros and Cons

Interpreters have been invaluable to researchers in a wide range of fields, yet their contribution to interview-based studies remains under-analyzed. Not much is written about working with interpreters (Temple 2002), even in the much more established methods literature on ethnography (Borchgrevink 2003, 97).

While ethnographers of yore might have ventured into their field sites speaking nothing but their own language (Winchatz 2006, 84–85), expectations today have changed. Ethnographic standards put a premium on the researcher being or becoming fluent in the local language. Fluency represents entrée into the world of one's research subjects. Without facility in the local language, the researcher is effectively shut out from this world, with no way to understand "how natives think, how they perceive the world, and what assumptions they make about human experience" (Spradley 1979, 20). Another advantage to fluency is the richness of data one can collect through direct interviews (Devereux 1993, 44) and the rapport one can build through daily interactions (Francis 1993, 90). Without fluency in the local language, one is cut off from everyday life.

Standards in political science seem to be similar when it comes to interviews, though perhaps for different reasons. Direct interviews are better, one assumes, because one-on-one communication will be smoother and clearer than three-way communication; and the researcher will have better control over the interview working alone rather than through an interpreter. Competency in the local language may also help the researcher to establish trust with people, since it demonstrates both her seriousness about the project (John Donaldson, personal communication, March 16, 2010) and respect for the people in her research site (Devereux 1993, 44). In certain regions, fluency may simply be so common among specialists that not speaking the local language (e.g., Spanish for Latin Americanists) would call into question the researcher's professional competency.[1]

For many projects, direct interviews may indeed be better than working with an interpreter. Research topics or sites might be sensitive; initial trust may depend on the researcher demonstrating proficiency in the interviewee's language; and a third party might shape the interview in ways the researcher did not intend and cannot control. An interpreter might distort responses to such a degree, for example, as to diminish rather than facilitate communication. There is also the issue of cost. Many graduate students and scholars may not be able afford professional interpreters, especially for extended periods of time.

These concerns are well-founded and important to consider; but they should not overshadow the potential advantages of working with an interpreter. All research involves trade-offs. Whether one chooses to work with an interpreter or not, the researcher should consider a range of issues rather than simply assuming that conducting interviews with an interpreter will produce low-quality data.

For many projects, it may not be practical for the researcher to conduct interviews on her own. There may be multiple languages spoken locally, or the project might include sub-communities that speak their own language. Most Latin Americanists, for example, speak Spanish but not necessarily Quechua or Mixtec. Learning a new language is a time-consuming process, and, depending on the project, that time might be better spent attending to other research tasks (Thøgersen 2006, 44).

While hiring a professional interpreter might be too costly, it is also possible to work with an interpreter who has not been professionally trained, but who is willing and able to learn. Hiring a nonprofessional does put the onus of training on the researcher, but it also brings down costs and makes it possible for even those on limited budgets to work with an interpreter over extended periods. In Rwanda, for example, all researchers, including graduate students with limited funds, work with interpreters, some for months at a time.

Choosing not to work with an interpreter also presents risks. An English-speaking researcher who does not feel comfortable working in the local language might unwittingly gravitate toward those who speak English and avoid those who do not. This might not matter in some situations; a researcher seeking the official views of a Czech ministry, for example, might obtain the same response from an English-speaking representative as a Czech-speaking one. For other projects, however, talking only to those who speak English might skew the selection of interviewees in ways that compromise the project. In some places, talking to people who are comfortable speaking English might mean interviewing only the most educated, thereby excluding women, the poor, or certain age cohorts. My "under thirty" interpreter in Sarajevo had learned English entirely on her own (by listening to American music and watching American movies on TV), but many older Bosnians, including heads of civil society organizations and senior faculty at the local university, may not speak any English at all. Interviewing only English-speakers might also mean talking with people who grew up abroad. In the years following the war and genocide in Rwanda, talking with English-speaking Rwandans generally meant talking to Rwandans who had spent their entire lives outside the country.

Conducting interviews in the researcher's (rather than interviewee's) language also might compromise the reliability and richness of the data. An interviewee with limited English will have limited ways to express himself. He may stick with what he literally knows how to say, leaving aside more complicated stories, ideas, or commentary. Other data may be lost as well, such as concepts that do not translate easily into English, or registers and moods that communicate different degrees of formality, politeness, respect, and even hierarchy. Working with an interpreter also presents challenges, but the main advantage is that it allows the interviewee to talk in the language in which he thinks and feels, thereby expanding the possibilities for self-expression and the range of potential interviewees with whom the researcher can communicate in a meaningful way.

Rethinking Language Proficiency

The decision to work with an interpreter is usually based on a researcher's own assessment of her proficiency in a particular language—whether she feels sufficiently fluent to conduct interviews in that language. But language proficiency is a matter of both degree (Devereux 1993, 45) and context. One can be fluent in one context (shopping for food) but not in others (in-depth discussions about the complexities of the legal system). Language proficiency is thus not only a question about the researcher's abilities; it is also a question about the project itself—what languages and types of fluency the project requires. Researchers should consider the following points when assessing the language needs of their project.

First, "textbook fluency" may not prepare the researcher for everyday forms of communication, particularly among those who did not go to university or even secondary school. As Thøgersen (2006, 111) notes in the case of China: "Non-native speakers of textbook Chinese run into language problems as soon as they leave the protected world of educated informants." In other words, being fluent in classical or formal forms of the local language might not make the researcher fluent in everyday forms of the language. If the research design calls for talking to people other than the most educated, then textbook fluency may not suffice.

Second, vocabularies can be highly specialized. One can be fluent in some domains but not in others. I am a native English speaker who is fairly proficient in French, yet I am not fluent in French slang and am unfamiliar with terms related to medicine. Hence, if I were to do a study of urban youth in Paris or health care programs in Guinée, I would need to become fluent in the relevant vocabularies or work with an interpreter until I gained such fluency.

Third, many words and ideas do not translate easily across languages or cultures (Temple 2002, 847). With the demise of apartheid in South Africa, a Zulu phrase had to be invented for the term "democracy" (Cole 2010, 73). When terms such as "democracy" are imported wholesale into other languages, their meanings may shift according to the local context and thus differ significantly from how the researcher understands the terms (Schaffer 2006).

Fourth, meanings and usage can vary even within the same language. Any American who has traveled to the United Kingdom knows firsthand how different British, Irish, and Scottish English can be from American English. It is not just a matter of accent, which by itself can make one type of English unintelligible to another's ears; it is also a matter of usage. The same word can mean different things—for instance, "jumper," "bonnet," and "boot." References, too, are culturally rooted, so that idioms and metaphors in one type of English may have little meaning in another. I once sat in a meeting with three software managers in Manchester, England, and came out having understood only half of what my colleagues had said. Urban and rural dialects of the same language can also vary to the point where rural idioms may not make sense to urban speakers and vice versa, even within the same country (Cole 2010, 73). Thus, even if a researcher is fluent in the local language, she may still need to consult with a local who can "translate" local references and idioms so the researcher can be sure she understands what people are saying. It might also require budgeting time to become acclimated to the local language, even if that language is ostensibly the researcher's "own."

Fifth, languages also vary in their complexities and nuances. What makes a language difficult for nonnative speakers to learn is not only grammar and pronunciation, but also how people convey meaning. In some languages, meaning is conveyed through inflection and context, rather than word choice, tone, declension, or conjugation. In Kinyarwanda, for example, the same verb (*gushaka*) can mean "to want," "to desire," "to need," and "to look for"; the same word (*i*) can mean "to" and "from"; and some verb tenses are expressed through inflection rather than conjugation. These linguistic nuances make it difficult for outsiders to master Kinyarwanda as speakers and listeners. Devereux makes similar observations about the language spoken in his research site in northeast Ghana. During a study of the economics of hunger, he discovers, much to his dismay, that the same word (*kom*) is used to express all forms of hunger, from mild pangs to widespread famine (Devereux 1993, 48). Devereux must then rely on his interpreter to translate the precise meaning speakers intend when they use this word. As Devereux (1993, 45) points out, "*knowledge* of vocabulary is not *understanding* of meaning" (emphasis in original).

Sixth, language competence does not make a person culturally competent. Early in my fieldwork in Rwanda in 2004, I realized that even if I did speak enough Kinyarwanda to conduct interviews myself, I would still need an interpreter because I would not have been culturally competent to make sense of people's responses. So nuanced is the language that even scholars with quite good proficiency in Kinyarwanda still work with interpreters.

In sum, language proficiency is not a straightforward concept. What it means to be proficient in the relevant languages will depend on the project, the type of interviews, and the type of interviewees. For those fluent in textbook versions of the local language, an interpreter might be useful for understanding more colloquial or spoken forms of the language. For languages or cultures that are difficult for outsiders to master, working with an interpreter may add crucial insight into nuances in meaning, even if the researcher has a working knowledge of the local language. For situations where the researcher has general competency in the local language but lacks familiarity with certain vocabularies, dialects, or expressions, an interpreter may not be necessary for interviewing, but may be helpful for going over interview tapes and transcripts to make sure the researcher has understood what people said in their interviews and how they understood the questions.[2]

Working with Interpreters

Good interpreters do much more than simply render spoken words from one language to another; they also can play a vital role "interpreting" in the methodological sense—in helping the researcher make sense of what people say by calling attention to background knowledge that gives meaning and context to people's words.

In this way, interpreters can serve as valuable collaborators in their own right. They can provide a second set of eyes and ears. They can pick up on different cues, both verbal and nonverbal. They can provide insight into people's responses, behaviors, attitudes, and body language during interviews. They may notice details that the researcher misses. My French-Kinyarwanda interpreter in 2004, for example, noticed right after one interview that the man we had just interviewed had given the same names for his parents as another man we had recently interviewed in the prison. My interpreter deduced that the two must be brothers. This was a significant realization, since the man we had just interviewed never mentioned having a brother in prison, which suggested a strategy of evasion on his part (Fujii 2010).

In some settings, translating may be the least important task that the interpreter performs. In war zones, for example, interpreters can occupy dual roles—that of interpreter and guide, ensuring not only communication, but also security. American journalist Peter Maass (1996) traveled all over Bosnia in the early 1990s during the first two years of a very bloody war. During that period, he worked with a few different interpreters. According to Maass, the English language skills of his interpreters were much less important than their instincts about safety—what was safe to do and where it was safe to go. In Iraq, Maass chose interpreters for the same reasons (Peter Maass, personal communication, June 3, 2012).

French journalist Jean Hatzfeld's experience underscores the importance of an interpreter's instincts about safety. In the final pages of his book *Une saison de machettes* (*Machete Season*), Hatzfeld relates a story of how his interpreter led the two out of a potentially deadly situation while Hatzfeld was conducting interviews in Rwanda at the end of that country's four-year civil war and a genocide that had claimed the lives of half a million people (Des Forges 1999). Hatzfeld was following the wave of Rwandans fleeing westward toward the border with then-Zaire (now the Democratic Republic of the Congo). Going through the Nyungwe forest, Hatzfeld became curious about stories he had heard that some Rwandans had taken to living in the forest, rather than fleeing across the border. His curiosity prompted him to turn off the main road. He and his interpreter followed a path into the forest and came upon a group of men with machetes nearby and monkey meat on the grill. Hatzfeld's interpreter quickly warned Hatzfeld that the men were *Interahamwe*—that is, former militia who had been largely responsible for the recent mass killings.

Hatzfeld and his interpreter got out of their car and approached the group of men. The men asked Hatzfeld for news of the war. The conversation continued haltingly; then the atmosphere shifted abruptly. The group of *Interahamwe* stood up, grabbed their machetes, and began to encircle Hatzfeld and his interpreter. The two men slowly backed up to their car, jumped inside, and fled the scene. The *Interahamwe* hacked at the fleeing vehicle, disappointed that their "prey" had gotten away.

The scene that Hatzfeld describes is one of the most chilling passages in the book. What is clear from his retelling of this incident is the critical role his interpreter played in reading the situation correctly. Hatzfeld's interpreter accurately identified these men not as refugees, but as militia who were more than capable of killing them. Without his interpreter's instincts, the two may well have lost their belongings, their vehicle, and possibly their lives (Hatzfeld 2003).

Though I was not working in an active war zone, I also came to value my interpreters' instincts about safety and security. I came to trust my interpreters through my earliest experiences working with them. At the very start of my research in Bosnia, my interpreter in Sarajevo introduced me to a wide range of intellectuals and leaders of civil society organizations. These were people she thought I should meet so that I could get a sense of the range of perspectives people had about the war. One reason I came to trust her was that after several meetings, she would tell me about her personal experiences with the people we had just met. Sometimes these experiences were negative, but she had never let on either before or during the meetings. Instead, she let me discover for myself what information and perspectives various people offered.

It was this same interpreter who gave me advice about traveling to one of the former prison camps that the Bosnian Serb army had set up in areas it controlled during the war. I was staying not far from one of the camps and wanted to visit. Before going, I asked my interpreter if she thought it would be all right if I made the trip by myself (going by cab). She advised me not to go since I spoke English (an indication I was American) and there was nothing in the vicinity but this former camp, so there was no way to camouflage my trip as anything but a "fact-finding" excursion into an aspect of the war that was still highly contested. The combination of an American "visiting" a former concentration camp in the Republic of Srpska did not bode well for my safety, she explained, given recent events where visitors had been attacked. I followed her advice and decided to forgo the trip.

In addition to keeping researchers safe and sound, interpreters also can serve as interlocutors. My interpreter in the Krajina region of Bosnia, for example, was extremely valuable as an interlocutor because she had grown up in the small village where I was doing research and knew many of the people still living there. Because she had known these people most of her life, we were able to gain access in a very short period of time.

Interpreters can also become key informants. My interpreters in Bosnia and Rwanda all became informants through the numerous informal conversations we had over meals or waiting for an interview. During my first field trip to Rwanda in 2004, I discounted these exchanges and became frustrated with what I mistakenly considered to be "down time." I later came to realize that these exchanges formed as much a part of the fieldwork as any formal interview. More recently, I have come to value the stories my interpreter in Rwanda has begun to tell me in the car and over lunch. Her stories have provided extremely valuable insight into the larger (regional) power structures that were in place during the 1990s. These insights are all the more valuable because I have come to trust her so much and because they come from her own, firsthand experience working with and observing various authorities in the volatile period leading up to the 1994 genocide.

Finally, interpreters can provide invaluable local knowledge. Local knowledge might include insight into the possible meanings behind specific expressions or idioms; the stories surrounding well-known figures or places; and the customs and practices that define different kinds of relationships. So invaluable is local knowledge to my current work that I have even hired an "interpreter" in my U.S. research site in Maryland, where language is presumably not an issue. I have come to rely heavily on my Maryland research assistant for her extensive local knowledge about people, places, history, and culture. Her "fluency" in names, places, and dates allows her to converse more easily with interviewees and to establish rapport with people much more quickly and effectively than I would be able to working on my own.

In sum, good interpreters can play multiple roles throughout the research process. In addition to interpreting during interviews, they can also bring insight, perspective, and instincts that may be critical to the researcher's ability to navigate the field safely and soundly and to make sense of what people *mean*, not just what they say, in interviews.

Finding the Right Interpreter

What makes a good interpreter? From the discussion above, it is clear that language ability alone does not make a good interpreter. So what criteria should researchers use to look for an interpreter? Many, if not most, of the qualities that make a good interpreter are the same that make a good (local) research assistant. Here are a few to consider.

First, a good interpreter is someone who can navigate many different types of relationships. To the extent that research involves interacting with all kinds of people—from the lowliest bureaucrat to the highest official and many in between—one quality to look for is the interpreter's ability to talk easily with people from a wide range of social strata and to treat these people with similar levels of respect and friendliness. It is important to notice whether an interpreter feels uncomfortable or hesitant in certain surroundings or tries to differentiate herself from those around her, through how she dresses, talks, or behaves. One of my colleagues in Rwanda, for example, worked with an interpreter who insisted on wearing her nicest city clothes to conduct interviews with poor women living in a very rural area. Her interpreter's style of dress accentuated an already pronounced difference in social status between her and the interviewees, which made it even more difficult for my colleague to build rapport with these women.

A second, equally important quality is the interpreter's ability to put other people at ease. If potential interviewees feel uncomfortable around the interpreter, they will likely feel uncomfortable around the researcher. If they find the interpreter too haughty or officious (or, conversely, lacking in competence and integrity), they may well view the researcher in the same light.

A prisoner in Rwanda whom I interviewed several times recently confirmed my belief that people's comfort level with my interpreter was key to the quality of the interviews I conducted. At the end of one interview cut short by rain, this man commented (without my having asked) that the reason he was willing to talk so openly was because of my interpreter. I followed up this remark at a subsequent interview, asking whether his willingness to talk with us was because of his trust in me or my interpreter. Without hesitating, he said that it was because of my interpreter—that everything depended on the interpreter. He also claimed that my interpreter was the reason that other prisoners were willing to talk to me as well. While there is no way to verify his claim, I felt gratified that he confirmed a belief I had long held—that "everything" did indeed depend on my interpreter's ability to win people's trust.

One way to assess an interpreter's ability to put people at ease is to observe how she talks to others and how others respond to her in turn. Does the interpreter use the same manner of greeting toward everyone or only those of certain social status or rank? Does she chat as easily with the minister's secretary as the minister herself? Does she assert herself at the right moments and back off when necessary? The researcher also might take note of how the interpreter acts with the researcher. Does she show too much or too little deference or treat the researcher as a colleague? I myself prefer working with interpreters who see their role as equal partner, rather than subordinate or employee. Establishing a more equal relationship with an interpreter acknowledges the unique skills and knowledge that the interpreter brings to the project.

A third quality is the interpreter's ability to translate others' words without letting her personal feelings color how she translates. A good interpreter is someone who can talk with bankers in the morning and thieves in the afternoon without giving the slightest hint of her own personal views about either profession. This type of neutrality may be difficult to discern. If the researcher has any doubts about the accuracy of the interpreter's translations, she might try to tape interviews, then go over them with another interpreter afterward.[3] If the researcher simply has questions about certain translations, she can discuss these with her interpreter later. I use the time spent transcribing the data as an opportunity to discuss specific interviews in greater depth with my interpreter and to raise questions I may have had about particular responses or translations.

In some cases, interpreters might draw their own personal line in terms of what kinds of interviews they are willing to do. I worked with an interpreter in Bosnia, for example, who told me at the very beginning that he would find it too difficult to translate perpetrators' words in the first person. If an interpreter's reservations are known ahead of time, it may be possible to work around them. In Bosnia, I could have hired a different interpreter for interviews with perpetrators. What is not possible, however, is to "correct" interviews after the fact, especially those inexorably shaped by the interpreter's personal judgments, dislikes, or commentary.

A fourth quality is the interpreter's instinct for the kind of research one is doing. Does the interpreter fit the project? Does she understand the nature of the project, including the kinds of people the researcher wants to interview and the topics the researcher wants to probe? Does she understand the researcher's concerns regarding time limitations, budget, and institutional review board mandates?[4] My own research involves talking to people living in rural areas who do not occupy positions of power of any kind. With this type of project, I need to work with someone who understands the importance of obtaining informed consent and who does not insist that informants be paid for their time, since I do not pay for interviews. An interpreter who does not respect (or believe in) these requirements could doom my project, by misrepresenting the terms for interviews, for example, or by violating our ethical obligations to minimize risk and harm to interviewees.

A fifth quality is the interpreter's ability to give and take direction. During the course of fieldwork, the interpreter and researcher will likely take turns leading and following. The researcher should not feel like she has to make all the decisions; neither should the researcher assume that her interpreter is an expert in social science methods. What is ideal is for both parties to remain flexible and able to take direction from the other. I frequently solicit my interpreters' advice about field strategies—how to locate certain people, how to plan logistics, how to approach certain people. Their feedback is invaluable because fieldwork is such an all-consuming process that it is easy to lose sight of alternative ways to accomplish even the simplest tasks.

A sixth criterion to consider is the positionality of the interpreter vis-à-vis the researcher and potential interviewees.[5] Positionality refers to the way others identify or make sense of the interpreter and, by extension, the researcher. Choices regarding gender and age may be critical to the success of a project. A study focused on women, for example, might proceed better with a female rather than male interpreter, especially if the researcher is male. Similarly, a study of youth may call for an interpreter of similar age to the demographic group of interest.

Researchers should not approach issues of positionality as a checklist of desired characteristics, however. Interviewees and interlocutors will read subjectivities differently in different contexts. The same interpreter whose youthful appearance leads people to talk openly in one context might lead people to refrain in another. An interpreter's insider status might produce quicker access but make people more hesitant to talk about sensitive issues with someone from the same community.

One should also be careful about applying "standard practices" from one research setting to another. In Bosnia, for example, colleagues advised me to hire a Serb interpreter to talk with Serbs and a Muslim interpreter to talk with Muslims. In Rwanda, I received just the opposite advice. A Rwandan colleague advised me to find an interpreter whom interviewees could not easily type as Hutu or Tutsi. In general, the skills of an interpreter will always be more important than any putative social categories he or she might occupy. The researcher simply needs to be aware that people in any research site will try to categorize both the researcher *and* interpreter; and how people read these subjectivities can shape who agrees to being interviewed and what people are willing to say in an interview.

Finally, researchers should pay attention to the level of overall professionalism that an interpreter brings. These qualities include trustworthiness, reliability, and intelligibility. Trustworthiness has to do with the interpreter's ability to keep all confidential materials and exchanges confidential. If a researcher has any doubt about an interpreter's commitment to maintain confidentiality, the researcher should find another interpreter, because ethical practices are a fundamental responsibility of all field researchers (Fujii 2012).

Reliability has to do with the interpreter's standards of professional conduct. Does the interpreter arrive on time and prepared to work, or is she habitually late? Does she meet deadlines? Does she follow through on tasks the researcher has given her? Given the multiple roles that interpreters can play in the research process, it is imperative that the researcher can count on him or her. An unreliable interpreter is not just a nuisance; he or she can derail a project, by causing the researcher to miss appointments, for example, or by making the researcher appear unprofessional to potential interviewees.

Intelligibility has to do with how well the researcher and interpreter communicate—how well they understand each other. Intelligibility does not reduce to language abilities. I have worked with Rwandans and Bosnians whose English skills were quite good, but the communication remained quite poor.

Conversely, I have worked with Rwandans whose French was very limited, but our communication was always excellent.

To locate potential interpreters, scholars might consult with researchers who have worked in the same region or community or have done similar types of studies in the same country. These colleagues may be able to give insight into the reputation of various interpreters and the going rates for interpreters, which can vary considerably. It may also be possible to advertise for an interpreter. In Rwanda, I put an ad in the weekly newsletter of the United States embassy that went out to all embassy staff, including Rwandan staff. With Facebook and other online social media, researchers might be able to obtain recommendations even before arriving at their field site (though I would strongly advise any researcher to spend face-to-face time with candidates before hiring anyone).

Finding the right interpreter may involve some trial and error. Initial meetings with interpreter candidates may reveal whether there is an initial fit, which in my experience is more important than prior experience. My first interpreter in Rwanda fit me and my project extremely well, even though all her prior work experience was with nongovernmental organizations, not interpreting for solo researchers. During this initial meeting, the researcher also may be able to tell—by the questions the candidate asks or the comments she makes—how well the candidate understands the nature and goals of the project.

Following interviews of candidates, the researcher might hire the most promising candidate for a single day or afternoon to help the researcher accomplish a variety of project-related tasks, such as meeting with contacts or visiting sites relevant to the project. After I first arrived in Rwanda in 2004, for example, I hired one interpreter to go with me to various genocide memorials and another to visit potential research sites. After spending a whole day or afternoon with a candidate, the researcher should have a fairly clear idea whether the candidate is someone with whom the researcher can spend long days traveling, commuting, waiting, sitting, conversing, and interviewing. Fieldwork can be exhausting, and working closely with an interpreter who is not a good fit will feel like a burden rather than a help.

Once the researcher has hired her interpreter, the first task is to train or orient the interpreter to the researcher's specific preferences and needs. The researcher should explain the nature of the interviews she is conducting (structured? semi-structured? open-ended?) and what she is looking for in the data. The researcher should also specify how she wants the interpreter to translate. Does the researcher expect simultaneous translation? If so, this will be difficult for nonprofessional interpreters, especially when the word order between target and base languages is quite different (Cole 2010). Is paraphrasing in the third person sufficient, or does the researcher need first-person translations that are faithful to what the interviewee is saying? In my own research, I was interested not only in what people said but also how they said it, so I wanted the translations to be in first-person voice and to be as faithful as possible, even when interviewees repeated themselves or meandered (Fujii 2009, 2010).

One way to begin working with a new interpreter is to do a series of practice interviews. In Rwanda, I did practice interviews with people who worked in the homes of colleagues and with Rwandans who worked in the building where I was living. My interpreter and I did these interviews as we would a real interview, starting with full introductions and an oral consent protocol. When issues arose, my interpreter and I could address them immediately, such as my preference for first-person translations and asking people for first names only, to help protect identities.

Researchers should also be clear about what they want translated. Should the interpreter only translate interviewees' answers in formal interviews, or should she translate the "small talk" that takes place before and after each interview? Should she translate only their final response and ignore any spontaneous colloquy that arises? For example, in both Bosnia and Rwanda, my interpreters regularly interject clarifying questions during interviews. Whenever I hear my interpreters do this, I ask them to translate their prompts so I can capture those in my notes. I also have to be explicit about when I want them to translate conversations that fall outside the formal interview. Sometimes I am content to be left out of these informal exchanges, and at other times I want to be let in so I can follow the conversation.

The researcher also might think about terms or words that she does not want translated. For example, there are several words in Kinyarwanda, like *Interahamwe* or *Igitero*,[6] that I did not want translated. Because these were key terms in the local vocabulary of war and genocide, I wanted to hear how and when people used these words. Finally, researchers will work more effectively with interpreters if they study the local language. Even beginner proficiency in the local language can help. At the very least, it can help assure the researcher that the interpreter is translating faithfully. It may also help the researcher to follow the general contours of what a person is saying. I once sat in on a conversation between my interpreter and a close friend of hers. I was interested in finding out whether her friend might agree to be interviewed later, but first my interpreter and her friend began catching up on the latest news. As the two talked, I found that I could follow the gist of the conversation even with my very basic Kinyarwanda. This allowed the women to speak freely without my constantly interrupting them to ask for translations.

In this chapter, I have argued that research designs and interview strategies should not be constrained by which languages the researcher speaks fluently.

When a project involves interviews in a language the researcher does not speak, she might consider working with an interpreter, rather than forgoing that particular project or spending years trying to master the language. A good interpreter brings much more than added fluency. He or she can bring added perspective, knowledge, and access, and help to keep the researcher safe and sound. A good interpreter, in short, brings benefits that even the most fluent scholars will find valuable.

8

THE PROBLEM OF
EXTRATERRITORIAL LEGALITY

William Reno

Judicial agencies in some countries have become involved in identifying and prosecuting individuals who committed, ordered, incited, assisted, or otherwise participated in genocide, torture, or extrajudicial killing, the recruitment and use of child soldiers, and a variety of other acts beyond these countries' borders. International organizations such as the International Criminal Court (ICC) now pursue such individuals across borders too.

The extraterritorial investigation and prosecution of those who commit war crimes and serious violations of human rights is a positive development from the point of view of strengthening global norms of governance. Countries with strong judicial institutions and rule-of-law traditions assist in bringing justice to people in war-torn societies, especially those where state institutions have collapsed or are very weak.

But this practice also affects the capacity of social science researchers to conduct fieldwork and to use interviews to collect data in war zones. Researchers now have to consider whether the information that they collect from interviews can be used as evidence in prosecutions of their research subjects. In a few cases, extraterritorial investigations and prosecutions may affect the researcher: foreign governments sometimes criminalize interactions with research subjects whom officials have classified as terrorists. These legal concerns have to be weighed against the benefits of obtaining, through interviews and direct observation, first-hand information about informants' motivations, activities, and political views; and against the obligations of researchers and their home institutions to protect informants.

These developments may shape how certain places are studied. Academic researchers (and journalists) may conclude that it is easier to engage in self-censorship or to err on the side of caution, avoiding sensitive topics and groups. Fears that governments will apply statutes selectively leave the specter of legal entanglements hanging over the researcher's head, even if these concerns were not present at the time that the research was conducted. This leaves field researchers to guess whether their own activities or activities of their research subjects will fall under the scope of these extraterritorial legal measures, potentially impoverishing academic and public understanding and debates surrounding groups involved in conflicts. The prudent scholar may favor quantitative studies based on data from a large number of cases (and which can be conducted from a desk) over interpretive and comparative studies based upon direct contact with people who participate in the events under study and requiring mastery of the languages that are needed to speak directly (although see Fujii, this volume) with these actors.

These legal changes started to appear in the late 1990s and gathered force after the September 11, 2001, attacks on New York and Washington, DC. New technologies have allowed informants to become aware of the full range of foreigners' interests in their activities. These technological changes also shape subjects' assessments of the risk of sharing information with researchers as subjects become aware of how a wider array of outsiders judge their actions. As the next section demonstrates, this has been a recent and swift development, with serious implications for understanding issues of vital international importance.

Communication then and Now

I conducted interviews and observed local militias on the Sierra Leone–Liberia border in the late 1980s and early 1990s. The topic of the study—informal governance and the manipulation of access to illicit markets as a tool of political authority—involved people who later joined the National Patriotic Front of Liberia (NPFL), members of anti-NPFL militias on the Sierra Leone side of the border, and individuals who joined various factions of the United Liberation Movement of Liberia for Democracy (ULIMO) as the war unfolded. Conducting research in war zones in the 1990s required assessing local risk in order to ensure one's personal safety and to approach potential informants in ways that did not bring them unwanted attention from other actors.

Wartime precautions, in this regard, were just more-intense versions of precautions that one needed to take in a country where politics often involved violence and personal risk. Informants needed to be protected from harm from their own government, political factions, rebels, or from private militias or other violent groups who might use the interviewee's words as evidence of disloyalty or opposition. Coding interviews to make the identification of individuals impossible was essential. Consent had to be procured on an oral basis, as signed consent forms could be used against informants if those documents fell into the wrong hands. The use of handwritten notes and the absence of recording devices encouraged some informants to be more forthcoming. Writing notes in pencil, so that informants could inspect and then erase what they felt might pose a threat to them, and the sharing of contact information gave informants multiple opportunities to withdraw consent if they wished; these strategies underscored the researcher's concern for confidentiality. In any event, the bulk of the informant's and the researcher's concerns focused on how information could be used or misused in the immediate political and social environment.

Direct contact and discussions with principal actors was, and continues to be, essential for the study of the organization and behavior of armed groups in wartime. This can extend to living with some of these groups so as to maximize opportunities to observe their behavior and hold repeated in-depth discussions with participants. This intensity of engagement is necessary to understand the micro-politics of armed groups. It can help to uncover nuances such as the dynamics of the "security dilemma" facing many participants. In these instances, members of armed groups act aggressively toward neighbors on the assumption that their neighbors' preparations for warfare signal aggressive intent, even when the neighbors may believe that they were only taking prudent steps to defend themselves (Snyder and Jervis 1999). Close observation of this sort has implications at empirical and theoretical levels of investigation; it can generate new explanations for the appearance and uses of violence and for the variable processes of recruitment, for example. Interviews and direct observation also help to uncover other important elements of wars that might seem trivial or marginal from a macro-level perspective, such as the different uses of intimidation, mechanisms for identifying and recruiting followers, the relations between mechanisms to discipline fighters and preexisting social networks, the origins of armed groups and the effects of these origins on groups' relations with noncombatants, and the development and evolution of group commitments to political ideas.

Since warfare in 1990s West Africa was largely a consequence of the collapse of state institutions and the splintering of national armies into armed factions, it did not produce clear front lines or consistent demarcations among specific armed groups. Categories such as civilian, military, and rebel are not absolute in this kind of war (Kaldor 2001). In these wars, many individuals, including informants, shift from one category to the other, including from victim to perpetrator and back again. Individuals can benefit from these wars at the same time that they suffer terrible personal tragedies. An armed group may be considered by many noncombatants as a protector of their community at the same time that it preys upon other noncombatants. Explaining how and why individuals and organizations act in particular ways and the complex choices that they face is integral to understanding how these wars begin, how they unfold, and how they end in Africa and elsewhere in the world. Interview research and direct observation may be more appropriate methods for illuminating key relationships and processes in these contexts. At the very minimum, close-in research of this sort can play an important role in generating questions and questioning categories at more macro levels of investigation.

These wars tend to be particularly nasty; they also have unfolded in ways that blur conventional categories and challenge assumptions about wartime processes and relationships. Some of these more sensitive issues may be better addressed through close observation and interviews. Awareness of this fact has grown recently, at the same time as changes in technologies and legal regimes have complicated these approaches. For instance, approximately one-third of the entire population of Liberia sought refuge in foreign countries in the first four years of that country's war (1989 to 1993), with many more internally displaced. The use of children as combatants was widespread. A large postwar survey in Sierra Leone found that, among the many thousands of people who were forcibly recruited, 50 percent were age fourteen or younger, and a quarter were eleven or younger. Some of these children committed human rights violations during the war. Revolutionary United Front (RUF) fighters who fit the internationally accepted definition of children—a person under eighteen years of age—committed almost one-fourth of recorded human rights violations, including forced displacement, abduction, arbitrary detention, killings, looting, torture, forced labor, and sexual abuse. Even what remained of Sierra Leone's national army counted within its ranks one child perpetrator for every 11.89 adult perpetrators of these acts (Conibere et al. 2004).

During the 1990s, wars of this type, particularly those in Africa, tended to be seen from abroad as curious barbaric affairs that were of limited consequence, except as unfortunate humanitarian disasters. In the same year that the UN completed its withdrawal from Somalia and Rwanda's genocide occurred, the journalist Robert Kaplan (1994, 57–58) described Africa as receding behind a "wall of disease" that enclosed a nightmarish, Dickensian spectacle of burgeoning slums teeming with violent young men. "The coming upheaval," he wrote, "in which foreign embassies are shut down, states collapse, and contact with the outside world is through dangerous disease-ridden coastal trading posts will loom large in the century we are entering." His vision was of a continent abandoned to its own devices and foreign disregard for the actions of those who participated in these wars, outside of the attentions of concerned diaspora communities, humanitarian agencies, and a few scholars. Kaplan presented his accounts of African wars as sober realism, emphasizing volatility and threat that justified small nodes of Western military power to maintain watch and to ensure that the chaos could be contained.

Kaplan's West Africa really was informationally isolated. Communication was difficult through the 1990s, and this limited the flow of information. A telephone call from Freetown to the United States required journeying to the central telephone office to book a line. A six-minute operator-assisted call in 1990 cost $15 (in 2012 dollars). Telegrams were still received, with messages typed on stationery marked "On His Majesty's Service" bearing the colonial crest of King George VI. Television broadcasts ended in the late 1980s, and radio ceased shortly after. By 1990, electricity was rare in the capital city. Access to international news was through battery-powered shortwave radio. The British Broadcasting Corporation's *Focus on Africa*, daily at 5 p.m., was the only reliable source of accurate war news. This program was beamed to Africa and was not widely available to people outside the continent, except in brief summaries in BBC's *Focus on Africa* magazine.

At first, no UN observers or peacekeepers were present to monitor human rights abuses and to produce public reports about them. The few NGOs that monitored events produced only hard copies of their reports, a rare few of which were passed from hand to hand among intellectuals in the capital. The International Crisis Group, now a major source of information and field-based analysis for conflicts around the world, did not exist before 1995.[1] An oft-heard complaint from Sierra Leoneans and others in war zones in Africa was that the international community had abandoned them. It was common to hear in the mid-1990s that foreign governments and international agencies intervened in Yugoslavia's wars but did not care if Africans killed each other.

This isolation was short-lived. By 2002, mobile phone service reached Sierra Leone's capital and provincial centers. Liberia's president, Charles Taylor, was a partner in a telecommunications operation that brought mobile telephone service to that country in 2000. Calls to the United States from Liberia that cost $1.25 per minute in 2000 had dropped to 40 cents per minute by 2004 (Anonymous 2009). By the mid-2000s, mobile phone SIM cards were available for under $2 in many African countries. The appearance of voice-to-Internet protocol (VoIP) services in the late 2000s drove prices even lower. Even a call on a mobile telephone from Somalia to the United States cost only several cents a minute by 2011. In larger urban areas, "business centers," often really small shops, began to offer international call services for a few cents per minute and low-cost access to the Internet for those without computers of their own.

Internet connectivity has been slow to develop in comparison to global trends, with one Liberian of every two hundred counted as a regular Internet user by the end of 2010. Connection rates were much higher in other parts of Africa, with 9.2 per hundred connected in Uganda, 9.7 per hundred in Kenya, 11.8 per hundred in Zimbabwe, and 28.3 per hundred in Nigeria (International Telecommunications Union 2011). The reach of other media also has grown. Al Jazeera, BBC, and CNN broadcasts inform the discussions of many intellectuals, businesspeople, and officials and are even incorporated into local broadcasts in some countries. For those with higher incomes, increased bandwidth capable of delivering video has begun to compete with satellite television. The SEACOM cable in 2009 brought high-speed Internet to East Africa, and with it came Internet-delivered HDTV, peer-to-peer networks, and the capacity to rapidly download books, large data sets, and other materials. These new media and the technologies that support them make it easier for Africans to find material about them produced by others and to become familiar with the wide range of views of others about conflicts in the region.

This rapid easing of communications means that key actors in these wars now possess the means to become aware of and investigate the developing risks that international attention to extraterritorial justice may pose to them. In practical terms, knowledge of these developments has had a chilling effect on the willingness of some informants to share information. Some cite fears that prosecutions would include low-level figures—or some actual low-level figures perhaps view themselves as higher-level figures who could be targets for prosecution. Concerns among informants that "the future is uncertain" or "one cannot be too careful" intrude into interviews. These concerns may be overblown in some cases, but they are based on solid foundations, as I demonstrate in the next section.

The Criminalization of War in Africa: The Impact for Interviewees

Innovations in communications coincided with an increase in international attention to war crimes and crimes against humanity in Africa. This attention brought more-vigorous condemnation of such behavior and calls to prosecute perpetrators of abuses, including torture, the use of child soldiers, and the use of rape as a tactic in warfare. People in Africa are increasingly exposed to information about this international concern. Even if they do not have access to the Internet, they can follow news of UN investigations, read NGO reports, and find in their local newspapers other information printed from websites. United Nations radio stations in Liberia, Sierra Leone, Congo, and Côte d'Ivoire have carried programs that focus on these issues.

Growing international attention has been part of a global move to criminalize the conduct of war in Africa. This move away from the passive determinism of observers like Robert Kaplan is based upon a liberal conviction that an end to impunity for past misdeeds will empower citizens to take a more assertive role in politics and will deter others from committing such deeds in the future. This approach toward war is articulated in terms of the pursuit of justice against all perpetrators of serious human rights violations, whether governments, community groups, or rebels, regardless of justifications for their uses of violence. This shift was rapid, gathering force after 2000, and clashed with ideas among people in conflict zones about responsibility for atrocities, rationales for self-defense, and appropriate uses of violence. The UN-mandated report *Responsibility to Protect* declared that "the defense of state sovereignty, by even its strongest supporters, does not include any claim of the unlimited power of a state to do what it wants to its own people," and that "good international citizenship" compelled responsible international actors to use threats of international prosecutions of perpetrators of human rights abuses, crimes of war, and crimes against humanity to punish and change bad behavior (ICISS, 2001, 8).

Previously, grievous abuses commonly went unpunished. For example, during the 1971–1979 rule of Uganda's President Idi Amin, state security forces killed between a quarter and a half million Ugandan citizens (International Commission of Jurists 1977). This situation was widely known to the international community; certainly many Ugandans knew that their government was taking a murderous course. High-profile victims of state-sponsored murders included a former prime minister, the Anglican archbishop, the vice chancellor of the country's flagship university, and members of Amin's cabinet. When these crimes were committed, Amin served as chairman of the Organization of African Unity (1975–1976), and Uganda had a seat on the UN's Commission on Human Rights (1977–1979). Military and security forces under the command of Somalia's President Siad Barre (1969–1991) attacked citizens in northern Somalia in retaliation for their alleged support of the Somali National Movement (SNM) rebels. Over several months in 1988, this campaign killed about fifty thousand people, from a total regional population of approximately three million. About four hundred thousand took refuge across the border in Ethiopia, and 1.5 million others were displaced inside Somalia (Gilkes 1989). Though these events were widely known, the recipients of this information were compartmentalized; there was very little coordination among them, and certainly there was no overarching process that included prosecution for misdeeds.

Leaders of the SNM and other insurgent groups with whom this author has spoken have complained about this earlier lack of coordinated global attention. They stress that their uses of violence before and after 1988 were in the defense of their communities against a state campaign that nearly all label as genocide, intended to exterminate or drive out the several million northerners, in retaliation for their opposition to the regime. They point out that Siad Barre was a U.S. ally in 1988; at the time, his regime received weapons from the U.S. government, despite criticism among U.S. legislators of Barre's terrible human rights record. Their distinction between unjust and just uses of violence initially led informants to speak very openly about their own roles in these rebel groups. But closer international scrutiny of issues such as the uses of child soldiers began to have a chilling effect on conversations. Through the media of satellite television and the Internet, former participants in the struggle against the old dictator took note that the outside world might view as criminal their mobilization of sixteen- and seventeen-year-old youths to fight against a government that had attacked their community and uprooted half the region's population.

More generally, extraterritorial prosecutions initially focused on a few state officials in Africa who were alleged to have committed the most serious violations. A Belgian court in 2001 convicted and gave fifteen-to-twenty-year sentences to four Rwandan citizens for their involvement in Rwanda's 1994 genocide. The decision of a Belgian judge in 2000 to issue an arrest warrant for the Democratic Republic of the Congo's standing minister of foreign affairs for his role in human rights abuses in that country's war that began in 1996 signaled a more determined effort to bring alleged perpetrators to justice, regardless of their official status. Even though the International Court of Justice ruled that this high-ranking official was immune from prosecution by virtue of the sovereign prerogatives attached to his office, dissenting judges on that bench wrote of the need to consider serious human rights violations as subject to universal jurisdiction (International Court of Justice 2002). Much as universal jurisdiction has been applied against piracy, this case, despite its reversal, put incumbent officials on notice that they risked being held accountable in foreign courts for their actions, even if they claimed to act in defense of a home community, a regime, or a sovereign state. Prudent state officials who face rebellions and insurrections that threaten their regimes now have to take into greater consideration the international scrutiny of their actions, and they have to consider whether their responses could lead to serious legal problems later.

A more serious challenge to incumbent state officials appeared with the March 7, 2003, indictment by the Special Court for Sierra Leone (SCSL) of Liberia's President Charles Taylor for crimes against humanity and for violations of international humanitarian law, including the use of child soldiers, sexual slavery, abductions, and looting. This was the first instance of a sitting head of state facing a serious indictment for war crimes and crimes against humanity. The SCSL was created as an ad hoc tribunal jointly by the UN and the Sierra Leone government to prosecute all those who bore "greatest responsibility" for war crimes and crimes against humanity committed after November 30, 1996, during that country's war. The court indicted only thirteen individuals for charges of war crimes and crimes against humanity—five from among the leadership of the Revolutionary United Front (RUF) rebels; three from the government-supported Civil Defense Forces (CDF), including a former interior minister; four from the Armed Forces Revolutionary Council (AFRC), a breakaway segment of the national army; and Liberia's President Taylor.

The SCSL criminalized the conduct of war on all sides. The indictment of Taylor defined his support for the RUF rebels as a criminal conspiracy, a "common plan . . . to gain access to the mineral wealth of Sierra Leone, in particular diamonds, to destabilize the Government of Sierra Leone in order to facilitate access to such mineral wealth and to install a government in Sierra Leone that would be well disposed toward, and supportive of, the accused's interests and objectives in Liberia and the region" (Special Court for Sierra Leone 2006, 10). United States political pressure and indirect regional and international support to anti-Taylor rebels forced Taylor into exile in Nigeria in 2003. In March 2006, Nigerian authorities arrested Taylor, and he was transferred to the SCSL in Sierra Leone to face these charges.

Although the great majority of Sierra Leoneans believed that Taylor bore significant responsibility for their country's terrible war, the trial of CDF leader Hinga Norman for war crimes drew protestors who argued that "Chief Hinga Norman stayed to confront the rebels and renegade soldiers. . . . Without his contribution and tenacity, the rebels would not have come to the peace table and would have still been in the city, killing and maiming at will" (Beecher 2003, 3). Though responsible for numerous violations of human rights, the CDF battled renegade government soldiers and RUF fighters who had launched "Operation No Living Thing" against the population of the capital in 1999. Over the course of one week, rebel fighters killed about 250 policemen and targeted law offices and other institutions of public order (Commonwealth Human Rights Initiative 2002). As Norman's indictment was made public, the CDF's second-in-command offered to help stem incursions of Liberian fighters, reflecting the opinions of many at that time that the CDF was better able to protect the country than was the government army (International Crisis Group 2003).

By the mid-2000s, it became more difficult to gain the cooperation of well-known wartime figures to sit for interviews, as some feared that information about their wartime experiences could expose them to the glare of potential prosecution. This was a very rapid shift, as I had no trouble speaking with a former head of the AFRC in 2001, shortly before he became the target of UN sanctions and before he was indicted before the SCSL. The operation of a Truth and Reconciliation Commission between 2002 and 2004—the same time that SCSL proceedings were gathering steam—to "create an impartial historical record of violations and abuses of human rights and international humanitarian law related to the armed conflict in Sierra Leone . . . to address impunity, to respond to the needs of the victims, to promote healing and reconciliation and to prevent a repetition of the violations and abuses" (Special Court Task Force 2002, 3), convinced many that talking about one's activities during the war, even if in defense of one's community or valorous in one's own eyes, would attract unwanted attention.

The Shift to Victimhood

It became apparent in the conduct of interviews that some informants who previously expressed pride in their wartime roles had become keen to highlight their roles as victims of violence. For those who research the micro-politics of conflict, nuances in the uses of violence and research subjects' shifting roles during conflicts are central to addressing basic questions about wartime processes. It is not unusual, for example, for fighters who have been forced to join armed groups to become leaders and assert initiative in these positions. Most fighters act on a variety of motives. It is important for researchers to be able to gain an understanding of how the salience of motives shifts, how armed groups frame individuals' choices, and how contexts shape later accounts. But it is very hard to address the basic questions surrounding the nature of the recruitment of individuals to armed groups, their discipline, and the nature of these groups' organization when informants are anxious to avoid any discussion of these matters and particularly their own experiences with them. Victimhood provides a comforting and safe coda to wartime experiences when it becomes risky to express pride or satisfaction in wartime conduct.

The new narratives of victimhood may be due to more than a shift in the international or domestic legal climate, and the related search to identify perpetrators. After 2000, the number of foreign social scientists studying child soldiers and female victims of wartime atrocities surged; this may have provided cues more generally to people to depict their involvement in the war primarily as victims. Some of the more well-funded studies, asking people about their involvement in wartime armed groups, involved the deployment of local research assistants to conduct surveys in a manner that may have encouraged respondents to associate these requests with official investigations, or to expect that certain kinds of answers would generate monetary rewards. The international provision of relief and development aid or at least promises of future assistance to wartime victims provided material incentives to individuals to highlight their status as a victim in return for assistance or the distant promise of reparations. Among the more enterprising former commanders and other wartime actors, a few found employment as "post-conflict consultants" and lead their own NGOs to assist foreign researchers and aid agencies. This situation creates multiple layers of wartime accounts among informants, focused as much on present discourses as on past events.

Some Sierra Leoneans condemn the postwar prosecutions in their country. A former community defense force member whom I encountered continued to express pride that he killed RUF rebels in defense of his community at a time that the national army was in disarray and the UN intervention force was yet to be. He observed that extensive postwar trials of key figures occur only in the world's poorest countries ("Never Bush, never Sharon") where desperate governments have little choice but to serve as stages for foreigners to act out their desires in exchange for financial and political support. He observed that foreign consultants conducted most of the background research for the Truth Commission report and that the SCSL spent about $30 million a year to eventually prosecute ten people at a time when the country's entire domestic justice system operated on a budget of less than a million dollars.

Defining War and Crime

Recent investigations and prosecutions highlight changes in how Sierra Leoneans and the international community define war apart from crime. It is commonplace in academic literature and among some policymakers to frame discussions of recent conflicts, particularly in Africa, as ones that "involve a blurring of the distinctions between war (usually defined as violence between states or organized political groups for political motives), organized crime (violence undertaken by privately organized groups for private purposes, usually financial gain) and large-scale violations of human rights" (Kaldor 2001, 2). The SCSL's indictment of Liberia's Charles Taylor for a criminal conspiracy to divert Sierra Leone's diamond wealth for personal benefit and to overthrow its government through RUF proxies shows this blurring of the distinction between war as the activity of states and armed groups in contention and war as an epidemic of personal criminality (Collier 2000).

Previously, researchers seeking interviews had to pay attention mainly to how the state in which they worked defined crime. Those for whom state definitions of criminality held little legitimacy because their governments were corrupt and predatory were often eager to talk about politics. One could be woken at night as enthusiastic interlocutors showed up at the door to present their views and opinions. Under those conditions, even some state officials were loquacious, confident that their positions placed them beyond the reach of the law. Interviews of this sort often involved frank discussions and yielded valuable information. Confidentiality was essential, but more to protect informants from personal rivals or local strongmen than from the legal system or foreigners' scrutiny.

Rebels across the continent were available for interviews, too. In the tradition of the anticolonial and antiapartheid rebels who exhibited their "liberated zones" to foreign visitors, many rebels were keen to talk to journalists and academics to convey the righteousness of their grievances and goals. Visits to areas under the control of the Sudan People's Liberation Army before the 2005 peace agreement, for example, afforded a glimpse of a "liberated zone," the idealized vision of the SPLA-ruled society as the rebel group would have outsiders see it.

The conflation of crime and war, however, leaves much less room for these kinds of interactions when even "victory" (i.e., seizure of state power and the mantle of sovereignty) might not shield victorious fighters from foreigners' legal designs. Moreover, the suspicion among many informants and potential informants that the international community really behaves tactically in the application of legality, only against the weak, causes informants to weigh more heavily the future risks associated with revealing information, even if there is no apparent current risk. Like the Sierra Leone informant described above, they may feel that international agencies and foreign diplomats will pressure local officials who are too weak (and too desperate for international support) to defy requests to prosecute foreign-defined misdeeds.

Inconsistencies in international definitions of war and criminality were especially marked in the case of Liberia; they serve as a warning to incumbent officials that they could become subject to a sort of *ex post* application of laws. As late as 2000, UN Secretary-General Kofi Annan thanked Liberia's Charles Taylor for his help in negotiating the release of UN peacekeepers taken hostage (United Nations Security Council 2000a, par. 67). Around the same time, a UN investigating team was preparing a report that concluded that Sierra Leone's rebels were financing their campaign of violence through the trafficking of diamonds to Liberia in violation of UN Security Council resolutions. This was a trade "that cannot be conducted without the permission and the involvement of Liberian government officials at the highest level" (United Nations Security Council 2000b, par. 2), a conclusion that had been widely shared by most researchers and many people in these two countries for years. But by 2000, it was unclear in international diplomatic circles whether Liberia's head of state should be treated as a criminal or as a leader with sovereign immunity.

One could argue to this point that the threat of prosecution only concerns "kingpins" and therefore is a limiting factor only in interviews with these upper-level state officials and rebel leaders. Yet the activities of Liberia's Truth and Reconciliation Commission have changed that calculation, at least in that country. Commencing operation in June 2006, the commission was mandated to "document and investigate the massive wave of human rights violations that occurred in Liberia during the period January 1979–October 2003," identify victims and perpetrators, and to make recommendations to the government for prosecution (Republic of Liberia 2009a, 2–3). This investigation was undertaken with help from U.S. legal and investigative consultants and with support from U.S. federal agencies, and was not hindered by the Liberian government's low bureaucratic capacity or scarcity of resources. The U.S. Department of State's Office of War Crimes Issues (from late 2009, under the direction of the former prosecutor of the Taylor case before the SCSL) has worked closely with West African governments, international institutions, and nongovernment organizations to assist in similar investigations of wartime crimes.

The decision to include the investigation of "economic crimes" in Liberia was intended to attack the corruption that was widely considered to be one of the root causes of the war. The report noted that "a single definition of economic crimes remains elusive" but drew upon other countries' laws prohibiting "illicit enrichment" (Republic of Liberia 2009b, 4, 6). This investigation into "economic crimes" produced a list of sixty-four alleged perpetrators and twenty-one ministries, foreign firms, rebel groups, and local companies, accounting for a substantial part of Liberia's formal and illicit economy over the past quarter century. Eight leaders of warring factions were recommended for prosecution, as were ninety-eight "most notorious perpetrators." In addition, fifty people were recommended for public sanctions.

The Liberian commission's focus on "economic crimes" followed the UN's investigations into wartime commercial dealings that led to travel bans and asset freezes of individuals accused of dealings with armed groups (United Nations Security Council 2003). Many of the individuals on the commission's list were already sanctioned under the UN Security Council's provisions and had been identified by name, beginning in 1999, in a series of UN Panel of Experts' reports on violations of Security Council sanctions and embargoes.

This focus of internal and international agencies addresses factors that are widely known to be complicit in the promotion of conflict. Armed groups, including those on the government side, may have been heavily dependent on resources from illicit trades (e.g., in "blood diamonds"); limiting or eliminating this commerce was critical for reducing the level of violence in war-torn societies. Alongside this very real problem lay the difficulty of interviewing key actors in a conflict when many of them had been labeled as criminals on domestic and UN lists. Researchers face the additional complication of interviewing people who do not fit easily into most standard research subject-protection protocol categories. For example, does one ask for research leave to interview a "war criminal" when one wishes to interview the leader of a rebellion that uses sixteen-year-olds to help fight against an oppressive government? This potentially asks institutional review boards (IRBs) to make determinations about whether a group consists of "freedom fighters" or "criminals." This is much like the dilemma of deciding whether African National Congress operatives who put bombs in public places in the 1980s and incited children to attack security forces were guilty of war crimes or were leaders in the liberation of their country from the scourge of apartheid (or both).

In any event, interviewing key actors in a war in a country like Liberia, with about three million inhabitants, is impossible if one eliminates from consideration the names that appear on domestic commission and UN sanctions lists. While one finds among targeted individuals people with names like Blood Sucker War Boss, Black Diamond, Young Killer, Chinese Jabber, and so forth (who also may be valuable informants), these lists also include serving legislators, the sitting president of the country, and nearly everyone who operated a significant business in Liberia since 1979, whether foreign—a gigantic rubber concession, an American evangelist's commercial schemes—or local. Unfortunately, Liberia has been a very corrupt country for a long time. Achieving success or prominence and protecting one's legitimate concerns from predatory officials has nearly always involved some element of complicity with corruption. Prosecution for wartime crimes risks the same kinds of open-ended, wide-ranging expansion in a country where about 8 percent of the population was killed and a substantial portion of the rest fled a fourteen-year conflict that involved numerous factions, local self-defense forces, foreign intervention forces, and many other actors.

These investigations create obvious disincentives for people to grant interviews. Some may be suspicious that researchers will volunteer or be forced to give information to investigators. The practice of commissions and courts in Liberia and Sierra Leone to cite the published work of researchers in justifying their conclusions enhances this suspicion. Investigators do, in fact, contact researchers for interviews and recruit them as expert witnesses. Contact usually comes not from a member of a Liberian or a Sierra Leone commission but instead from American lawyers. In their efforts to assist commissions, the interrogators seek confidential information from interviews and documents. The researcher should note that university research subject-protection protocols protect the confidentiality of interviews. In any event, notes and confidential interview transcripts appear to be immune from subpoena or other efforts to compel the researcher to provide specific information. Thus far the burdens of the extraterritorial extension of legality (and its incorporation into domestic justice systems) have focused on laws and processes that (potentially) target informants. But the complications of research in conflict zones takes on other dimensions if one's own national legal system criminalizes contact with some of the principal actors in wars.

The Criminalization of Contact

The extraterritorial reach of the law can affect the researcher in other ways. Prior to the September 11 attacks, the study of wars (and journalists' reporting on them) required professional contact with a variety of foreign groups, the great majority of which were ignored by the U.S. legal system. The USA Patriot Act, signed into law on October 26, 2001, criminalizes the provision of "material support or resources" to proscribed groups and claims extraterritorial jurisdiction (United States Code 2006). Since the intent of the statute is to hinder these groups' unlawful activities, a nervous researcher might be left with uncertainty as to whether the dissemination of information in scholarly publications, from in-depth interviews with members of these groups, intended to gather information about members' motivations, activities, and political views, constitutes "material support" if such a product could be seen as supporting a group's political position or otherwise advancing its claims. Moreover, it is not clear that a scholar's close contact with a proscribed group would fit under the rubric of the statute's exemption from prosecution of people who act "entirely independently of the foreign terrorist organization" (section [h]), given that such groups are likely to exercise significant direction over the researcher's activities in areas under their control.

It is highly likely that most U.S. federal prosecutors have better things to do with their time than pursue scholars who have contact with proscribed groups such as Colombian rebels and paramilitaries, various Palestinian organizations, and important groups such as Hezbollah that are included on lists of terrorist organizations.[2] (Other countries, including the United Kingdom, also compile such lists.[3]) But it is not beyond the realm of possibility that a scholar whose work reaches a conclusion that is at odds with official policy—for example, that dialogue with a group might be a more effective method of deterring violence than launching a politically controversial military campaign against it—could attract official scrutiny.

Two serious challenges to research emerge in light of the more general criminalization of members of some armed groups. The first challenge lies in the scholarly need for extended discussion with informants to include the sharing of analyses and a depth of observation that exceeds the demands of gathering purely technical data. The second challenge concerns the researcher's reliance on the armed group for protection while conducting field research.

Many scholars insist on intensive interaction, particularly if they question the notion that field researchers can be present as neutral observers or that findings can be restricted to technical commentary (see, for instance, MacLean, chapter 3 of this volume). Scholars of social movements in poor countries and those who study marginalized and disadvantaged groups propose as an alternative a "participatory action research" in which communities that are the focus of research share in formulating research questions and participate in analysis (Kemmis and McTaggart 2008; MacLean, this volume). Field research that sheds light on the inner workings of armed groups and the processes of war also may involve direct observation and extended interactive interviews with participants, often on multiple occasions and through contacts that can span years. The careful researcher will question subjects to gain an understanding of different perspectives among members of these groups and to comprehend how contexts shape how informants engage in political action. This effort to "get into the heads" of informants helps scholars to identify biases in research designs and to formulate new questions that address previously unseen relationships and processes.

This approach rests on the assumption that the scholar and informants share a critical perspective on the social interactions that are central to the study. Interviews can take the form of discussion in which the researcher presents his or her views and the views of other scholars who write about important elements of armed group organization and behavior, such as the recruitment and the discipline of fighters. Discussions about discipline, for example, typically involve comparisons of different groups as informants survey their successes and failures and weigh their own experiences against the records of other groups. Many commanders of armed groups have well-thought-out opinions and analyses of American counterinsurgency strategies in Iraq and Afghanistan, for example. Satellite television, Internet, and telephone services also bring them information about the strategies of insurgents who fight U.S. forces. Many informants have access to (and often read) open source scholarship and think-tank reports about contemporary conflicts. For example, I have encountered commanders in Sudanese and Somali armed groups who have recent publications, including one by David Kilcullen (2009), who was an important adviser on counterinsurgency to the commander of U.S. forces in Afghanistan. Some of the commanders of groups in these places fought guerrilla campaigns for as long as a quarter of a century. Through those years of experience, they have developed a keen professional perspective on and interest in the activities of those who fight in other contexts. Discussions about these works and about other conflicts shed light on the thinking and perspectives of these informants. This interaction also could be construed as aid to such fighters in developing their own analysis, a sort of advice that might constitute "material support." Fortunately, none of the groups to which these informants belonged appeared on U.S. or other authorities' lists of proscribed groups.

This close social interaction with subjects contains elements of what Paulo Freire (1982) termed "conscientization"—a shared inquiry into the social life of the organization. Freire advises that researchers ought to be disposed to relearn things that they thought they already knew and to challenge different narratives, or, in social science terms, to carefully test hypotheses and challenge various theoretical perspectives and explanations. In terms of the study of conflict, this can involve focused efforts to share in the informants' perspectives.

Prosecutorial activities, however, can shape these informants' perspectives *ex post*. While during and after the 1991–2002 conflict in Sierra Leone, truth commissions and official investigations were eager to hear stories about the victimization of women and children, these bodies were not interested in hearing about women's heroism or about community support for the recruitment of adolescents as fighters—important perspectives to understand how armed groups operated in that country's conflict. Engaging members of the RUF—still on the U.S. terrorist exclusion list in 2004, two years after Sierra Leone's conflict ceased—would have been critically important for addressing questions as basic as why tens of thousands of young men and women joined this armed group; why some fought in particularly brutal ways while others did not; how and why this group managed to maintain close personal connections to some members of the military that was supposed to fight it; and what happened to members after they left the group. Engagement of this sort, even after a peace agreement and demobilization, might cause concern among foreign government officials who watch for people who they think are advancing the cause of proscribed groups.

The researcher's need for basic protection in conflict zones further entangles the researcher in the milieu of the research subject. Border hassles, mistreatment at checkpoints, small arms in the hands of children, and the threat of kidnapping require the researcher to anticipate the risk of personal harm associated with interviews in conflict zones. Harm can include the physical and psychological damage associated with regular contact with traumatized populations and the stress connected to constant concerns about safety. Traveling in rebel groups' "liberated zones" exposes one to the threat of state-sanctioned violence. These hazards require constant gathering of information to assess risk and often careful readings of social interactions among members of armed groups that can be used to provide protection for the researcher.

Protection in conflict zones, particularly for a lone researcher or small research group, usually comes from close association with key individuals or groups.

The researcher identifies a relationship that is not limited to a simple reciprocity between researcher and local protectors (who also are informants). Honor, vendetta, and clan reputation offer important avenues for protection in places where central state authority does not hold sway. Thus the host's incentive to protect the guest from harm is found in the host's concern to maintain reputation and status within the host's own social hierarchy, rather than a direct obligation to the guest. Protection of this sort does not allow a researcher to act entirely independently of the armed group, as one's access is contingent upon one's relationship with the armed group and the social structure in which it is rooted. Thus people in Somalia and the Caucasus's Kabardino-Balkaria, two conflict zones separated by considerable geographic distance and cultural difference, share what are ultimately similar folk aphorisms: "A guest is a gift from God," and "The guest is the prisoner of the host."

This manner of protection is important in places like the Caucasus and Somalia to avoid kidnapping, and, in the former, abuse at the hands of corrupt state security forces that are suspicious of foreign visitors. Threats of vendetta deter potential attacks, however remote this possibility may be, as those who contemplate such actions would have to consider the possibility of retaliation against their family members. Hospitality is essential for avoiding hotels ("collection points for kidnappers"). Having to pay a bill for hospitality is a sign of weakness and alerts observers to the customer's lack of a strong local protector. One generally does, however, have to pay for other forms of protection, such as escorts with automatic weapons that various authorities in Somalia require of foreigners when they travel outside of towns.

Extensive social interaction of this sort has been an important ingredient of security when studying wars in Africa. It involves balancing trade-offs. Traveling solo or in a small group allows one to shed the accoutrements of status and power (white SUVs with international organization logos, armed security) that inhibit interaction with armed groups; but it requires the compromises associated with having to live according to the host's terms. Living under such terms, though, is essential for the sorts of interactive learning that Friere and others promote. It is also an essential element of anthropology; Clifford Geertz (1977) notes that "anthropologists don't study villages . . . they study *in* them" (22). Political scientists must similarly be able to communicate with the people and groups that they study if their research questions require intensive and repeated social interactions within the armed group.

Could an official investigator become suspicious of such scholarly activities? It is left to the scholar to try to guess whether a group will become proscribed or whether the interaction will be seen by others as criminal. Rather than being left to guess whether activities fall within the Patriot Act's statutory scope, for instance, many researchers will err on the side of caution and restrict their communications with these groups. They will engage in self-censorship, much like the informant who censors comments to avoid the attention of truth commissions and tribunals. The guessing game is more serious for informants who now view a world in which more combatants are targets of domestic and international efforts to prosecute them for wartime deeds. The actual threat to a particular informant may not be great, in reality; the important point, however, is that this potential informant sees a threat that was virtually unknown until fairly recently and that has quickly gained visibility.

Much of the argument in this chapter is premised on plausible concerns among scholars and informants about the risks associated with extraterritorial extensions of legality to pursue individuals or to address armed group behavior. The concerns generally do not involve large-scale government efforts to suppress contact between scholars and informants. Nonetheless, these concerns appear to be justified when one considers the continued expansion of international efforts to criminalize the conduct of war. The U.S. Department of Justice's Office of Special Investigations assists in identifying suspected perpetrators of human rights violations in other countries. The office's principal mandate is to focus on alleged perpetrators who have obtained U.S. citizenship and to take legal action to revoke it. These investigations frequently reach into the countries in which wars were fought. Other Department of Justice offices and the Department of Homeland Security have been involved in collection of information overseas. For example, the prosecution in Miami of Charles ("Chucky") Taylor Jr. under the U.S. Federal Extraterritorial Torture Statute (18 USC § 2340A) for acts of torture committed in Liberia between 1997 and 2003 involved investigations of individuals in Liberia who were involved in that country's war.

This is not to argue that holding perpetrators of crimes against humanity and war crimes accountable for their actions is a bad idea. Inevitably those who suspect that they have committed crimes will become reticent to speak about them. This will make the study of conflicts more difficult, even as it also may signal positive changes in how violent conflicts unfold in the future. The more immediate concern for those who study wars in which these violations occur and who interview people who may have committed these crimes, however, is that protecting informants will become much more challenging in the face of new uses that governments have for scholarly information, or in the (albeit unlikely) event that one has to defend oneself from legal action if a group appears on a list of terrorist organizations. This risk will continue so long as governments are tempted to extend the reach of laws to suppress or punish harmful behavior. Another terrorist attack in Europe or North America on the scale of the September 11 attacks would likely accelerate this trend, exposing those with contacts to groups that are even peripherally related to perpetrators to increased scrutiny. This tendency should be weighed against the genuine need to learn more about these groups, protect research subjects, and to reduce pressures for self-censorship.

Part 3

PUTTING IT ALL TOGETHER

The Varied Uses of Interview Data

9

CAPTURING MEANING AND CONFRONTING MEASUREMENT

Mary Gallagher

A common assumption among political scientists is that qualitative methods are better at getting at "meaning," sometimes described as "depth over breadth," while quantitative methods are superior in various types of measurement, offering, for example, more reliable data and the ability to make broad generalizations across a population. This chapter argues that this is, quite often, a false dichotomy. Accurate measurement requires understanding the meaning, and context, of the social phenomenon one is studying. Conversely, the ability to convey meaning is more powerful when one can make confident statements about how far and wide one's findings travel and the limitations or constraints of the research. The importance of understanding the meaning and context of social phenomena should encourage political scientists to employ qualitative interviewing as a normal and regular part of the research process, even when the bulk of the project is grounded in quantitative analysis.

Such a recommendation is now commonly called a "mixed methods approach" or a "multiple methods approach." It is fashionable for graduate students and established scholars to adopt this approach in their research, as indicated by the 2008 name change of the Qualitative Methods Section of the American Political Science Association to the "Qualitative and Multi-Method Research" Section. Much has been written recently on the advantages (and vices) of combining qualitative and quantitative methodologies. In the fall 2009 issue of the section's newsletter, a symposium "Cautionary Perspectives on Multi-Method Research (MMR)" was convened to debate further the limitations of MMR, which followed a similar newsletter symposium in 2007. Many of the critics pointed to examples of MMR that used qualitative methods (most often case studies) in conjunction with regression analysis to increase the validity of the causal effects posited in the statistical research. Qualitative methods, often applied to supply "causal mechanisms," are then lined up with statistical findings as further proof that the relationships uncovered in the quantitative data are indeed correct. In other words, qualitative research provides "proof" that a correlative relationship is causal. However, as these authors correctly point out, there is no assurance that causal mechanisms uncovered in a single or a few case studies are in fact the same causal mechanisms that explain statistical correlation. A story of causal mechanisms uncovered in a case study does not make the statistical relationship more valid, though it does provide a possible, usually logical, accounting for how X is related to Y. The same critique applies to arguments that advocate case study research as a supplement to formal theories (Goemans 2007).

The argument presented here is from a different perspective, one that takes the use of qualitative methods to be integral to quantitative research, in particular survey research. The use of diverse methodologies improves the overall robustness of the project by making up for deficiencies in each approach. For the sake of space and time, this chapter focuses on the contribution of interviewing to survey research. This is also the contribution that tends to be overlooked in a discipline that highly values quantitative research. It should also be noted, however, that this is not necessarily a new or currently uncommon approach. Many political scientists do incorporate some interviewing into their research projects. However, it is not often recognized as an important facet of the research design, and the way in which the interviews contribute to other parts of the research project is underemphasized. Overlooking its importance and contributions can lead to neglect of the how-to of good interviewing in graduate student training, methodology courses, and in the writing of effective dissertation prospectuses.[1]

This approach also questions the assumption that a researcher's interest in "meaning" necessarily falls into a subjective/hermeneutic/interpretive approach that rejects positivistic statements of empirical reality. There is an important role for interpretive research that can then be applied to social science questions of cause and effect, comparison, and generalization. Indeed, as the title indicates, I argue for the importance of understanding meaning and context when involved in attempts at accurate measurement and analysis.[2]

The chapter examines these questions at three different junctures during the research process: the development of a survey instrument, the analysis of survey data, and the situating of research results in a particular sociocultural context. I end the chapter with some recommendations for effective interviewing techniques and strategies.

Qualitative Interviewing and the Formulation of Appropriate Survey Questions

Semi-structured, qualitative interviewing of informants can play an important role in the survey research process, most importantly at the point when the survey questionnaire is designed and post hoc, when the survey data is analyzed. This is not to ignore other strategies that are used to improve survey research, such as pilot tests and comparisons with methods and strategies in previous surveys on the same subject. Qualitative interviewing is most critical when the field site of the survey is new, when the research topic is not well developed theoretically, or when the survey is extended to field sites of different cultures and languages from the original survey, which requires not only translation but also changes in question wording and context. But as the examples below demonstrate, qualitative interviewing can be useful even when these special conditions do not apply.

Breaking Down Linear Concepts

Many concepts developed in social science are measured in a linear fashion: support for an individual government, support for a political system (such as democracy), growth of rights or legal consciousness, or value shifts toward democratic and liberal values. Even if the relationship that is uncovered is not linear—for example, support for democracy might be nonlinearly related to income—the notion of support moves linearly from low support to high support. In the case of my research project, I was interested in the increasingly common belief (among the media, scholars, the government, and social actors) that Chinese citizens' "legal consciousness" is rising rapidly as China undergoes rapid economic and social change. People are more aware of the law, they are more likely to invoke their legal rights, and they are more likely to initiate disputes to protect these rights. Some macro-data such as the number of disputes, the use of courts, and the growing legal profession are used as indicators of this phenomenon. Admittedly, "legal consciousness" (or sometimes "rights consciousness") is a somewhat frustratingly vague concept, but it has a long pedigree in law and society studies (Engel and Yngvesson 1984; Ewick and Silbey 1998; Merry 1990). The word "consciousness" indicates some kind of internal belief or value structure that the researcher must dig to reveal. However, despite the problems of this term, it is not only commonly used in the law and society literature; it is also a fashionable term in China—法律意识 (falu yishi) or 权利意识 (quanli yishi). It is sign of modernity, of legality, of a shift away from "rule of men" to "rule of law." It was something that I wanted to understand, and it was something I wanted to measure in the sense of knowing who was more likely to have "high" legal consciousness.

My fieldwork began before all the funding was in place, so I developed a qualitative project that included fifty in-depth, semi-structured interviews with legal aid recipients from a large legal aid center in Shanghai affiliated with a well-known law school. The legal aid center specialized in workplace disputes, but it did not have a means test for legal aid. The center chose cases from the very large number of people who visited it on a daily basis for free legal advice. Out of nearly ten thousand visits per year, the center had a budget to litigate forty to fifty cases. With one of the legal aid center's volunteers, I selected cases randomly (not in the statistical sense, but in the messy sense) from the files in the office, contacted the recipients, and asked them to participate in a post-dispute interview. All but three of the informants contacted accepted. Although this group of legal aid plaintiffs was not representative of the larger Shanghai population, not to mention China, I believed that interviewing them would yield important insights about rights consciousness in China and about the dispute process. Generalization, at this point, was not only out of the question; it also was not my main goal. By oversampling, in effect, those people who had chosen to use the legal system to resolve their workplace dispute, I gained insights from, arguably, the most "legally conscious" subset of the population.

When funding did become available for survey research work, just as the fifty interviews were coming to an end, my colleagues and I began to work on the survey design. In the absence of those interviews, I believe that we would have gone about finding ways to capture and measure legal consciousness in a straightforward process, with a strong assumption that this concept would be captured in an additive way by examining legal knowledge, attitudes toward the legal system, and reported behavior. However, the interviews with legal aid recipients had completely changed my notions of what it meant to be "conscious of the law." From the general literature (overwhelmingly drawn from the American context), legal consciousness is often interpreted as the propensity to frame social interactions in a legalistic way and to look to the legal system as the proper place for the negotiation and resolution of disputes. Out of this literature one could envision a battery of questions that investigate the fundamental "measurable" aspects of legal consciousness: legal knowledge, attitudinal questions regarding trust and confidence in judicial institutions, and behavioral questions related to dispute resolution, either actual or hypothetical.

In the end, the survey did ask questions of these dimensions (knowledge, attitude, and practice). However, I no longer believed that these questions would deliver simple measures of high or low legal consciousness. While interviewing legal aid recipients, I noted very high levels of legal knowledge and awareness.

They had learned from their disputes and could speak easily about different reso-lution procedures, difficulties of the evidentiary requirements, and how one le-gally forced implementation of a court order. They scored "high" for legal knowl-edge. On the other hand, given their frequent negative experiences with judicial institutions and professionals, they tended to have very low estimation of the courts in terms of quality, efficiency, and fairness. Unlike the subjects studied in Kritzer and Voelker (1998), familiarity did indeed seem to breed contempt of the court. High levels of awareness and knowledge did not equate with high levels of trust or confidence. Finally, in terms of behavior, these respondents were more cautious of future legal battles. While some individuals took pride in their new-found knowledge, and while their experience led some respondents to the law again, other respondents spoke of the sacrifices in time, money, and mental health that they did not fully appreciate before their first case. They tended to be more cautious toward future interactions with the legal system compared to more naïve, but optimistic, first-time plaintiffs.

The problems with measuring a phenomenon are probably more extreme when the researcher is interested in a vague concept such as legal/rights con-sciousness. However, one can envision similar issues arising when attempting to measure attitudes toward more straightforward concepts such as democracy or democratic elections. Clearly as well, these problems might be more extreme in developing or transitional countries like China where institutions are weak or in flux. But they are not limited to those places. The effect on the survey and how I thought about the survey was profound. A "knowledge, attitude, and practice" survey of labor law consciousness would not amount to a simple formula of high levels of legal knowledge + positive attitudes + greater propensity to sue = high legal consciousness. While I remained interested in all three aspects (and in their relationship to other variables like education, gender, and age), I realized that they should be analytically separate while I also explored relationships between them, as well as the mediating effect of the respondent's prior legal experience.

Understanding Motivation and Rationality

The qualitative interviews with legal aid recipients also enriched my perspective on motivation and the reasoning that plaintiffs undertook when they went ahead with the dispute. Clearly, our sample of recipients had strong selection effects. It behooves researchers to think carefully about what is unique or special about their population in comparison to the general population. I was generally inter-viewing people without the economic means to hire a private lawyer. I was also interviewing only those who had decided to pursue a legal dispute. I could not find out about the much larger group of aggrieved workers who had simply given up. But in finding out what their calculations were, I could better grasp the range of motivations that came into play when deciding to sue one's employer.

Political scientists have in the past spent a lot of time debating the nature of rationality, even whether human beings should be analyzed with strong assumptions of rationality, particularly of the economic kind (Friedman 1996; Green and Shapiro 1996). The interviewing process revealed the equally fundamental problem of understanding the complex but ultimately rational calculations that arise when risky behavior can be costly not only in terms of economic costs, but also in terms of reputational costs, opportunity costs, and costs to one's well-being given the stress and anxiety of a legal dispute. I did not fully appreciate these additional noneconomic costs until the informants themselves recounted the entire dispute narrative with special attention to concern over one's reputation among coworkers and future potential employers, over the time and energy devoted to digging up evidence, finding willing witnesses, and filing briefs, and over the mental health costs that emerged when they received threats and were subject to retaliation from angry employers. As with the complications that arose in measuring legal consciousness, these revelations shifted my focus away from a concern with the economic costs of the dispute and led to more complicated questions on the survey regarding the respondent's evaluation of additional noneconomic costs, such as time, retaliation, and social discrimination or embarrassment.

Within the informant pool at the legal aid center, there were also enough people with long, arduous, ultimately unsuccessful suits to prompt additional questions about motivation. In many cases, the potential economic benefits of a successful suit did not seem to balance out the large costs of time, money, and energy. As these interviews were semi-structured, the narrative of the dispute was told in their own voices, with little prompting from the interviewer. Commonly used phrases and exclamations began to resonate as different people with different problems used similar language to explain motivation that was difficult to understand when considering the low payout and the high costs. "I wanted an explanation" [我要一个说法 (wo yao yige shoufa)] was one such phrase. There is a lot to this phrase. Probably not coincidentally, it was used in the famous Zhang Yimou movie *The Story of Qiu Ju*, about a poor peasant woman who travels to different levels of government bureaucracy seeking justice for her husband who was beaten by a local Communist Party cadre. I believe this saying has some similarity to the American exhortation to "have one's day in court." In both contexts, it is a citizen's attempt to receive a public reckoning of a private dispute. For many of these plaintiffs, it was an ethical position. Based on the strong conviction that wrong had been done, they demanded that the Chinese state give an explanation. Respondents presented this principle as adamantly opposed to cost-benefit analysis and often in defiance to economic rationality.

Unexpected Answers to Typical Questions

In addition to the question of motivation to pursue the legal option, I also was interested in the decision to use legal aid services, which was a relatively new institution in post-Mao reform China. In the semi-structured interview form, I had questions that asked about the decision to use legal aid, whether the informants had tried other avenues first (private for-fee lawyer, trade union representation, extralegal petitioning, and the like). I also asked several questions related to how the informants chose this particular legal aid center. In both cases, unanticipated answers to these questions significantly influenced the survey design that followed.

The legal aid services provided by this center were completely free, and I fully anticipated that the financial calculation of free legal services would be the most critical factor for my informants. In asking these questions, however, many of the informants, while acknowledging that the financial constraints on them were important, spoke almost as often about the nonmonetary aspects of legal aid. In particular, they spoke about the benefits of psychological support, as if the legal aid volunteers were both legal and mental health counselors; the educative value of being taught "how to talk" and how to articulate their claims in a way that courts would recognize; and even the value of having a public space where they could share their troubles and find others from society with similar complaints.

These responses required that we widen our survey questions to include broader aspects of the value of legal aid. Given that the household survey would capture only very few legal aid recipients in the general population, we also had to make sure that we included possible substitutions for these effects—for example, the role of friends, family, and coworkers. In this way, we had to recognize the strong selection effects in our qualitative interview data but still incorporate some of the insights learned for work on a much broader population.

These discoveries not only improved the survey; they also led me in a different, more ethnographic direction. I began to use my time in the legal aid center, at court, and with the volunteers as opportunities for participant-observation of this "public sphere" effect of the center and its growing network. My "data collection" work was certainly not limited to those times when I was engrossed in several hours of informant interviewing. These interviews, however, sharpened my perspective in what could otherwise be a very bewildering, open-ended part of the project.

In the questions regarding the decision to use this legal aid center in particular, I was very surprised to learn that the broad majority discovered the center through the official, traditional media outlets of Shanghai. My initial assumption that word of mouth would be the primary source of information was wrong; word of mouth was proven to be less important than information gleaned from the pages of the local evening newspaper. The legal aid center depended on the advice columns and articles that ran in the local papers or in other cases that were broadcast on local radio stations. The importance of the traditional media raised many fascinating questions and introduced new opportunities for data collection, including news content analysis, interviews with journalists and editors, and eventually, an entirely new section in the survey that asked questions about media consumption. The importance of this finding is elaborated further below when I discuss the contributions of interviewing to understanding the context of one's research.

Survey Analysis and Interviews

As discussed in the previous section, qualitative, semi-structured interviews can provide valuable insights on specific theoretical concepts, on the context of cost-benefit analysis, and on the characteristics of the population that might have been overlooked in their absence. These interviews made important, perhaps crucial, contributions to the survey that followed. While serving this important, complementary function for the survey research, the insights provided by the interviews also opened up new avenues of research, on the role of the media and on the nature of the Chinese legislative process.

The interviews also played an important role in the analysis of the survey data. The survey, undertaken in the spring of 2005, was a four-city household survey with about four thousand respondents in total. One of the key motivations of the survey was to understand what kind of person is inclined to take a workplace grievance to the legal system for resolution. Given what we had learned in the interviewing stage, we had already realized that knowledge of the law, attitudes toward the law, and propensity to use the legal system (behavior) could not be used in an additive sense as indicators for "legal consciousness." Instead we would examine these indicators separately to understand the effects of media consumption, legal experience, and other predictable variables, such as age, gender, education, and work history.

Analysis of survey research relies on statistical techniques, usually multivariate regression, that attempt to explain variation in a dependent variable using various models of independent variables combined with control variables. Understanding the nature of the relationships between the independent variables and taking into consideration the potential for omitted variable bias are critical aspects of data analysis. In our own work on the survey of legal mobilization among Chinese workers, one key dependent variable was the propensity to use the legal system to solve a workplace dispute. This behavioral variable could then also be linked with prior legal experience and attitudes toward judicial institutions. As indicated by research in other contexts, propensity to use the legal system may be closely related to socioeconomic status and education. Higher levels of income and education give confidence to plaintiffs that a legal battle can be paid for and won. Highly educated, wealthy plaintiffs may feel that they can take on the economic risk of a lawsuit, but they might also feel confident that the chances of winning or losing have been reasonably weighed, given their high levels of education and grasp of the legal process. Other variables such as gender, age, work history, and ethnic/racial identity also might be important factors determining an individual's propensity to use the legal system. In China, the policy-driven inequalities between urban citizen and migrant worker would also play a role, in most cases discouraging migrants from bringing cases to the state's attention. Various hypotheses regarding these relationships were drawn up for the original survey project's funding application to the National Science Foundation.

However, as with the writing of the survey, the intervening ten-month period of intensive interviewing had prompted me to think about other possible relationships between propensity to use the law and these individual-level variables, as well as some important institutional effects, such as workplace history both pre- and post-reform. In particular, my research assistant and I were struck by the huge differences between younger and older workers in the nature of their workplace disputes, their modes and strategies for resolution, and their responses to the dispute resolution processes of the state and courts. These dramatic differences appeared to be related to age, but given the dramatic shifts in China's political and economic system pre- and post-reform, these differences also were the product of changes in China's education system, differences of political socialization, and a transition from socialist to capitalist workplaces across different generational cohorts. An age variable in multivariate regression analysis might be sufficient to show differences in how individuals reacted to workplace strife, but we would not have had the requisite contextual knowledge to interpret our findings without the in-depth interviews. Moreover, we might have inaccurately attributed these effects as a function of age difference in and of itself, rather than using age as a marker between two radically different political generations.

Combining these two research methods also highlighted some of the difficulties of "mixing methods" to buttress findings in a cumulative way. While we had a better grasp of the generational differences that seemed important in shaping our informants' reactions to the legal system, we did not have the ability, the budget, or the time to explore this deeply in the survey. Given the strict restrictions on survey length, we could not ask detailed questions about work history. Questions about workplace ownership, while superficially straightforward, were often not straightforward in practice when so many workplaces in China had been merged, acquired, or restructured during the transition process. At times it seemed that the survey respondents themselves were unclear about their workplace's ownership status.

Second, my notion of "political generation" was difficult to explore statistically beyond the age differences because it was a complicated amalgamation of individual and institutional characteristics. Those from the socialist generation of pre-reform workplaces were likely to have low levels of education (a function of school closure during the Cultural Revolution), were socialized into the rhetoric of class struggle and sacrifice for the nation, and had entered the workforce through the socialist system of state assignment into permanent jobs with extensive welfare benefits. Younger workers from the post-socialist generation did not have their education interrupted by political campaigns, were socialized in the era of "rule of law," economic development, and social stability, and were hired into firms that did not guarantee long-term employment, not to mention extensive social benefits. While individual variables like age, education, and workplace characteristics might yield some limited insights into this relationship, much of our analysis and interpretation of the meaning of the findings relied on the qualitative interviews. While this heightens the importance of the interviews, it also reduces the external validity of the findings, given the restrictions due to selection bias and a relatively small sample size.

Understanding the Sociocultural Context of Political Phenomena

Survey research in political science, especially in comparative politics, is used increasingly to compare common phenomena across many different political or national contexts. The Asia- and Euro-Barometers and the World Values Survey are some of the best-known survey projects that entail extensive cross-national comparison, but there are many other smaller-scale projects as well. Common subjects of interest include political and social values, voting and political participation, attitudes toward inequality, trust in government institutions, social capital, and ethnic cooperation and conflict. Such comparison is not only necessary for theory development and testing; it also can yield interesting and important insights regarding variation in political phenomena.

Qualitative interviewing can provide insights into the specific contexts of these increasingly common political phenomena. In some cases, the qualitative data can reduce overgeneralization by demonstrating important differences between superficially similar political behavior, for example when political behavior is voluntary in one context, but coerced in another. My interviews with legal aid plaintiffs proved many insights on the nature of mediation in the Chinese legal system, which while not usually overtly forced, is strongly encouraged through judicial behavior and career incentives for labor bureau and court officials. In democratic legal contexts, mediation is assumed to be voluntary between the two parties, but in authoritarian legal systems, there may be formal and informal institutions that coerce plaintiffs into accepting a mediated settlement.

In my project on Chinese workers' legal mobilization, the discovery of the important role of the traditional media is the best example of how qualitative interviews provide critical context to common political phenomena. I had not anticipated the important role that the traditional media would play. The data provided by the qualitative interviewing led to the expansion of the survey's section on media consumption and to a secondary project of content analysis of media outlets. More important, however, it led to new theoretical questions regarding the roles that media outlets play in authoritarian countries. There are a number of possible causal explanations for this media effect: that Chinese propaganda institutions are surprisingly effective in influencing attitudes and behavior; that the media is independently mobilizing citizens to use the legal system; or that coverage of these issues in the Chinese media unintentionally encourages workers to pursue legal options. These explanations are not mutually exclusive, but understanding the mechanisms at work was necessary to add meaning to the qualitative and quantitative data that showed a strong role for media consumption.

Different causal mechanisms also have different implications for theory development regarding the nature of China's authoritarian state, which continues to rely on the media for propaganda work even while commercializing and diversifying the media sector. Working with a colleague who had done intensive interviewing with media professionals, combining our own interview data, the survey research, and content analysis of media outlets, led us to argue that commercialization and diversification of the media had improved the public's reception of media messages (Stockmann and Gallagher 2011). However, due to strict government controls over political content and editors' self-censorship, the overall message did not change significantly. Content stayed true to the propaganda message, while the delivery changed. In the end, we argued that authoritarian states could commercialize and transform their media sectors without giving up on the media's role in political socialization and social control. Media commercialization did not necessarily lead to the media's political liberalization.

Our conclusion in this project did not rely on any single method or data source, but rather was the result of analyzing large amounts of different types of data and using qualitative interviews with legal aid plaintiffs, journalists, and editors to understand the process of media content production. This qualitative dimension was critical to the development of the argument that the media was more effectively delivering the state's own propaganda messages and *not* acting in an independent or liberalizing capacity.

Strategies for Effective Use of Qualitative Interviews

In this section, I offer some general recommendations, on the assumption that many strategies and techniques for effective interviewing need to be tailored to the particular subject of inquiry, the research site, and the time and budgetary constraints of the individual researcher. I will focus on three general areas: preparation for interviewing, choosing an interview style, and using triangulation methods to reduce error.

Preparation for Interviewing

For the graduate student entering the field for the first time (and often doing interviews for the first time), the most important steps are not to underestimate the difficulty of interviewing and to prepare oneself well ahead of time for the challenges. This preparatory work is also important in increasing the validity and reliability of the interview data. Preparation includes taking classes in qualitative research methods. If these classes are not offered in one's own department, one might find similar courses in sociology, anthropology, or some professional schools, such as schools of public health or social work.

A researcher also should think carefully about what kinds of people should be interviewed (also see Bleich and Pekkanen, Lynch, this volume). If at all possible, one should strive to interview many people in the same position, to allow comparison and to learn about the possible variation that might occur, for example, in implementation of a policy between one town and the next. In my project, I consciously chose to dedicate a large part of my time to interviews of fifty people from a single legal aid center in Shanghai. Options such as interviewing different plaintiffs from many centers, or interviewing plaintiffs without legal aid, were rejected in order "to control" some aspects of the research project. For example, through one center, I controlled for variation in the quality of legal aid. I knew with confidence that plaintiffs had all received high-quality and consistent legal aid and advice from the staff. I also knew that most of their grievances were related to the reforms of the state sector in the early part of this century. We could not say much about the dispute experiences of most migrant workers. These constraints did prevent generalization, but they also allowed me to focus on comparison in other ways and with fewer distractions.

Though it may seem obvious, it is valuable for the researcher to realize ahead of time that getting, scheduling, and completing a large number of interviews is exhausting. When you are interviewing elites who are busy and think themselves to be very important, it also can be humiliating. It is best to be prepared and not to think of this part of the research project as less important or less difficult than other, more overtly rigorous stages. Training does not need to be all inductive, instinctive, or "on-the-job." One can be (at least somewhat) prepared for this stage and more confident of the results at the end. Courses on qualitative research also will provide good strategies and processes for collecting, storing, and analyzing interview data. Most courses will also include significant instruction in how to achieve these research goals while protecting informants' privacy and anonymity.

Choosing an Interview Style

Semi-structured interviews can be done in a variety of different ways. One can treat the interview like a survey but with only open-ended questions. This strategy might be effective for interviews with elites or government officials. One has access to them for a limited period of time and probably has very specific information to learn. Appearing organized and efficient is a good strategy for this kind of interview. If the interviewee seems more inclined to be chatty and engaging, then the researcher can veer off the text to gather new data and have more of a conversation. If the interviewee is very professional and distant, one should appear to respect this reserve and gather the information as efficiently as possible. For these interviews, being prepared, knowledgeable, and professional is important.

For more ethnographic interviews, however, a semi-structured, survey research–like approach might be too distant, too structured in your own vocabulary and language. It might reduce dialogue rather than encourage it. In my interviews with legal aid plaintiffs, I found it most helpful to begin with a simple question, "How did the dispute begin?" This usually led to an interviewee-directed conversation and allowed them to set the pace and the nature of the interview. I could ask clarifying questions or follow-up questions based on the questionnaire in front of me, but I also could hear the person's experience of the dispute in their own words, not mine. This strategy worked in large part because I myself was affiliated with the legal aid center; since the plaintiffs trusted the staff at the center, they were more likely to trust me. Ethnographic interviews also require preparation and a level of professionalism, but it is also important to reduce the distance between the interviewee and the researcher and to allow for more open-ended (and interviewee directed) exchange. This is particularly important if the researcher is interested in understanding key concepts and vocabularies (the discourse) of the target population.

Triangulation

Interview-based research findings are often distrusted in social science because there is little confidence that informants tell the truth. It merits pointing out that dissemblance can occur in nearly every mode of data collection in social science research. If human beings are our subject of inquiry, there will be incentives to lie, hide, or present only part of the story. This can occur in survey research, in interviews, in archives, and in macroeconomic data compiled by governments or interested parties. It is also unlikely that lying or biased answers are random, but instead it is likely that they pose real risk of systematic bias in the research findings.

"Triangulation" sometimes means a mixed-methods approach in which one method is used to check the results of another. "Triangulation" also can be used to mean the checking of one source against another to reduce the danger of deception in the data sources. For example, one can check interview data against archival data, or check one interview response against the response of another source. Although social scientists often criticize works for being "journalistic," good journalists are usually held to a very high standard for the sourcing of information. These triangulation methods can be very useful to an interviewer if the interviews are being used to acquire facts or objective data. In the case of my own research project, triangulation was more important in interviews with elites (government officials, lawyers, academics, trade unionists) than it was with the legal aid plaintiffs. For the most part, I was interested in their subjective experience of the legal process and their decision-making process along the way. I was not interested in making any normative judgment, nor did I care if some of their responses were not objectively "true." For example, many plaintiffs suspected corruption between legal officials and their former employers. They made allegations about bribes and favors, but often without any evidence to back up such a claim. It was important for me to know how deeply embedded expectations of corruption were, but less important whether or not corruption had actually occurred.

Triangulation also can be used during an interview to encourage an informant to talk about difficult or sensitive issues. For example, a Chinese local government official, interviewed about labor problems, might be very reluctant to talk about his own locality's challenges. It sometimes helps to note in the interview that local officials from another area (of course you would not reveal their identity) had mentioned similar issues. This not only shows to the informant that you are knowledgeable about the issue (and harder to deceive for that reason), but it also demonstrates that these problems are not unique to his locality or office. China scholar Dorothy Solinger (2006) describes this as the difference between her "smart and dumb faces" in interviews. That is, she strategically sometimes appeared to be ill-informed so that the respondent would take more time in filling her in on crucial details (Solinger 2006). In the example above with a recalcitrant government official, the strategy is the opposite. The interviewer uses previously gained information to make the respondent aware of the interviewer's level and depth of knowledge. This strategy makes it easier for the respondent to divulge sensitive information.

Much of what I have discussed in this essay is not novel. In much research in comparative politics, it is not uncommon for such a combination of methodologies to be used. It is, however, an area that is underemphasized and neglected in graduate student education and in the research design of projects. While one might spend several paragraphs or pages in a prospectus or grant proposal discussing the ins and outs of sampling, survey questionnaire design, and pilot testing protocol, qualitative interviews are often mentioned in a cursory way as supplemental to these other endeavors. I have argued and demonstrated here that qualitative, semi-structured interviews can provide critical information for the development of survey questions and for analysis of survey data, and also on the sociocultural context of political phenomena. In these ways, interviews can provide essential meaning to the concepts and variables that one is measuring.

ELITE INTERVIEWING IN WASHINGTON, DC

Matthew N. Beckmann and Richard L. Hall

Like many political scientists before us, we have seen much of Washington. Our interviews have taken us up and down Capitol Hill, inside the White House, and all over K Street; we have met with members of Congress, top congressional aides, and senior White House and cabinet officials, as well as with scores of lobbyists. We have attended a fund-raiser surrounded by congressmen; a Hay-Adams breakfast surrounded by lobbyists; and a private tour of the West Wing with a presidential aide—all without paying a dime. Along the way we have heard wonderful anecdotes about Washington's work ways, about the personalities and politics involved in the day's biggest issues. Tourists would be jealous.

But, of course, tourists we are not. In fact, the very trappings that make insider interviews enjoyable can often (and insidiously) diminish their social scientific value. In the pages that follow, we detail lessons we have found useful *as political scientists* interviewing elites in Washington. Many of these lessons are not new with us, nor are they relevant to all kinds of interviews, many of which have purposes different from our own: interviewing "informants" to recover otherwise unobservable behavior and decisions.[1] Still, by connecting our basic methodological principles with specific practical advice, including illustrative examples, we hope to add to this literature by detailing the strategies we have employed to gather valid data through face-to-face interviews. We conclude by echoing the calls that inspired us: we encourage those who study Washington to go and (effectively) interview those who work there.

The Practitioner and the Political Scientist

Many a Washington practitioner has an impressive title and distinguished ré-
sumé, and more than a few work from an awe-inspiring office that underscores
their status. They know lots about the day's policy issues, potential solutions,
budgetary trade-offs, parliamentary machinations, as well as the politics associated with each. They also know the other players involved. Perhaps it comes as
no surprise, then, that academics can find themselves a bit bedazzled when interviewing Beltway insiders inside the Beltway. Even an experienced interviewer
will often feel an instinct to assume a deferential posture, asking the respondent
rather docile questions like "What do you do?" and "Why do you do it?"

If the purpose of one's interviews is to examine the actors' understanding of
themselves, this is perfectly appropriate; if not, an interviewer should resist this
pull toward passivity. The reason is simple: like most people, those who work
in the nation's capital are so busy doing their jobs that they rarely stop to think
systematically about how they do them, much less why they do them as they do.
Such is why psychologists have long viewed subjects' self-reported behavioral
explanations as dubious, if not altogether unreliable (see Nisbett and Wilson
1977; Wilson and Dunn 2004). And perhaps more problematic for inferences
generated by this class of interview questions, respondents may not even provide
accurate summary *descriptions* of their behavior.

This is a warning bell John Kingdon sounded in his classic study, *Congressmen's Voting Decisions*. Discussing his methodological approach, Kingdon observed that although a legislator may "have no difficulty in articulating" theories
to explain his voting behavior, those explanations "may or may not have a relationship to his actual votes" (Kingdon 1981, 12). One congressman Kingdon
interviewed, for instance, lamented how little he knew about most issues on
which he was asked to vote: "So you seek out fellow members who are of the
same philosophical bent as you and who are on the committee that heard the
experts and considered the legislation. You rely on them." That the member did
so is entirely plausible, of course. However, Kingdon's evidence suggested that it
was simply inaccurate: "The fact is that on four of the five specific votes which I
explored with him, this congressman did not rely on fellow members" (12). To
be clear, Kingdon's point about interviewing would not be different if his
respondent had relied on his colleagues in four of five, rather than one in five,
of the votes; the broader lesson is that the member's general reflections did not
capture variation in what he did or why he did it in the cases being studied.

Given that political practitioners are not political scientists, we should not ask
them to play the part. Interviews whose primary aim is to reveal general theories

or recover central tendencies are likely to prove unreliable at best, misleading at worst. Our experience shows that elites' narratives emphasize those policymaking elements they seek to affect, not those they cannot, regardless of the latter's importance relative to the former. In practice this means improvised accounts that overstate the significance of individuals (rather than institutions), personalities (rather than incentives), and processes (rather than contexts).

Acknowledging Washington elites' capabilities and limitations leads to our central thesis: interviews with elite informants work best when designed to extract systematic information about practitioners' *actual behaviors* on *specific cases* in the *recent past*. Stated somewhat differently: we have found our theoretical and empirical objectives are best served by focusing the interview on elites' strengths (i.e., knowing what they did in a specific instance) rather than their weaknesses (i.e., making empirical generalizations or espousing theoretical explanations).

That being said, stating a research objective is easier than achieving it, and articulating a research strategy is easier than implementing it. Successfully executing interview-based scholarship requires careful consideration at each step of the process: case selection, respondent sampling, interview structure, question wording, answer coding, as well as interviewer style. Let us now turn our attention to each.

Anchoring the Interview

Nobody in Washington works on a typical case. Lawmakers work on specific bills, each with a particular legislative history; bureaucrats work on specific rules, each with a particular regulatory history; presidents work on specific appointees, each with a particular nomination history; justices work on specific cases, each with a particular judicial history; and on and on. As we see it, the case-specific nature of capital elites' work is a defining feature of their decision-making and behavior. So while Washington practitioners may or may not accurately depict what happens in a "typical" case, the people who worked on a particular bill, rule, appointee, or case know exceedingly well their actions in that specific context.

Given the nature of their recollections, our first practical point about conducting elite interviews is especially important: gathering valid data is greatly facilitated by tailoring it to the respondent's work on actual cases. By focusing the interview on the concrete and particular, the interviewer taps the respondent's recollection of events and actions that can be described in language that has identifiable, real-world referents. Much like anchoring vignettes in mass interviews (e.g., King and Wand 2007), such questions mitigate problems associated with interpersonally incomparable categories.[2] When it comes to Congress, for example, what can we say about differences across legislators if respondents base answers on different cases: a noncontroversial resolution (e.g., post office naming), a major, controversial domestic bill (e.g., economic stimulus), a budget resolution, an appropriation bill, or even an executive nomination?[3]

Another key benefit of building interviews around specific cases is that it allows us to nail down each respondent's role in that case. For instance, on a given issue, we know whether a member of Congress was chairperson, committee member, or backbencher. This is especially valuable considering that Washington elites, when left to their own devices, will naturally envision situations where their office was especially involved. Indeed, off the top of his head, a congressional aide will almost always invoke cases where his boss was on the committee of jurisdiction, not those where she was a backbencher. So a second important advantage to anchoring interviews around specific cases is that it avoids the Lake Wobegon problem (where everyone is "above average").

Considering that elite interview data are best when about existent cases, carefully selecting those cases is critical to the study's success. Accordingly, researchers should assess potential cases in the context of the broader population from which they come (or could come). Indeed, precisely because interview data should be collected at the respondent's level of analysis, it is important to be clear about what inferences a particular anchoring case can or cannot credibly sustain, regardless of the n. In this respect (among others), Baumgartner et al.'s systematic, interview-based, hundred-case study of lobbying sets a standard to which all of us should aspire (Baumgartner et al. 2009; also Leech et al., this volume).

Getting the Right Respondent

Having established the interview's substantive focus (and having completed the homework that choice entails), the researcher will already have a good sense of the controversial issues, key players, and critical junctures. Now the task turns toward actual interviewing, where the first assignment is deciphering whom to interview. Fortunately, compared to other areas explored throughout this volume, Washington provides a favorable environment for interview-based research. Not only are its participants relatively easy to identify, but also they tend to be concentrated within a few square miles, which makes interviewing large numbers of them a real possibility. Thus the population of interest will often be small and proximate enough that sampling proves unnecessary; in other cases, one may need to sample, ideally with a probability sample, but potentially with a purposive one (see Lynch, this volume).

Given that knowing whom to interview depends principally on the research question and corresponding population of interest, there is little more for us to say about the theoretical side of respondent selection. On the other hand, part of fulfilling ultimate theoretical and methodological objectives is successfully traversing corresponding practical realities. When it comes to interview-based research, two of the most pressing practical realities are those of *identifying* and *landing* the right "informant"—a term we use to denote either observers of events in question or the participants themselves. On this, we do have some thoughts.

Identifying the Right Informant

In addition to a vast array of good news sources—for example, the *Washington Post*, *Roll Call*, *The Hill*, *CQ Weekly*, *National Journal*, plus scores of online outfits—interest groups, think tanks, lawmakers, and executive branch officials all offer pronouncements that clarify the capital's current debates. Even seemingly minor or noncontroversial matters—for example, esoteric regulatory matters—almost always spawn "talking points" from a handful of lobbyists, lawmakers, and bureaucrats. By culling from these various public sources, a diligent researcher can construct a preliminary list of potential informants. It is important to note, though, that this is very much a preliminary list, which will be wrong or incomplete, or both, in important ways. The basic reason is that public sources tend to overemphasize high-profile entities while underplaying smaller groups, run-of-the-mill public officials, and, most important, staffers of all stripes.[4]

Given the limits of publicly derived respondent lists, the next step toward identifying the right informants is conducting background interviews. While we will highlight background interviews' benefits in several respects, at this point the relevant one is that these initial interviews provide a catalog of players and, better still, the specific "point people" for each case.

Before turning to our strategies for "landing" interviews with desired respondents, it is important to note that one should keep probing for potential additions to the sample. At the conclusion of every interview, we ask, "Before I leave town, are there any other people I need to talk with in order to get the full story?" In our experience, respondents are happy to help.[5] And while the obvious names come up early and often, a little informed probing—for example, "What about the auto industry? What was their role? Were any of their people working on this?"—can quickly yield a comprehensive, precise target list.

Landing the Right Informant

To be sure, identifying informants is far different from interviewing them. Everyone in Washington is busy, and more than a few view outsiders with a skeptical eye. Actually, depending on the research topic and potential interviewee, getting the desired respondent to return a call or an e-mail can be the hardest part of doing interview-based research inside the Beltway.

But difficult is not impossible. As a matter of fact, we have had remarkable success at landing interviews with Washington's preeminent policymakers or their aides. Our approach reflects a simple, overriding strategy: start with a "toehold" respondent and then "snowball" through social networks to get the others. The corollary: avoid cold calls, which are easy for respondents to ignore (see also Goldstein 2002).

TOEHOLD RESPONDENTS

As noted above, background interviews are essential for learning details about the case under study and the politics surrounding it, as well as for identifying appropriate interview targets. But background interviews' value extends further: a second benefit is they often serve as a toehold for proceeding through the sample, through the study. Whenever someone suggests additional potential respondents, we follow up by asking if we might "mention you as a reference" with any of those people. When they allow their name to be invoked, which they regularly do, it greatly improves response rates. This is why we try not to contact a targeted respondent until we have a close colleague to cite as motivation for doing so.

The importance of name-dropping begs an obvious question: how does one land the initial background/toehold interviews? Here we have two pieces of advice. First, look for preexisting connections with the relevant elites: your university is in their state/district; you both went to the same college; your university's government relations office knows them; your former students work there; and so on into the distance. The more direct the connection, the greater the chances it will work.[6]

Our second piece of advice about landing background/toehold interviews is to start with people who are well informed and well connected, but also not in-sample interviewees. So if one ultimately wants interviews with congressional officers, the background interviews should be with lobbyists; if one ultimately wants interviews with lobbyists, the background interviews should be with congressional officers. Our rationale is that refusals are more likely early in the process (before the researcher taps into a social network), so it is best if these early interviews target nonessential interviewees.

SNOWBALL RESPONDENTS

Once a handful of toehold interviewees agree to serve as references for subsequent respondents, then the interviewer can begin snowballing through the sample, typically starting with less-important respondents. But how? That is, how, in practice, does one get a targeted respondent to agree to an interview? First, we start with a brief e-mail introduction about a week before heading to Washington, which offers a little background about the investigator and study, highlighting the case(s) of interest. This summary should state the study's "academic" aims and "off the record" protections. It should also explain, "I got your name from [source], who said my study will be better if I had the chance to meet you." The e-mail also should tell the respondent to expect a follow-up call in the next week.[7]

After the introductory e-mail comes a crucial phone call, the first direct personal contact between researcher and respondent. The phone pitch, which should be practiced regularly, largely shadows the e-mail. It crisply introduces the researcher and the project, with a specific explanation of the respondent's role therein. Additionally, the caller will want to be prepared to answer the following frequently asked questions: "How did you get my name?" "How do I know you are who you say you are?" "What do you want to know?" Finally, we sometimes have had respondents say they want to do the interview right then, over the phone. Because phone interviews do not allow for paper-based measures (which we discuss below), one must be ready to explain why a face-to-face meeting is needed.[8]

Conducting the Interview

Beltway elites are quick to tell outsiders, including academics, "how Washington really works." Therefore, unless the researcher enters prepared and remains vigilant, the "interview" can quickly mutate into a half-hour tutorial on Washington realpolitik. As we explained earlier, we believe such impromptu lay-theorizing rarely proves profitable, which is why we focus our (non-background) interviews elsewhere—toward gathering valid data. Befitting this unabashedly positivist objective, our interviews are relatively structured, only loosely conversational. We very much treat the experience as an interview, where we ask precise questions and seek precise answers. In the following section, we explicate our interview schedule, start to finish.

The Introduction

After quick pleasantries, we begin by quickly reaffirming what was said in the introductory e-mail and over the phone. We introduce ourselves, our project, our objectives. Beckmann, for example, began his interviews on presidential-congressional interactions thus:

> First, let me thank you for taking the time to talk with me. As I mentioned over the phone, I am a political scientist at the University of California, Irvine. My goal in this research project is to better understand the interactions between White House officials and members of Congress regarding tax policy. Because these interactions occur largely behind the scenes, I'm trying to talk to as many people in the mix as possible to get a better sense of how these interactions play out. So again, thank you for your time.

Before pivoting to the interview's substantive focus, we first take a moment to reaffirm our confidentiality policy, which we hand over as a signed letter (on official letterhead).[9] We believe this part of the interview is important for a number of reasons, not the least of which is that it helps establish rapport with the respondent. A sample letter is included in this book's appendix.

One point in the letter warrants further discussion: we ask to record our interviews. Interestingly, and bucking our initial expectations, few respondents objected to our doing so. Perhaps this is because most respondents have practice dealing with reporters; perhaps it is because our confidentiality policy puts them at ease. Regardless, having conducted scores of recorded and unrecorded interviews, we firmly believe recording devices do not inhibit respondents, nor do they distort the information respondents provide. And the benefits of recordings are substantial: they ensure accuracy, capture colorful anecdotes, and, most important, free the researcher to engage in the interview rather than furiously attempt to transcribe it.[10]

Transitioning to Substance

The next portion of the interview turns to its substantive focus. This is the moment when the researcher shows he or she does not need a civics lesson. In fact, we start this section by asserting, "Because it is nice for me, as an academic, to be as concrete as possible, I want to use a couple of specific issues as case studies. . . . I have read up on each of these and know the nuts and bolts about what happened, as well as the basic contours of the debate." From there we characterize some of the cases' most important features, junctures, etc. This preface material attempts to both establish our informational bona fides and put the interviewee on his or her heels a bit. Actually, we hope the respondent ends this piece of the interview thinking something along the lines of, "Well, if you know all this, what do you want from me?"

In the next sentence, we reveal the answer to that question and reach the heart of the interview. We explain in greater detail what we want the interviewee to share. Using Hall's study of Washington lobbyists as an example, at this juncture the interviewer would explain, "What I don't yet know is the type of information that doesn't get into the news. . . . As such, I am hoping you can help unpack more precisely what types of conversations go on between groups affected by the legislation and the lawmakers who worked on it. . . . So, to start, how about we talk about your position on [the issue] as it first got started. What was your group's take on [the issue] as the debate got under way?"

Measurement

After the respondent's open-ended introductory exposition, we transition to a more focused question-and-answer period. This portion of the interview is the most important; it is where we collect valid data about the respondent's behaviors for the particular case(s) under study. Though theoretically banal, the techniques and measures we use here are operationally innovative. Indeed, if this chapter leaves any lingering impression, we hope it is that traditional social science standards are not necessarily incompatible with the elite interview research design. On the contrary.

As we have explained, our approach to elite interviews emphasizes the interview more than the elite. In practice this means that we see relevance in mass surveys' long-standing measurement concerns and, in turn, adopt their best practices for mitigating them. So although we certainly tailor our script to fit the nature of face-to-face elite interviews, we nonetheless draw upon familiar lessons regarding the order of questions, the wording of each, as well as the range and forms of answer-options. The result of weaving together these various elements, we believe, is uncommonly good data on how Washington works.

FIRST, THE ORDER OF QUESTIONS

Because Beltway actors are not plagued by "non-attitudes," the order in which questions get asked is less important in elite interviews than in mass surveys. A particular line of questions will not induce a civil servant to alter her analysis, a lawmaker to change her opinion, a presidential aide to recast her behavior. They know what they think, what they did, and answer accordingly. That said, interview question order does matter in at least two ways. First, it is useful to structure questions in a way that encourages respondents to bring the researcher's substantive focus to the "top of their head." Such was the motivation of the open-ended introductory question mentioned above, which cast lobbyists back to the "beginning of the debate." The second important point about the question order is more pragmatic. Because interviews sometimes end abruptly, it is important that the interview efficiently proceed to the most important sections.[11]

SECOND, THE QUESTION WORDING

As with the question order, Washington elites' extensive information and considered views render them fairly impervious to minor variations in interview questions. There is, however, one important exception to this general rule: it is important to use plain, simple language—or, alternatively, no scholarly jargon.

Hall's experience developing a measure of lobbyist-lawmaker interactions underscores the importance of question wording. Talking with a sample of lobbyists about their strategies regarding a recently completed environmental bill, he initially asked each, "On this particular issue, which legislators were you lobbying?" This seemed to be a clear, reasonably concrete question, which did yield reasonably consistent answers from a range of organizations. "You go after the guys in the middle," reported one. Another seemed incredulous that we would even ask: "The undecideds, of course, the 'threes' " (referring to a five-point scale from "strong supporter" to "strong opponent").

Yet as effective as this "lobbying" question seemed at first blush, answers to a subsequent question—one that asked lobbyists to estimate the number of "contacts" the lobbyist had with members on the relevant committee—suggested a problem. Specifically, while answers to the first question indicated most lobbying interactions occur with so-called centrists, results to the follow-up question showed the vast majority of conversations were between lobbyists and their strongest legislative allies. When Hall went back to one of the interviewed lobbyists and inquired about the discrepancy, the discussion quickly revealed what happened:

> LOBBYIST: Sure, we worked a lot with our allies.
> HALL: But that isn't lobbying?
> LOBBYIST: Sure, I think it is [but] I didn't think that you did. Most people think that lobbying is when the push is on, and you have to get the votes.

In light of this new information, he dropped the case, threw out those interviews, and changed the question wording, dropping all references to lobbying and asking simply, "How many face-to-face or phone conversations did you have with someone in each of these offices?"[12]

THIRD, GETTING COMPARABLE ANSWERS

There is a widespread perception that elites will not tolerate the confines of more typical survey respondents; they will not submit to standardized, closed-ended response options. As a result, even researchers who have taken painstaking care structuring their interview schedule and wording their questions have tended to end up with markedly varied responses, which do not permit easy comparisons across individuals, much less across cases.

Happily, it turns out the conventional wisdom regarding elites' delicate sensibilities is false. When respondents find the answer options "make sense," which good answer options should, they do not just use them, but do so with great care. If anything, our experience showed that offering closed-ended response options to specific questions helped organize respondents' thinking in ways that encouraged them to make interesting distinctions or add interesting extensions. But even if they had not, the essential point remains: standard methodological measurement matters can be—indeed, should be—as fundamental to elite interviewers as they are to survey researchers. This means carefully deciding whether the conceptual elements of interest can best be operationalized as nominal, ordinal, or interval measures.

Again, that more quantitative approaches can be effectively used in elite interviews is a critically important finding. However rich and interesting, general narratives arising from participant interviews have the feel of "just-so" stories. It is hard for the skeptical reader to tell what standards of evidence are being applied and, in turn, assess whether the researcher's thesis is supported, refuted, or some of both. That interview-based research has not had greater impact on contemporary scholarship on American national institutions is probably due to concerns about falsifiability (or the lack thereof).

As a final point about measurement, one feature of our interviews implicit in the discussion above is useful to state explicitly: we have respondents indicate their answers on a paper form. The appendix to this book depicts one such form, which Beckmann employed to have Senate staffers quantify presidential-congressional interactions during the 2001 tax cut debate. Beyond the obvious benefits of ensuring the respondent understands and answers every question, forms like this also focus respondents' attention, which directly serves the methodological objectives discussed above. Better still, the nature of paper forms helps efficiently move the interview along, since it defines when the respondent is "finished" with each question, as well as helping define a "complete" interview as one in which all the forms are filled out. We believe carefully designed paper forms offer an effective (and efficient) way of collecting valid data—our foremost goal for doing the interview in the first place.

Interview Intangibles

There are several intangibles important to successful elite interviewing in Washington—elements not easily explicated but still consequential enough to consider. Among these, rapport is the most obvious. As we say, there is no formula for establishing good rapport, and much depends on how the respondent feels about participating in academic research. That said, two controllable ingredients seem to help: the first is knowledge; the second is interest. When the interviewer is knowledgeable about Washington—at the level of *Roll Call* or *The Hill*—the respondent is more likely to treat the interviewer with collegial courtesy, which means following the researcher's lead through the interview. Second, the more the interviewer demonstrates interest in the respondent's answers, including but not limited to the researcher's narrow objectives, the more motivated the informant is to offer more information. Of course, a healthy dose of gratitude never hurts.

If an interviewer can get face to face with the interviewee, things usually proceed smoothly. But usually is not always, and a second intangible interview "skill" involves handling these difficult situations. Again, we do not have any magic keys to share, but it is worth saying that we are not easily dissuaded. If the respondent does not want to put her answers to paper, we ask if she could answer a few aloud (while we write); if the respondent expresses uncertainty, we acknowledge that imprecision is inevitable and then encourage "reasonable approximations." We take similar tacks when confronting comparable headwinds.[13]

Finally, researchers should remain cognizant that access to Washington elites is a public good—one today's scholars ought not spoil for tomorrow's. Here we echo Richard Fenno's admirable ideals, espoused in the appendix to *Home Style* (1978), about conducting himself in a way that would not inhibit future researchers' ability to follow in his footsteps. These points being so important, the last interviewer intangible we highlight is one's fidelity to the broader scholarly community. At the most basic level, this requires living up to confidentiality agreements, not divulging private information with other informants or colleagues, and no winking or nodding. Additionally, we believe researchers should not editorialize publicly about information learned from private interviews as political scientists. This means not serving as news sources or policy advocates (e.g., an op-ed writer or congressional witness) for the cases under study.

Elite interviews provide opportunities to learn about political actors and events in contexts one cannot observe and whose parameters may be difficult to infer. Interview-based research has thus been indispensable to studying Washington politics for over a half century. Until fairly recently, in fact, the inaccessibility of sources other than interviews meant that whole areas of scholarship were impossible without them.

Consider, for instance, the study of congressional committees. Until the early 1970s, almost all committee markups were held in "executive session." Similarly inaccessible were the records they generated: transcripts of the debates; amendments offered and passed; the roll of the yeas and nays; the procedural legerdemain and partisan wrangling that characterize committee processes; and the role individual committee members play. The classic studies of committees by Fenno (1966, 1973), Manley (1970), and D. Price (1972) would thus have been impossible without extensive interviewing on Capitol Hill. The same point applied to almost every other topic of American institutional scholarship. Bauer, Pool, and Dexter's (1963) magisterial study of business lobbying was heavily interview-based. So too Kaufman's study of the Forest Service bureaucracy (1960). The research for Neustadt's *Presidential Power* (1960) relied on interviews with numerous observers in and around the White House and Capitol Hill. That these books remain classics in the study of American institutions demonstrates the potential value of interviewing for political science inquiry, especially when written records are incomplete and behavioral data thin.

The fact that institutional processes in national politics are increasingly transparent—their records more accessible (even downloadable), codable, and quantifiable—has not diminished elite interviews' value. On the contrary, the brighter public spotlight that now shines on formal decision-making stages frequently serves to push Washington's players deeper into the informal decision-making shadows. For only in backroom, off-the-record venues can presidents and lawmakers, lobbyists and political appointees readily partake in the wheeling, dealing, and compromising that hallmark their chosen professions. If anything, many of the capital's most important decision-making arenas operate in obscurity precisely so behavioral data are not easy to trace from afar.

In the literature on Congress, for instance, House-Senate conference committees operate inside a proverbial black box and remain largely impenetrable without systematic interviews. The same is true for presidential-congressional interactions regarding executive nominees, for lobbyist-lawmaker relations on legislation (and beyond), or for virtually all manner of bureaucrats' deliberation or decision making. Because systematic records are virtually nonexistent for the many important activities that occur outside of official venues, opportunities for elite interviewing in Washington abound, and great will be the intellectual payoff as political scientists harness this potential effectively.

LESSONS FROM THE "LOBBYING AND POLICY CHANGE" PROJECT

Beth L. Leech, Frank R. Baumgartner, Jeffrey M. Berry,
Marie Hojnacki, and David C. Kimball

Interviewing is the most flexible of research methods. It can be useful in situations where the researcher is a newcomer to the topic area and knows almost nothing at all, as well as for researchers with extensive experience on a topic. Interviewing can be used to "soak and poke," providing ethnographic or interpretive insights, and interviewing also can be used to collect quantitative data for hypothesis testing. The main methodological requirement is that an exchange of information take place between a researcher and an informant or research subject. Perhaps because interviewing methods are so flexible, it is sometimes hard to know which rules are necessary and which rules can be bent.

In this chapter, we take a close look at a project the five of us recently completed. It relied heavily on information attained through more than three hundred interviews with lobbyists and policymakers in Washington (Baumgartner et al. 2009). A discussion of the methods used in that project provides a useful starting point and examples for talking about interview methods more generally. Here we will take a look at the methods used in that project, and also at the reasons why we chose the methods we did, pitfalls to look out for, and the circumstances under which another researcher might choose to use an alternate method.

Political scientists are often most familiar with the mass survey interview. Although technically an interview because it is spoken and takes place between two people, the survey interview follows the rules of standard survey methodology and thus is not much of a mystery to political scientists (see, e.g., Fowler 1993; Frey and Oishi 1995). These interviews tend to be highly structured, requiring informants in most cases to give responses within predetermined categories, such as "disagree," "somewhat disagree," "somewhat agree," or "agree." The resulting data emerge already coded into usable form for data analysis, and tend to be prized for hypothesis testing because the results are so easy to compare. The problem is, of course, what if the researcher asked the wrong questions or did not provide an important category of answer? The results may be reliable across informants without being valid. Although they are more easily replicable than other types of interviews, survey interviews with close-ended responses may miss the point and may overlook important opportunities for learning from the research subjects.

On the other side of the interviewing world, researchers in fields such as anthropology and sociology have written extensively about ethnographic or interpretive methods of interviewing (e.g., McCracken 1988; Spradley 1979; Werner and Schoepfle 1987). Ethnographic and interpretive interviewing techniques often leave it to the informants to decide what is most important to tell the researcher. Ethnographic interviews are best when very little is known about the subject at hand or when the goal is to get a true insider perspective on a topic or situation. Because such interviews allow the subject to direct the course of the interview, they are not usually very useful for hypothesis testing—there simply isn't enough consistency across the interviews.

Much less attention has been paid to the type of interviewing that political scientists most often refer to when they discuss "interview methods": semi-structured interviews with elite informants (for a notable early exception, see Dexter 1970). This type of interview strikes a middle ground between the formal standardization of the mass survey and the informant-led anarchy that ethnographic interviewing can sometimes result in. The term "semi-structured" covers a broad range of approaches between those two extremes. In the semi-structured interview, which is the type of interview used in the Lobbying and Policy Change project, a general set of questions are determined by the interviewer beforehand, but the questions are virtually all open-ended and provide the interview subject with a substantial amount of leeway in how to answer them. This form of interviewing provides some of the benefits of more open-ended, ethnographic interviews, while creating an interview transcript that can be coded for hypothesis testing as well, since similar questions have been asked of all interview subjects.

Most semi-structured interviews are conducted with "elites" of one kind or another. Informants in political science interviews often hold positions of power or authority within government. This type of interviewing is useful, however, whenever the subjects of our interviews hold expert knowledge about a topic, regardless of whether those subjects are technically "elite" in a sociopolitical sense. If we (as researchers) are bothering to interview using open-ended questions and allowing the subjects to answer as they wish, we must think highly of their ability to tell us something we didn't already know. We are treating them as experts in their field—whether that field is political beliefs of urban youths (when interviewing an urban youth) or social norms in the Senate (when interviewing a senator).

The Project

The Lobbying and Policy Change project was based on a random sample of ninety-eight policy issues in Washington during the last two years of the Clinton administration and the first two years of the George W. Bush administration. We tracked each of these ninety-eight issues over a four-year period, looking at which issues moved forward and which died, and which advocates inside and outside of government were involved. The goal was to examine the role that interest groups played in the resulting policy outcomes and what role interest group resources played in which groups succeeded and which did not. We suspected that political scientists had a one-sided view of what lobbyists do and how successful they are, because most researchers select on the dependent variable, choosing to study well-publicized issues on which interest groups had been reported as being influential. Our interviews allowed us to consider issues that had not been highly publicized and that often were little known, even inside the Beltway.[1]

We used the interviews in this project for two basic purposes. First, we used the interviews to collect information about policy activity by interest groups and public officials that was not part of the public record—that is, to collect background information about our policy issues that was known only to the participants in that issue and therefore could not otherwise be collected. Second, we used a subset of our interviews to devise the sample of issues that we studied, as we will discuss in the next section. Information from the interviews was used both qualitatively[2]—to provide colorful descriptions and quotes in our chapters and to help us understand the background of the issues—and quantitatively. We used information from our interviews (with substantial help from graduate and undergraduate coders) to code more than one hundred variables at the level of the "side" of the issue and more than thirty variables at the level of the issue itself. That information was combined with an extensive array of data collected from secondary sources on interest group resources and expenditures and on issue salience and outcomes, then used to help us analyze which sides got the policies they sought, and why.

Sampling

Our goal was to analyze a random sample of national issues in which interest groups were involved. Unfortunately for us, no sampling frame or list of all possible issues exists from which to sample. Sampling randomly from all bills introduced before Congress wouldn't work: most bills get no attention from interest groups or anyone else, and past research also suggested that interest groups often are active in agenda-setting lobbying, working on issues that have not yet attracted government attention and so therefore may not appear on a list of bills. We solved this problem by using our interviews to help us sample.

We began by drawing a random sample of one hundred interest groups active in Washington from the federal lobbying registration reports, which lobbying organizations file with the House and Senate. The sample was weighted so that organizations that were more active were more likely to be selected. We interviewed a lobbyist at each of the organizations and asked him or her to identify *the most recent issue* on which they had spent time. Those familiar with survey research methods may recognize this method of issue selection as being essentially the same approach that is used when a survey interviewer asks to speak to the person with the most recent birthday. Both randomize which issue is selected, although in our case it purposely gives greater weight to issues on which the lobbyist was spending greater amounts of time. If the lobbyist was working on more than one issue, we asked the lobbyist to talk about the issue that was related to the most recent phone call he made or paper that crossed her desk, regardless of how important or not important is was or what stage of the process it was in, as long as the issue would potentially involve the federal government. Each issue identified by one of those one hundred lobbyists became one of our case studies.[3]

The ninety-eight issues we studied thus provided a randomized snapshot of what interest groups in Washington were working on during the period of our fieldwork (1999–2002). The weighting and selection process meant that issues that were of concern to hundreds or thousands of interest groups during the time of our study were much more likely to be selected, but it also meant that issues that were more limited in scope also were selected into our sample, in proportion to the number of organizations working on them. As with virtually all social science sampling methods, our approach faced threats to randomness. Informants could have ignored the request to talk about the most recent issue and instead talked about the most interesting one. From our resulting list of issues it did not seem that this was the case, but the possibility remained. Our approach led to issues that were largely Congress-centered, since lobbyists in the Washington offices of interest groups tend to be Congress-centered (advocacy efforts aimed at the bureaucracy are usually handled by experts in the field who often do not self-identify as lobbyists, even though talking with government officials is a large part of their jobs). Still, the result was the closest to a pure random sample of targets of interest group lobbying that has ever been devised.

Is random selection necessary or even important for interviewing? The answer, as with all aspects of research design: it depends on what you want to know (also see Lynch, this volume). It is important for researchers to consider what data they seek and what threats to inference are posed by their proposed methods. If the researcher wants to use the subjects of the interviews as the units of analysis for hypothesis testing, then random selection is of great importance. For instance, Kingdon (1989) wanted to be able to describe the voting processes common to all members of Congress, and he therefore interviewed a random sample of congressmen about a sample of issues. Likewise, Aberbach, Chesney, and Rockman (1975) randomly sampled civil servants and lawmakers in each of their countries, so that they would be able to speak about the belief systems of bureaucrats and politicians overall. Non-random selection greatly limits the ability of the researcher to generalize beyond the people he or she has interviewed.

Interviewing is time-consuming, and random selection sometimes is not practical. This is one (although certainly not the only) reason that we almost never see random selection used in interpretive, "in-depth" interviewing. So some researchers end up treating their interviews as case studies, rather than as units of analysis for hypothesis testing. If the interviews or interview subjects themselves are being treated as non-randomly selected case studies, however, the rules of case selection should be applied to the selection of the research subjects (see, e.g., Geddes 1990; Mahoney and Goertz 2004). Examples of using elite interviews as case studies include research that focuses on just a few individuals (e.g., Lane 1962; Fenno 1978) but also would include Reeher (2006), despite the fact that he interviewed seventy-seven state legislators. Both Fenno and Reeher selected their subjects purposefully to be "representative" of the legislative bodies in question. Although Reeher's overall sample should have been large enough to rely on randomization to make his sample representative, that sample was split across three states, raising the possibility that random sampling might have left him with an unusual mix of legislators in one or more states.

Researchers choose the case study approach over random selection sometimes because gaining access is difficult, or because small numbers make randomization impractical. Still, there is always the danger in purposefully selecting individuals based on important descriptive variables (party, seniority, region, or policy area) that the researcher will overlook variation on some unknown variable that may prove important. For instance, "ability to get along with others" is likely to be a trait that affects the success of lawmakers, and yet it is not a trait for which it would be easy to select purposefully. Non-randomly selected samples may be biased in ways about which we remain unaware.

On the other hand, if the interview subjects are not themselves the topic of the study, but rather are being used as expert sources of information about some other unit of analysis, random selection might not even be advisable. Instead the researcher would want to purposefully select the individuals who are likely to know the most about the topic and talk to them. For the book *Disarmed*, political scientist Kristin Goss used historical documents, websites, and snowball sampling to identify the most prominent gun-control activists; she attempted to interview as many of them as possible (Goss 2006). She used these seventy interviews to provide historical background for her analysis of the limited gun-control movement in the United States. Notably, she did not attempt to use these interviews to assess individual motivations for participating in efforts to advance gun control: for that she used a survey administered to a random sample of participants at a national gun-control rally.

In our study of advocacy in Washington, the primary unit of analysis was the *issue*, and it was important for us to initially have a weighted random sample of lobbyists so that we could identify a random sample of issues. Once those ninety-eight issues were identified, however, random selection of lobbyists and government officials was not the way to go. Our subsequent 216 interview subjects were *not* chosen at random, but rather through a modified snowball sampling technique aimed at finding the interest groups and government officials most centrally involved with the issue at hand. The ninety-eight lobbyists who each identified an issue that became one of our cases also were asked to name the other major organizations and government officials working for and against them, and to summarize those other actors' points of view about the issue. We used this information to identify "sides" of the issue, and we tried to interview at least one representative of each side. We asked the same snowball identification questions in our subsequent interviews to make sure that no side had been missed. In most cases this meant that we interviewed two interest group "sides" and one government official for each case, but some cases were more complex, and up to seven sides were identified.

The take-home message is this: if the responses of the interview subjects are not themselves the unit of analysis—that is, if the researcher is using the subjects as expert witnesses about some outside phenomenon, such as what happened in a particular policy case—then random selection very well may not be an important factor. In eschewing random sampling, it is also important that the information being collected is generally agreed upon across experts on that topic. Informants' affect or emotions regarding a particular issue are likely to vary just as much as those of survey respondents. But if (as was the case with our study) the information being collected from the informant is more factual and likely to be viewed similarly by others involved in the case—When did the issue arise? Who was working on it? What did your side do?—the variation across responses will be lessened, and the importance of random sampling thus would be diminished.

Certainly there are always differences in perception, but in some circumstances it is better to select the person in the best position to be knowledgeable about a topic rather than to randomly select the respondent. In such situations, researchers need to triangulate and to ensure that the expert subjects are indeed experts and do not all share the same nonuniversal biases. For example, in our study we were careful to speak both to people who supported the policy proposal in question as well as to those who opposed it. If opposing sides agree on the facts of what happened in a case, that is a good check on the reliability of the responses. One of the ways we knew that we had interviewed enough people about an issue was when we stopped learning new facts about the case with our subsequent interviews (also see Bleich and Pekkanen, this volume). However, if the researcher hopes to analyze the responses at the level of the informants themselves, drawing inferences based on what they said about the world of all possible informants, then of course randomization becomes of critical importance.

Questions to Ask

Interviews are by nature a social interaction and, like most social interactions, usually begin with greetings and a brief amount of small talk about the weather, questions about how the lobbyist's day is going, or an observation about the striking painting on the wall of the office. But lobbyists are busy people, and we found that such pleasantries usually took no more than a couple of minutes. Next there was always a small amount of business to address. We would quickly remind our informants why we were there and what our project was about (the thirty-second version of that description), and remind them that we would treat whatever they said confidentially, so that neither they nor their organization could be identified through their comments.

Just a few minutes after arriving, the interview itself would begin. Once we had identified the issue, using the sampling process described above,[4] we began with a modified version of what is called a "grand tour" question (Spradley 1979. Here is the question as written in our interview protocol:

As I mentioned on the phone, I'd like to talk about your efforts on [*issue*]. What are you trying to accomplish on this issue, and what type of action are you taking to make that happen?

- *Probe about lobbying activities, lobbying targets.*

Grand tour questions are probably the single most useful type of question for elite interviews (for a discussion, see Leech 2002b). They ask informants to verbally walk the interviewer through an area about which they are expert. Interviewers could ask informants to "tell me about what happens in a typical day, from the time you arrive in the office to the time you leave" or ask a *specific* grand tour question, asking about a particular day ("walk me through what happened yesterday"). The first has the benefit of informing the researcher about what *usually* happens, and is perhaps best used if only a few interviews are being done. In our case, we were conducting hundreds of interviews on ninety-eight issues and preferred a specific grand tour question, asking informants to walk us through what they were doing on a specific issue. We were not worried that a particular issue might be "unusual" or difficult to generalize from, since we had all of the other issues to which to compare it. This gave us as the researchers control over what was being averaged, as well as the ability to see how issue context affected what the groups were doing.

Our interview protocols were short. We followed up that introductory question with just six other questions, asking about who else was working on the issue, arguments being used, obstacles faced, how the interviewee's organization used research, how the organization's government relations functions were organized, and what the interviewee's work background was. The interview protocol for government officials was only five questions long, dropping off the questions about research and government relations. Despite how short our protocols were, our interviews almost all lasted an hour (and could easily have extended longer had we not promised to take only an hour of our subjects' time). In fact, the answer to the first question often took up more than half the interview and made asking the subsequent questions on the protocol almost unnecessary.

Giving our informants the ability to respond at length in their own words was invaluable; it taught us things about the issues and about advocacy tactics that we might not have thought to ask. It also helped us to gain fuller cooperation and greater candidness from our informants. As Aberbach and Rockman (2002) have noted, open-ended questions allow "respondents to organize their answers within their own framework." They add, "Elites especially—but other highly educated people as well—do not like being put in the straightjacket of close-ended questions. They prefer to articulate their views, explaining why they think what they think."

This is not to say, however, that we allowed the interview to drift onto any topic that the respondent wanted. We went into the interview with a clear idea of the types of information we wanted to collect, and with scripted and unscripted follow-up questions, or "probes," to try to elicit that information. So if the respondent talked a lot about the organization's public relations campaign and media blitz on the issue, we might first ask, "Did your organization do anything else in relation to this issue?" General prompts, such as "tell me more," or "anything else?" are preferred, because they avoid putting words in the informants' mouths. But if even after the initial question and the follow-up probes the respondent still hadn't mentioned any direct lobbying of members of Congress, we would ask about that specifically, as we would about other common tactics that lobbyists use. So despite the brevity of our interview protocol, we actually asked a lot of questions. For such a short interview protocol to work properly, the interviewer must have a very clear idea about what information he or she needs to elicit by the end of the interview and be ready to follow up with specific questions if the general questions do not provide an adequate answer. And every once in a while there is an informant whose answer to the grand tour question is exceedingly brief: "Oh, we've been talking to lots of people on the Hill." If that happens, then the scripted prompts become a questionnaire, and the interviewer has at her fingertips a series of specific questions to ask the taciturn informant.

Although the rules of survey research demand that interviewers always ask the same questions in the same order (or in some cases in randomized order) and ask them in the same way, this is a rule that is meant to be broken in elite interviews. To facilitate rapport and encourage the most candid answers possible, we worked hard to make the interview seem more like a conversation than a survey. This meant that we did *not* read the questions directly off the interview protocol; rather, we asked something very close to those questions, but in our own words. It also meant that if the respondent had already talked about who was involved, arguments made, or impediments faced during the initial response to the first question ("tell me what you are doing on this issue"), then we would *not* ask the questions as written on the protocol. To have done so would have made it seem as though we were not listening to what the respondent was saying, and we would have lost rapport. Instead, we referred back to the previous answer, modifying the question accordingly. For example, we would say, "You mentioned that X and Y were working on this issue. Is there *anyone else* working on the issue?" There is a trade-off between loss of reliability across interviews and loss of validity within the interview itself. If an interviewer asks the exact same questions in the exact same way, reliability is increased, because we will know that the interview process experienced by each respondent was the same. But if the interviewer asks the same questions in the exact same way, ignoring the earlier responses of the respondent, the quality of the answers likely will suffer, and less accurate—less valid—responses will result.

Readers will note that our advice about open-ended versus close-ended questions is different from the advice given by Beckmann and Hall in chapter 10. As with most things in research design, the approach you choose depends on what you want to know and what you are willing to sacrifice. Beckmann and Hall's close-ended approach improves replicability and consistency across interviews, and it may make a greater number of interviews possible. It is an ideal approach for gathering non-public information for hypothesis testing when existing theory is strong and the researcher has a clear idea of exactly what information needs to be collected. Our approach allows for greater nuance, and it offers opportunities for theory building and for the interviewer to learn about things she would not have thought to ask. The trade-off is less replicability and consistency, as well as more time spent in each interview. For us and for our project, the trade-off was worth it, but each researcher must assess these trade-offs in light of what he or she wants to know.

At the end of each interview we added one final question: "Is there anything else you think we should know or that we forgot to ask about?" Although we occasionally got responses about such things as the importance of PAC contributions (about which we were gathering information from secondary sources and thus did not ask much about in the interview), more often than not we either got more background on the issue or were told there wasn't anything to add. This question was useful, especially during interviews in the early stages of the process, since it served as a check on whether our questions were adequate. We could have modified the protocol if we were alerted to a topic that we were in danger of missing.

It should be clear from what we have described that the researcher conducting such an unstructured interview must (1) have a clear idea about the information that needs to be collected; (2) understand the topic that the interview subject is discussing; and (3) be able to improvise and follow up on the fly. This kind of interviewing requires a lot from the interviewer; the quality of the interview will rise and fall with the capabilities of the person doing the interview (Berry 2002). This is another reason why semi-structured elite interviewing is relatively uncommon in political science compared to survey interviewing. Researchers for the most part have to do the interviews themselves. It is not possible—without risking the validity of the entire project—to hire a crew of undergraduates to do all of the interviews for you. Indeed, although more than fifty students worked on our project in one way or another, only two of our most senior graduate students, Timothy La Pira and Christine Mahoney, ever conducted interviews for us. La Pira and Mahoney, now both professors themselves, did the interviews for thirty-eight of our issues and, as their interview transcripts attest, easily held their own with any of the principal investigators on the project. But the people a researcher hires to help with interviews must be knowledgeable about the subject matter, they must be well-trained, and they must be smart and good interpersonally, or the quality of the interviews will suffer (also see Cammett, this volume).

Just because interviewing is a very flexible tool, not all types of questions are suitable for all types of purposes. Looking at our interview protocols, which are included in the book's appendix, the reader might note that, although we are not shoehorning our informants' answers into close-ended boxes, neither are we truly treating them as the final experts on the topic. That is, we are not asking them for their own analysis of the policy process. In particular, notice that we never ask "why?" Even though what we wanted to know was why some groups succeeded and some groups did not, we never specifically asked our informants to analyze why this occurred. This is not an accident. The questions we asked sought to have the informants describe the facts surrounding what happened, allowing the researchers to do the analysis of why. Certainly all our informants had their own interpretation of the events at hand, and we learned a great deal from those interpretations that fed directly into our discussion of the cases. In the end, however, we believed that people involved in a particular case may understand that case very well, but may not be best placed to generalize about the factors that affect policymaking more broadly. The influences in one particular case may be different from those in other cases. In addition, asking informants to provide their own theories for why things happened as they did risked coloring their subsequent factual responses. Informants might unconsciously begin to edit and select their answers to better fit the theory they were propounding. Therefore, our questions did not ask for theories of policy change, but rather focused in on our interviewees' experiences and interpretations of the events that they had witnessed.

Our approach is particularly appropriate when a large number of interviews are being used and the plan is to code the responses for hypothesis testing. On the other hand, if only a few interviews are being conducted, it may sometimes make sense to treat the respondent as a true expert and ask for his or her analysis. "Why" questions become an appropriate way of helping to understand a situation, using the insight of the informant as part of the political analysis of the project. Whether the interview subject is asked to analyze the situation or whether the interview questions are restricted to the straightforward and descriptive, the interviewers should avoid letting informants know what they think or what the research hypotheses are. The rule: avoid putting words in informants' mouths. Sometimes researchers may be asked what they think, or even what the working hypotheses are (remember, these are *elite* informants, and many are highly educated). When we were asked questions along these lines we simply explained that we could not talk about such things, because we did not want to risk influencing their answers; we also said that we would be happy to talk about it after the interview was over.

All but two of us tape-recorded our interviews in most circumstances. Of course, we asked permission (at the start of the interview, right after the small talk), and most of our informants did not mind being recorded. They tended to forget that the machine was even on. For those interviews that were not recorded, the interviewer took detailed notes and then typed up those notes *immediately* after the interview. The timing is critical. Memories decay rapidly, and a jotted note that makes sense fifteen minutes after the interview becomes cryptic after a day and illegible after a week. Even for those of us who recorded our interviews, we found that transcribing the interview immediately afterward was much easier than waiting until later. Recordings are not always of perfect quality, and while a muffled response might be intelligible when the interview is fresh in the researcher's mind, a few weeks later that answer may be impossible to decipher.

Interview time is precious—both to the researcher who has worked so hard to get access to the subject and to the subject who is volunteering his or her valuable time. It therefore is important not to waste time in an interview collecting information that is available elsewhere. As a result, in our interviews we did not ask any questions about the amount the organization spent on lobbying, the amount it spent on campaign donations, how many news stories were published about the issue, or basic background about the organization itself that was already posted on the organization's website. These were all types of information that we collected later, after the interview was over. A related point is the importance of doing one's homework about the group and about existing sources of public information *before* the interview, so that one knows what he or she needs to ask and what information is available elsewhere.

Coding for Hypothesis Testing

Although we used stories and colorful quotes from our interviews throughout our book, the primary use we made of our interviews was to transform them into quantitative data. Because we had so many interviews, so many variables, and so many student coders, it was even more important than it would usually be to have a clear system for recording notes from the interviews. The methods we used also would be helpful for a single researcher who was doing all of the coding him or herself. Memories are not reliable, and it greatly speeds the coding process to have all the information in standardized places.

We used a template we called an "Advocate Summary" to organize what we had learned in the interviews (see the book's appendix). These advocate summaries organized interview transcripts or interview notes into a series of topics on which our students would be coding who was involved, what arguments were used, what tactics were used, and so on. The interviewer took the interview transcript or interview notes and divided them up under the proper headings. Everything from the interview that related to tactics would be put under the "tactics" heading, regardless of where that information came up chronologically in the interview. When the student who was coding "tactics" accessed that advocate summary, he or she could skip right to that section and avoid rereading the entire summary (summaries often ran to a dozen or more single-spaced pages).

Coding close-ended variables from open-ended questions is not always easy (see Aberbach, Chesney, and Rockman 1975 for a discussion). Coders need to be well trained, relatively knowledgeable about the subject matter, and supervised frequently. For example, in an early check of the coding of the lobbying tactics data being done by an undergraduate, it was discovered that the coder did not understand that a reference by a lobbyist about "making visits on the Hill" referred to direct lobbying of members of Congress and their staffs, and so had not checked the "direct lobbying" box on the coding form. We had to start over with the tactics coding (fortunately only a few hours of coding time was lost—this is why constant checks are important!); the next time, we made sure that the coder was a graduate student who had experience working in Washington.

The coding task is, in essence, a form of content analysis and should be treated as such. The interview transcripts or transcribed interview notes are being treated as texts to analyze. Because interview questions were not always asked the same way or in the same order and because responses were open-ended, using this information to answer quantitatively coded questions involved interpretation by the coder. Clear coding rules, researcher oversight of coders, and tests for inter-coder reliability therefore become critically important (Krippendorf 2003; Neuendorf 2001).

All of the inter-coder reliability tests in the world, however, cannot erase the fact that the interviewing process as a whole is fraught with subjectivity because the human experience itself is so. Even if the coding process is completely replicable, the interviews themselves cannot be. Not only will there be differences in interviewing styles across interviewers, but there will be such differences for a single interviewer. We learn about ourselves as interviewers as we go along. Consciously or not, we evaluate how good a job we did after we completed an interview; we may alter our manner or expressions in future interviews in an attempt to do better.

Likewise, coding responses into yes/no or ordered categories may seem overly positivistic to some, given the subjective nature of politics. And yet, in many cases this was not a problem at all. An interest group either did or did not contact an agency about its issue. A press release either was or was not written. In other aspects of our project, there were more potential gray areas: might we have gotten a somewhat different list of "major actors" on the issue had we interviewed a different lobbyist? Might the list of arguments we recorded have been expanded if additional lobbyists had been interviewed? We worked hard to try to shed light into these gray areas, conducting additional interviews and making use of secondary source materials. For most of our issues, there was substantial agreement across the interviews as to which actors were central and which arguments were being used by lobbyists and policymakers to support or undermine the issue. Occasionally, however, very different points of view arose in the interviews, and so we did more interviews on that issue to make sure that we were not missing anything. For most of our issues, we conducted three interviews: one with an actor in favor of the issue, one with an actor on the opposite side, and one congressional or agency staffer centrally involved in the issue, usually as the source of the legislation or rule. But for those issues where conflicting versions of the issue, actors, and arguments arose, we conducted as many as fifteen interviews on the topic. In the end, we adopted a pluralist view of political reality: if one of our informants said the actor or argument was important, we included it in our analyses. Informants might have very different views about what an issue is "about" or why things turned out as they did. We did our best to acknowledge the potential truth in each version, at the same time noting the commonalities and coding what it was possible to code systematically.

Coding from interview transcripts is potentially problematic if the interview subjects have been promised confidentiality. Most of our student research assistants worked on collecting and coding data from publicly available sources. The select few who read our interview transcripts were given clear instructions about the need to keep the contents of the interviews confidential, and all went through human subjects training as well. Questions about confidentiality are important to consider when the project is being designed.

Comments that are attributed may be more believable to readers and may better document a moment in political history, because we know which important figure said what. In his book *House and Senate*, political scientist Ross Baker identifies by name most of the senators, representatives, and media representatives he interviewed. Only a few of his interviewees asked not to be identified (Baker 1995). Likewise, for *American Business and Public Policy*, Mark Smith attributed information he obtained in interviews with U.S. Chamber of Commerce officials to those officials by name (Smith 2000). While naming the officials adds authority to their comments, it also may limit the officials' willingness to be frank. Baker, for example, kept several of his interviewees confidential because of the sensitive nature of their comments (1995, 10, 19). We chose to assure all our interviewees that their responses would be treated confidentially and that our data would be reported in such a way that the interviewees could not be identified. Unfortunately, this has meant that even some of our quantitatively coded data cannot be released to other scholars, because individual interest groups could be identified through process of elimination and through hints dropped by the categorical responses. Our efforts to encourage frankness thus come at a cost for future researchers.

Elite interviews can be used for many purposes. They can be used to analyze the behavior of the elites themselves or to learn about a political process in which the elites have expertise. They can be used to gain ethnographic insight into the worldviews of elites or used as sources of quantifiable data for hypothesis testing. There are trade-offs in each choice. None is intrinsically better than the others, but the research design chosen should be appropriate to the questions the researcher hopes to answer. More interviews may lead to more data, but they may also mean that each interview has less detail. In-depth interviews may provide great insight, but those insights may not extend beyond the individuals who were interviewed. It is difficult to know whether insights from a handful of interviews represent the typical or the unusual and whether the patterns seen in those interviews would hold true for other individuals or other policy cases.

Our project worked to blend some of the benefits of in-depth interviewing with the benefits from quantitative analyses of data from many policy cases. Our interviews gave us first-person stories, impressions, and insights, but our probes and outline of what we wanted to learn from our experts also provided us information that could be quantified and compared across ninety-eight issues and hundreds of policy advocates. In the process, we heard an insider's perspective on the policy process 315 times. Many of the commonalities in these interviews were things that were volunteered by the informants, not specifically asked by us. For instance, we heard lobbyists and congressional staffers talking about each other as collaborators rather than adversaries to be convinced. We noticed how issues that were early in the political process tended to be about many different things and related to many different dimensions, while those toward the end of the process had been reduced down to "yes" or "no." Our research design and our interviews led us to study issues that we would not otherwise have known about—issues that are more representative of day-to-day interest group politics in Washington than the front-page issues political scientists often study. We would not have known, for instance, that clinical social workers were lobbying to be excluded from bundled Medicare payments to skilled nursing facilities, and we likely would not have chosen to consider the issue of who can be counted as a member of a credit union. And yet both these issues attracted a vast amount of interest group and policymaker time and had the potential to affect how millions of Americans experience nursing home care and qualify for credit union benefits.

While the number of interviews we conducted is too large for most research projects to undertake, the general approach of the project could be adopted on a somewhat smaller scale by any researcher. One of our graduate students from the project took the twenty cases on which she did interviews for us, combined them with interviews on twenty cases in Brussels, and wrote a dissertation and subsequent book on lobbying in the European Union (C. Mahoney 2008). Several additional replications of our project are under way in Europe and South Korea. Although interviewing is time consuming, it is possible (although exhausting!) to conduct two or three interviews in a day.[5] If the interviewer transcribes the interview him or herself, that means that—on average—each interview takes up a full day of the researcher's time. Still, that means that a summer or a semester is enough time to do enough interviews to make a research project.

There is no adequate substitute for fieldwork. Being in the place and talking to the people involved are critical in a project such as ours. The interviews we conducted led us to policy issues that we would not have known existed had we relied solely on published information. The interviews also provided insight into the decision-making process that is not part of the written public record. Not only were many of our issues too obscure to be researched from secondary sources alone, but also some aspects of even the most prominent issues—for example, who contacted whom, who was working with whom, how much time and effort was spent on lobbying—are not recorded in any public database or set of documents. Although news coverage of our top several issues—such as health care reform, and trade relations with China—did include some information about what was happening behind the scenes, that was not true for more than 90 percent of our issues. Even when published information was available, interview subjects often pointed us to resources we probably would not have otherwise found. We suspect that for many of the unanswered questions in politics, this is the case. If the information were easy to get, it would already have been analyzed and published. The good news, of course, is that interesting findings await the researcher willing to put the time in to find them.

USING INTERVIEWS TO UNDERSTAND RACIAL GROUP IDENTITY AND POLITICAL BEHAVIOR

Reuel R. Rogers

Mixed- or multiple-method research is all the rage in contemporary political science. Researchers are moving beyond the long-standing tendency to rely exclusively on quantitative research tools, such as large-n surveys or experiments, and combining them with qualitative approaches. Still-sovereign quantitative empirical strategies often share methodological space with in-depth interviews, focus groups, oral histories, and archival investigations. This mixed-method approach allows researchers to satisfy the demands for statistical generalizability and reliability that rule political science inquiry, without sacrificing the empirical richness, nuance, flexibility, and depth associated with qualitative studies.

Although this growing trend toward pluralistic methods is a welcome turn in political science, there are caveats worth noting. Many researchers employing this multi-method approach still too often relegate qualitative techniques, such as intensive interviewing, to a preliminary or supplementary role in their research programs. Qualitative investigation may be limited to an exploratory or speculative early step in a linear progression to more generalizable quantitative techniques. For example, political scientists who study public opinion often convene focus groups only as a means of testing questions that will appear on surveys. Likewise, researchers sometimes use qualitative approaches to provide supplementary snapshots of patterns revealed by the hard numbers.

In either case, qualitative methods are not nearly as integral to such research agendas as they could be. To the extent that interviews and other qualitative methods serve only to add empirical illustrations or context, researchers shortchange or fail to exploit fully their analytic value for addressing certain kinds of research questions and challenges. There are times in the development of an individual research project or even in the progression of an entire body of research when qualitative methods, such as interviewing and participant observation, should occupy a central place in our constellation of research techniques.

This chapter considers how intensive interviewing might serve such a role in the ongoing research on the political behavior of racial minorities in the United States. Contemporary research on race and ethnicity in American politics increasingly has had to take into account new, unfolding demographic realities. It is by now de rigueur to note that the immigration trends of the last half century have precipitated a sea change in the racial and ethnic composition of the American population. Recent newcomers to this country hail predominantly from Asia, Latin America, and the Caribbean. Together, they have expanded and diversified the ranks of the nation's minority population. Flat-footed minority categories, such as "black," "Latino," and "Asian," all have been stretched to encompass an increasingly diverse array of nonwhite, foreign-born groups. Changes in native-born minority populations also have added to the complexity of these categories. Consider for instance the economic, generational, and regional divisions that have surfaced among African Americans since the civil rights movement.

These new demographic realities raise questions about the explanatory power of key concepts, measures, and even theoretical frameworks that long have been used by researchers to understand minority political behavior. Although demographic transformations in minority populations have occurred at a furious pace, the approaches to studying them have been somewhat plodding or downright inertial. This problem is especially noticeable in the literature on the relationship between minority group identity and political behavior. Political scientists have relied for decades on a stock set of concepts and measures to describe and explain the causal link between racial group identity and various forms of political engagement, from voting to protesting. These concepts and the items used to operationalize them provided a great deal of analytic leverage for understanding the dynamics of minority political behavior, particularly among African Americans, in the first few decades after the civil rights movement. But it is unclear whether they remain as valid or meaningful today, now that sweeping changes have unfolded within the nation's minority populations, or whether they need to be reconsidered and reformulated, given these new demographic realities.

It is precisely at a juncture like this one that interviews can play an especially helpful role. Interviews are an indispensable source of data on minority populations, especially in light of the fact that these groups are still quite underrepresented in national surveys. But the value of interviews goes well beyond filling this persistent respondent gap. Interviews are particularly well suited for resolving questions about whether prevailing concepts and measures can be extended to emergent and changing minority populations or whether new formulations are in order. I begin with a discussion of the problems inherent in the existing conceptualizations of group identity and the corresponding measures in the literature on race and ethnicity in American politics. I then consider how interviews can be used to address these problems by offering opportunities to delineate, validate, and update concepts such as group identity, and the items associated with them. Finally, I provide a glimpse of how interviews might be used in this fashion with examples from my previous research on Afro-Caribbean immigrants.

The Politics of Group Identity

Scores of recent studies have considered whether the racial and ethnic labels typically ascribed to minority populations are meaningful political identities for nonwhite foreign-born newcomers to the United States. The key question is whether Asians, Latinos, and other nonwhite immigrants self-consciously identify as part of a recognized minority group and make political calculations on the basis of such identification. The prevailing assumption is that individuals who share an ascribed minority category, such as African American or Latino, are likely to feel solidarity with that in-group. Those bonds of solidarity, in turn, lead them to share common interests and to take political action in concert in pursuit of those interests (Lee 2007).

Of course, this assumption derives largely from the case of African Americans. A long line of research has shown that racial group membership has deep political significance among native-born blacks. Even as serious divisions have emerged in the African American population in recent decades, African Americans have continued to share common ground in their struggles with racial discrimination, to identify with each other on the basis of these experiences, and to rely on their shared group identity to make political decisions. In short, racial group identity has remained a powerful political heuristic for African Americans (Dawson 1994a, 2011).

Two concepts have occupied a central place in analyses of the political significance of African American racial group identity: group identification and group consciousness. Social psychologists were the first to establish and elaborate the distinctions between these two concepts (e.g., Miller et al. 1981; Tajfel 1981). Group identification is the simpler construct and only a first step toward the more complex group consciousness. It is an awareness of one's membership in a group and a psychological attachment to that group. Survey researchers often use a measure tapping "linked fate" to gauge racial group identification among

African Americans. The item typically asks whether a black respondent feels that what happens to her is determined by what happens to blacks as a group.

Group consciousness combines basic group identification with an ideology about the group's position in society and what should be done to improve it. Although both group identification and group consciousness can influence political behavior, group consciousness has more prescriptive implications. Among African Americans, group consciousness has been associated with dissatisfaction with the group's share of resources relative to whites, support for situational or systemic explanations for black inequality, government solutions to redress racial disparities, and mobilization by the group to correct these inequalities. Survey researchers rely on a set of items that ask about these specific beliefs and orientations to gauge group consciousness. They also often include items about the relevance of the civil rights movement and affinity for other disadvantaged minority groups.

Linked fate and group consciousness are now standard variables for understanding the political attitudes and behavior of African Americans. In fact, researchers have concluded that these group-based identities account for many of the distinctive patterns in African American politics, such as the high levels of ideological and partisan uniformity within the population (e.g., Dawson 1994a; Gay 2004; Hajnal and Lee 2011; Tate 1993). The general consensus is that these identities, while they may have weakened in recent decades, remain salient for African Americans because so many of these individuals continue to encounter prejudice and discriminatory barriers in their everyday lives.

Most studies exploring group identity and its political effects in immigrant minority populations rely on these same concepts that have had so much traction in the research on African American politics, specifically linked fate and racial group consciousness (e.g., Jones-Correa and Leal 1996; Junn and Masuoka 2008; Leighley and Vedlitz 1999; Lien 1994; Lien, Conway, and Wong 2004; Marschall 2001). Researchers also typically operationalize these constructs in roughly the same fashion as they have been measured in studies of African Americans. To the extent that heavily foreign-born populations, such as Asians and Latinos, are also racial minorities and subject to discrimination, it is not surprising that researchers studying these groups take their conceptual and analytic cues from the scholarship on African Americans. Yet it is not clear that the concepts for studying group identity apply equally as well to the political behavior of these other minority groups as they do to African Americans.

Several researchers have cautioned, in fact, against "the presumption of functional isomorphism" or commensurability between African Americans and other minority populations (Chong and Rogers 2005; Lee 2007). The boundaries and composition of many of these immigrant minority groups are still quite unsettled.

Millions of newcomers from countries throughout Asia, Latin America, Africa, and the Caribbean enter the United States each year. New arrivals, long-settled immigrants, and groups from a diverse mix of countries are lumped together under broad minority labels, making it difficult to delineate exactly who falls within the ambit of these groups. There is little basis for predicting that the diverse array of populations subsumed under these labels will cohere easily or inevitably into self-conscious political constituencies with common interests as African Americans have. The divisions of nationality, language, and religion within these broad racial or pan-ethnic population groupings are many, the bases for racial group solidarity within these populations are difficult to demarcate, and the shared experiences that might make for such solidarity are still taking shape or coming into focus (Lee 2007, 439).

Even if feelings of group solidarity emerge among these immigrant populations, the process may differ significantly from the case of African Americans. The challenges that they might face and the concerns that might unite them may be quite distinct from those that have been salient for native-born blacks. Even among African Americans, racial group solidarity and the political effects it tends to produce can no longer be taken for granted, in light of the class, generational, and other cleavages that have emerged in the population since the civil rights movement. The assumption that African Americans continue to share a common set of racial experiences, which forms the basis for their feelings of group solidarity and influences their political choices, has become less tenable in recent decades.

All these caveats raise questions as to whether the concepts and measures developed decades ago to understand the political significance of group identity in minority populations are still valid. Most of the survey research using these concepts to explore the link between identity and political behavior among foreign-born minorities has turned up mixed or null results (e.g., Jones-Correa and Leal 1996; Leighley and Vedlitz 1999; Lien 1994; Marschall 2001). On the one hand, these findings might suggest that group identity has little influence on the political behavior of these populations. On the other hand, they might be an indication that the concepts and measures that researchers employ to study group identity are of limited analytic value when applied to these immigrant minority groups.

The Role of Interviews in Understanding Group Identity and Political Behavior

In light of these conceptual uncertainties, in-depth interviews are a much more effective methodological tool than large surveys for analyzing the connection between racial or ethnic identity and political behavior among emerging foreign-born minorities and African Americans. The methodological advantages of interviews have been laid out quite ably elsewhere in this volume and in other works (e.g., Rubin and Rubin 2005). But it is worth considering why and how interviews might be particularly well suited for reconsidering established concepts and defining new ones—a step that seems to be warranted in the ongoing research on group identity and minority political behavior. Determining whether long-standing concepts such as linked racial fate and group consciousness still have currency with African Americans, or whether they are meaningful to foreign-born Asians, Latinos, or Afro-Caribbeans, requires careful, expansive investigation of the subjective understandings of individuals in these groups. The same kind of flexible probing is also necessary for determining whether alternative conceptualizations might capture more accurately new or emerging forms of political identity within these populations. In short, validating or reformulating concepts—especially with new or dramatically transformed populations—calls for the kind of open-ended querying and in-depth engagement with respondents that interviews allow.

Using Interviews to Update and Validate Group Concepts

Social scientists have outlined criteria for formulating and validating concepts (Gerring 1999; Lazarsfeld 1966). Depth and differentiation are among the most important criteria. Depth refers to the range of properties or characteristics typically associated with a concept (Gerring 1999). Concepts defined by a wide class of attributes have more depth and thus are considered more analytically powerful than those associated with a narrower class of characteristics. Differentiation, on the other hand, refers to how well a concept can be distinguished from similar ideas. As Gerring puts it, a concept's differentiation derives from "the clarity of its borders within a field of similar terms" (1999, 376). Plumbing the depth of a concept or determining how well it can be differentiated from others requires the kind of rich empirical evidence about individuals' thinking that interviews typically generate.

Consider the attitudes associated with group consciousness. The standard battery of items used to measure the concept among African Americans includes the following probes:[1]

- Do you think what happens generally to black people in this country will have something to do with what happens in your life?
- Do you think blacks have achieved racial equality?

- There is still so much discrimination that special programs to help blacks and other minorities are needed. Agree or disagree?
- Latinos, Asian Americans, and other disadvantaged groups are potentially good allies for blacks. Agree or disagree?

These items are worded to tap the politically animating dimensions of group consciousness: feelings of racial solidarity, dissatisfaction with the group's status, and commitment to collective strategies for improving it. Although such attitudes may have been the most salient properties of group consciousness among African Americans in the first few decades after the civil rights movement, it is certainly plausible that a whole new set of attitudes are now associated with any form of group consciousness circulating within the population. For instance, some recent studies suggest that African Americans are beginning to turn to neoliberal, market-based policies and group uplift strategies to combat racial inequality (Cohen 2010; Dawson 2011). These ideas contrast sharply with the government-centered solutions that have long been associated with African American racial group consciousness. In short, the properties of the concept may have changed over time. Yet surveys that rely on the same standard set of items cannot account for such changes.

In-depth interviews, on the other hand, are an effective research technique for assaying the depth of the concept or taking stock of its properties in its contemporary form. A series of open-ended interviews with minority respondents would be a useful starting point. In fact, some of the early evidence for the neoliberal turn in black politics comes from interviews (e.g., Cohen 2010). But the strategy needs to be purposive and systematic. Minorities who rate high on political engagement and awareness would be ideal respondents for this kind of exploratory inquiry, as they are more likely than others to have had exposure to the prevailing political ideas, messages, and frames associated with the concept. Not only would the right people need to be targeted, but they would have to be interviewed in the right places as well. The interviews would have to be conducted in locations with a politically active critical mass of the target population.

The main of objective of these open-ended interviews would be to prompt respondents to conjure the full range of political ideas or attitudes that they associate with racial group solidarity. With this carefully chosen sample, a researcher then could begin to generate a list of the most salient properties of the concept that seem to recur across interviews. Such a list compiled across a number of interviews could furnish enough detailed empirical evidence to lay the foundation for reformulating a concept such as group consciousness. The most salient properties of the updated concept could be translated into discrete items, which then could be tested in a conventional survey with a much larger sample of respondents.

Using Interviews to Study Ongoing Group Processes

Of course, this research strategy will be effective only if the meanings associated with the concept are familiar and settled within the population under study. For instance, even if group consciousness is still a relevant concept for understanding African Americans' political behavior, the meanings attached to the concept in more recent times may not be embedded firmly in African American popular opinion. Many of the dominant group beliefs embraced by race-conscious African Americans and captured in the items included on national public opinion surveys were the result of long processes of debate and contestation within the population (e.g., Dawson 1994a; McAdam 1982; Morris 1984). Indeed, it is only after such processes were well under way that these beliefs began to surface in national political discourse and show up as items on national surveys during the civil rights movement (Lee 2002; Lee and Willcoxon 2011). To the extent that such processes are again currently unfolding for African Americans in the post–civil rights era, it would be difficult to generate a definitive list of the properties associated with a concept, such as group consciousness, through a series of one-on-one interviews.

Yet an appropriately structured qualitative research program culminating with interviews is an effective method for capturing processes that are still unfolding or unsettled.[2] In the case of African Americans today, a researcher first would need to take stock of ongoing debates about group-centered political beliefs and strategies within the population. Such evidence might be gleaned through a number of qualitative methods, such as content analysis of articles in the African American press and online discussions in African American web forums. A more common approach in the scholarship on African American politics is to collect such data through focus groups and participant observation in civic networks. Recent studies by Cohen (2010) and Harris-Lacewell (2004) rely on this strategy; both convene focus groups to map dominant racial beliefs in contemporary African American public opinion.

Researchers should choose participants for such focus groups or select sites for participant observation with an eye toward capturing the various points of view at stake in any ongoing debates or discussions. Cohen (2010), for instance, is careful to strike a gender and sexual-orientation balance in the participants recruited for her focus groups with black youth on the topic of sexual attitudes. This kind of purposive sampling or site selection allows a researcher to structure the investigation in a way that captures the degree of contestation or disagreement about the content of group beliefs within the population. Focus groups and participant observation might be useful not only for cataloging such debates; they might also provide a revealing snapshot of how such debates are settled. Both approaches allow researchers to peer into how group processes unfold—how some group-centered ideas gain adherents, achieve dominance, and cohere into a full-fledged group consciousness within a population.

This kind of exploratory investigation ideally should be followed by interviews with group leaders or elites. The purpose of such interviews would be to clarify, delineate, and gauge the political resonance of the ideas and beliefs generated by the focus groups, participant observation, or one-on-one discussions with rank-and-file members of the population. Armed with the insights yielded by these other sources, a researcher could ask group leaders about whether the uncovered group ideas and beliefs are reflected in ongoing policy debates or deployed in po-litical campaigns. These kinds of questions would provide a rough, indirect mea-sure of the extent to which the ideas are circulating in the broader political dis-course. In short, a series of interviews with elites focused on any emerging ideas or beliefs would help to establish whether they are verifiable group ideologies that serve as a basis for consciousness-raising within a population.

This interview-centered research strategy for updating concepts, such as group consciousness, is not only useful for studying African Americans, who have a long history of debating group ideologies and turning to those ideologies to motivate political action. It also could work equally well with heavily foreign-born minority groups, such as Asians and Latinos, many of whom are newer to the country and might be unfamiliar with such group-centered, race-based po-litical beliefs. Interviews have particular advantages that also make them an ef-fective method for exploring and validating these concepts with these popula-tions. The open-ended format used in most interviews gives a researcher considerable analytic room to probe respondents' thinking to determine if cer-tain concepts are recognizable to them in a variety of frames or guises. This kind of deep probing through intensive interviewing is typically not possible within the confines of the standard survey format.

A survey might fail to uncover evidence of group consciousness in immigrant respondents because of limitations in question wording and the range of probes. In contrast, an interviewer may ask a respondent about a concept using a variety of probes or may pose multiple iterations of the same question to determine if the concept has resonance for respondents. Equally important, the conversa-tional style of an interview allows a researcher to discuss a concept in an idiom that is familiar or comfortable for the respondent. This dimension of intensive interviewing may be especially helpful with foreign-born minority respondents, many of whom are likely unfamiliar with the items survey researchers use to tap concepts such as racial group consciousness. For example, one item used to measure group consciousness is a standard question about whether the civil rights movement has benefited the respondent. For immigrant subjects who may not be as steeped in civil rights history as their native-born counterparts, an interviewer could pose the same question but also follow with a series of probes focused on the overarching principles and goals of the civil rights movement. This kind of deep, tailored probing allows an interviewer to cull more reliable evidence about a respondent's group-centered beliefs, especially if her views are not couched in the language of the dominant frames that show up on surveys.

What it means to be a member of a racially or ethnically defined group in the United States is itself an unsettled question for many foreign-born minorities. Asians, Afro-Caribbeans, and Latinos are all potential emerging political constituencies whose boundaries and intragroup bonds are still developing. Interviews can capture and document these intragroup processes as they unfold. During interviews, a researcher can induce respondents to clarify these political processes and outline the contours of the group-centered ideas that these processes generate. Interview respondents can give their own accounts of how they view themselves in relation to other group members and how they perceive the boundaries of the groups to which they belong. Such subjective accounts may bring new ideas and concepts to the attention of a researcher. Interviews therefore provide opportunities for discovering data that may lead to new or updated frameworks for understanding concepts, such as group consciousness, that revolve around how minorities define themselves and view the political world.

Likewise, interviews with heavily immigrant minority respondents might uncover evidence of new forms of group identity not captured by existing survey items. In such cases, researchers could turn to the strategy outlined earlier for cataloging and exploring emergent group-centered beliefs among African Americans. They should include questions about these new forms of group identity in interviews with both non-elite and elite respondents, to account for the dynamic top-down, bottom-up processes that generate group-centered ideologies. In addition to combining elite and non-elite interviews, researchers also should employ purposive sampling to generate a pool of interview subjects that reflects sufficient variation on theoretically relevant variables (also see Lynch, this volume). For example, interviews with Latinos or Asians should sample respondents along lines of nationality, region, or other variables that are theoretically relevant to the formation of group-centered beliefs. Relying on purposive sampling for such interviews enables researchers to draw stronger inferences about the depth, reach, and validity of emergent forms of group identity or group-based beliefs.

Using Interviews along with Surveys

Not only can interviews be used to explore and identify new or burgeoning forms of group identity and race consciousness in minority populations, but they also can be helpful in designing the items used to gauge these identities on surveys. Interviews can therefore serve as the first phase of a research program to catalog new forms of group identity and translate them into discrete items that can be incorporated into surveys. The flexible format of interviews gives researchers room to experiment with the question wording for different probes and to determine which formulations have the most transparency and resonance with respondents. These kinds of practical insights gleaned from interviews can guide researchers as they design and update surveys targeting minority populations.

Interviews also need not be relegated to the preliminary phase of such a research program, or serve only as a precursor to surveys. They can be employed quite productively as a follow-up to surveys that include panels of identifiable respondents. This strategy may be especially helpful when certain survey items, such as those addressing group consciousness or identification, generate nonresponses or yield confusing, impenetrable results. For example, if there are problems with existing survey items, then follow-up, intensive interviews with respondents can shed light on where the issues lie—whether it is a matter of question wording, question clarity, or a more substantive conceptual problem.

Finally, interviews also can be used to develop deeper or fuller explanations for statistical patterns or theoretical anomalies that appear in analyses of survey data. For example, survey results might indicate that some groups in a sample express higher levels of racial group consciousness than others. A researcher may formulate hypotheses that could account for this pattern but be unable to test them statistically, given the limitations of the survey data. Interviews with respondents from the same survey could serve as an alternative method for exploring these hypotheses, generating others, or fleshing out partial explanations deduced from the data analysis. Although interviews can aid in designing surveys and generating explanations for their results, perhaps their greatest utility lies in the data they can furnish for reconsidering and revising concepts, such as group consciousness, especially with minority populations that remain underrepresented on national surveys.

Afro-Caribbeans and Racial Group Consciousness

A study of Afro-Caribbean immigrants that I conducted several years ago provides some concrete examples of how interviews can be used to reconsider prevailing conceptualizations of racial group consciousness and uncover new or emergent forms of group identity in a foreign-born population (Rogers 2006). As blacks in the United States have become more socially diverse, political scientists have explored whether the emerging demographic divisions correspond to varying levels of racial group consciousness. Numerous studies, for instance, have considered whether middle-income blacks are more or less race conscious than their low-income counterparts (Dawson 1994b; Gay 2004; Tate 1993). Following this line of inquiry, one of the principal empirical aims of this study was to determine whether Caribbean-born blacks exhibit the same kind of racial group consciousness that researchers have found among their African American counterparts.

I conducted interviews with a non-random sample of fifty-nine English-speaking first-generation Afro-Caribbean immigrants in New York City between 1997 and 1999. New York is home to the largest population of Afro-Caribbean immigrants in the United States. There are 1.5 million Afro-Caribbean immigrants in the United States. Roughly one-third of these immigrants live in New York. I also interviewed fifteen Afro-Caribbean political and community political cal leaders.

I used an open-ended, structured questionnaire and employed snowball sampling to recruit participants. The respondents in the rank-and-file sample included thirty-five women and twenty-four men. They were predominantly middle-class and more politically active than the average immigrant. The majority resided in predominantly black neighborhoods in two New York City boroughs, Brooklyn and Queens. A handful lived in the Bronx. Most of the heavily immigrant neighborhoods where these Afro-Caribbeans reside are of slightly higher economic status than surrounding African American areas. Afro-Caribbeans, in fact, tend to outperform their African American counterparts on the standard socioeconomic indicators.

The interviews included a series of questions about racial group consciousness. I adapted the main probes about this psychological construct from two surveys of African Americans, the 1993 National Black Politics Study and the 1996 National Black Election Study. I also exploited the open-ended format of the interviews to supplement the standard questions with other probes. This additional tier of questions, several of which I formulated and reformulated while in the field, allowed me to depart from the relatively narrow battery of probes that has been used to measure group consciousness in survey-based studies. I took advantage of the open-ended format of the interviews to experiment with alternative formulations of standard questions and incorporate new ones that took the immigrants' distinctive experiences and emergent patterns in the interview material into account.

The interviews appeared to turn up the same mixed results seen in the survey research on racial group consciousness in other foreign-born minority popula- tions (e.g., Leighley and Vedlitz 1999; Lien 1994; Marschall 2001; Verba, Schloz- man, and Brady 1995). Most of the respondents did not evince the standard form of group consciousness that existing surveys have documented among African Americans. But the interviews uncovered evidence of what may well be a less fa- miliar, latent form of race consciousness in this black immigrant population. By taking advantage of the latitude that the interviews provided for follow-up probes and ad hoc questions based on emerging patterns in the data, I was able to move beyond conventional measures and identify the outlines of this alternative form of racial group consciousness. Although it does not fit the prevailing conceptual- ization of the construct in political science, it appears to carry similar significance.

Methodological and Analytical Challenges

Several expectations and concerns informed how I approached and structured the questions about racial group consciousness. First, I was mindful of the pos- sibility that the questions about the concept—particularly those based on con- ventional survey items—might fail to generate meaningful results. A handful of previous studies by other researchers had shown that Afro-Caribbean immi- grants tend to downplay their racial identity and emphasize their ethnic roots instead (Kasinitz 1992; Vickerman 1999; Waters 2001). Although none of these earlier studies examined racial group consciousness per se, it was reasonable to infer from their findings that Afro-Caribbeans might not subscribe to the racial beliefs and ideas associated with group consciousness.

Other factors also suggested that race-conscious beliefs might be sparse among these foreign-born blacks. As immigrants from predominantly black countries, Afro-Caribbeans are less steeped in a history of black-white racial conflict than their African American counterparts. Moreover, many of them migrated to the United States during the post–civil rights era, when the consciousness-raising events of the 1950s and 1960s had become objects of historical memory, and the most flagrant forms of antiblack discrimination had been eliminated. In this light, finding low levels of racial group consciousness among the Afro-Caribbean im- migrants in the study would not be entirely surprising.

My second concern was that the immigrants might express their race con- sciousness in a new or unfamiliar form—one that might not be readily elicited with questions based on the usual survey items. Lurking behind nonresponses or low ratings on the standard questions might be other, uncharted racial beliefs. The challenge, then, was to craft a set of questions expansive enough to account for the possibility that racial consciousness might take an alternative form among the respondents. Any new questions I devised would have to be informed by the foundational properties of the concept—even if I were unsure about the particular details of how it might manifest in this foreign-born population.

My final concern was how to verify that any new or alternative form of racial group consciousness uncovered by the interviews was meaningful in the wider Afro-Caribbean population. The challenge obviously was compounded by fact that the study was based on a small, non-random sample of respondents. Although interviews are extremely useful for exploring the subjective perspectives of respondents, their narrow sampling frame can make it difficult to test just how valid or generalizable the interview-based findings are in the wider target population. To compensate for these methodological limitations, I focused on confirming the internal, rather than the external, validity of any new findings. The strategy entailed looking for evidence among the respondents of common or shared understandings of any new racial ideas or beliefs uncovered by the interviews.

Interviews on Racial Group Consciousness

With these methodological concerns and analytic goals in mind, I began the inquiry with the conventional survey questions about linked racial fate and racial group consciousness. Of course, I adjusted and tailored some of the questions to account for the distinctive experiences of my foreign-born sample of respondents. For instance, in addition to the familiar linked fate items, I asked the respondents if they felt close to other Afro-Caribbeans and African Americans, and if they believed that their life prospects were determined by what happens to black immigrants and African Americans specifically. Below are some examples of the tailored questions about linked fate:

- Do you feel close to other immigrants from the Caribbean?
- Do you feel close to African Americans?
- Do you think what happens generally to black people in this country will have something to do with what happens to you?
- Do you think what happens to African Americans specifically will have something to do with what happens to you?
- Do you think what happens to other immigrants from the Caribbean will have something to do with what happens to you?

My questions about racial group consciousness included the standard probes about government solutions to racial inequality, coalition building with other disadvantaged minority groups, and the effects of the civil rights movement. But I also veered away from those familiar items to unchartered topics that might be associated with racialized thinking or consciousness among immigrants. My standard rule for the additional questions was to ask about contemporary political ideas or policies that not only might be salient to the immigrant population, but also were ripe for engaging or priming race consciousness. The questions did not focus on explicitly racial topics, but they certainly addressed subjects that were open to a race-based interpretation or understanding. For instance, I asked a number of questions that tapped policy preferences or attitudes typically associated with race-conscious African Americans, such as support for affirmative action and welfare programs.

I also included questions about racially fraught current events or kitchen table topics that were likely to be salient to the respondents at the time of the interviews. For example, I asked about community relations with police and about a couple of police brutality cases involving Afro-Caribbean victims that dominated local news headlines at the time. The cases fueled a great deal of outrage and galvanized demonstrations in black neighborhoods. They were the kind of episodes that easily might prime or foster some form of race consciousness among Afro-Caribbean immigrants. The rationale for incorporating these additional probes into the interviews was not simply to expand beyond the conventional survey items for measuring racial group consciousness, but also to include questions that could capture beliefs and orientations that might correlate with race consciousness in a black immigrant population. Here is a sample of the additional questions:

- Is racial discrimination against blacks a big problem in New York City?
- Have you ever participated in a demonstration or rally to protest against racism in New York?
- How are blacks treated by the New York City police?
- Is police brutality an important issue for Afro-Caribbean immigrants?

Many of the questions based on conventional survey items elicited answers that indicated low or nonexistent racial group consciousness in the respondents. Although there were exceptions, the immigrants simply did not subscribe firmly to the political beliefs that traditionally have been associated with racial group consciousness among African Americans. Most registered ambivalence about these beliefs, and some rejected them outright. Yet, at the same time, there was evidence of racial group consciousness in their answers to some of the additional probes that I incorporated. Perhaps not surprisingly, the respondents frequently registered their most race-conscious responses to questions about racially charged issues that were particularly relevant to the immigrant population. Questions focused on police misconduct and immigration reform repeatedly elicited racially inflected reactions from the respondents. One immigrant was certain that racial animus was behind recent episodes of police brutality:

> Quite a few of our own have been brutalized by police. . . . When the police pick on you, he doesn't care if you're from Africa, the Caribbean, India, or Harlem. . . . There are racist cops. I don't care what they say or how much they deny it.

Another put it this way:

> Racism is the biggest problem . . . police brutality [specifically]. . . . When you look at the problems, it's the same problem that all minorities face. You follow?

These opinions actually resonate with the orientations typically expressed by race-conscious African Americans. The notable difference in the respondents' views, however, is their preoccupation with issues and problems that hold more salience or relevance for them as immigrants. Still, there is no denying the traces of race-conscious thinking reflected in these responses.

What was more unexpected and harder to interpret was an unfamiliar form of race consciousness that surfaced in these interviews. I noticed in the early phase of my fieldwork that the respondents expressed their race consciousness in a transnational frame, with repeated references to their home counties. When discussing how they were faring in the United States or lamenting how racial obstacles were complicating their quest for a better quality of life, the immigrants often drew comparisons between the United States and their home countries. When they expressed their concerns about racism or their fears for teenage sons who might encounter renegade police on the streets, they invoked the possibility of returning to their home countries in the Caribbean. They discussed the prospect of returning home as a kind of exit option in the face of racial barriers in this country. Consider one typical example:

> Q: Do you feel affected by the recent cases of police brutality?
> A: It's so bad now even in my neighborhood. My teenage sons are always complaining that the police harass them. It's getting so bad that I feel like I should just take my family and move home to Trinidad. I think about it seriously more and more these days.

When these attitudes first surfaced in my early interviews, I did not know how valid or common they were. Nor did I know how to interpret them or whether they cohered into anything like an ideology or worldview that would qualify as a form of consciousness. The basic conceptual properties of group consciousness are plainly political: an ideology about a group's position in society and a prescription for what should be done to improve it. The interviews certainly did not allow me to verify whether these ideas cohere and circulate as a full-fledged political ideology for responding to racism and group status in the wider immigrant population. But they did enable me to probe these ideas further by adding questions that asked explicitly about the exit option and transnational frame of reference in the context of American race relations. I began to ask respondents if they had contemplated returning to their home countries and to specify what would prompt them to make such a decision. I even reinterviewed some respondents to pose these questions.

This strategy allowed me to ascertain how common these attitudes were among the pool of Afro-Caribbean interview subjects. Many of them pointed out that racial frustrations, particularly in their quest for socioeconomic mobility and security, might motivate them to undertake return migration. The respondents also routinely assessed their status in the United Status by drawing comparisons with life back home. Whereas African Americans draw comparisons between themselves and whites, Afro-Caribbean migrants compare their lives here with the ones they left behind. In both cases, the comparisons can lead to dissatisfaction with the racial disadvantages that blacks suffer in this country and a systemic critique of American inequalities. As these interviews with rank-and-file Afro-Caribbeans yielded more and more evidence of this transnational perspective among the respondents, it became clear that this alternative form of race consciousness had validity, at least in the interview sample.

I turned to my interviews with elite Afro-Caribbean respondents, elected officials and organizational leaders, to glean indirect information on how much currency this orientation has in the broader population. I asked them whether it was apparent in the attitudes and opinions of their constituents. Even more importantly, I relied on the elite interviews to help me understand the conceptual contours of the transnational perspective and the accompanying exit option that it appears to provide to Afro-Caribbean immigrants. One Caribbean-born city council member explained this outlook in detail:

> I go back to the psychological and emotional ties to the Caribbean. People feel that "I have an *option*. . . . If things don't work out here for me, I'll work, make some money, and go back home. If I don't get respect, or I meet prejudice, I can always pack my bags and go back home, where at least people will respect me."

The interviews with elites thus confirmed that Caribbean-born immigrants rely on their transnational ties to make broad judgments about inequalities in the United States, and that they turn to the exit option to cope with those inequalities. These interviews therefore were critical for delineating the distinctions between this unfamiliar form of group identity and the more familiar concept of racial group consciousness associated with African Americans.

It is difficult to classify or even recognize the transnational perspective and exit option documented in the interviews as evidence of race consciousness, at least according to the long-standing conventions of survey research on minority political behavior. Neither the transnational perspective nor the exit option comports with prevailing measures or definitions of race consciousness, particularly among African Americans. Yet the interview methods employed in the study allowed for an excavation of the political meanings that the immigrants derive from this less familiar form of group identity. As it turns out, these political meanings appear to be part of a coherent set of racial beliefs that are akin to the kind of ideological outlook associated with the concept of group consciousness.

Bringing Interviews into the Study of Racial Group Identity

It should come as no surprise that there may be new or unfamiliar, but politically significant, forms of group identity circulating among African Americans and other minority groups today. With their growing diversity, African Americans no doubt have more difficulty setting a coherent agenda on racial issues these days than they did in the past (Dawson 1994b, 2011; Reed 1999). Outlooks on the status of the group have changed, ideas about how to improve it have gone in and out of political fashion, and new ideas about which problems demand attention and how to address them are up for debate. In short, there is currently far less consensus within the population about which beliefs and positions count as politically viable forms of race consciousness. Likewise, the differences in nationality, class, and culture that divide foreign-born minority groups, such as Latinos and Asians, make it quite likely that various ideas about race, group membership, and group status are circulating within these populations. These ideas ultimately may lead to the emergence of new forms of race consciousness in these groups as well.

These developments pose new challenges for political scientists who study minority group identity. Specifically, researchers need to update and expand how we conceptualize and measure racial group consciousness among African Americans and other minorities to account for the increasing diversity within these populations. Current conceptualizations are too heavily influenced by the research on African Americans during the early post–civil rights period. The concepts and their corresponding measures should be revised to reflect recent changes in racial thinking within the African American population. To be sure, existing items for tapping group consciousness on surveys, such as the National Black Politics Study, still have considerable empirical value for understanding African American political behavior; but revisions are in order.

These existing items are perhaps even less helpful for developing a full understanding of the political significance of group identity among the growing numbers of foreign-born minorities now living in the United States. The probes designed to tap racial group consciousness on most existing surveys do not account for the distinctive experiences of these immigrant populations. Rather, they are based largely on the outlooks and orientations of native-born populations like African Americans. Consequently, foreign-born minority groups that have not had exposure to the beliefs tapped by the conventional measures are likely to appear less race conscious than their African American counterparts. Yet as the interview research on Afro-Caribbeans summarized in this chapter demonstrates, there are alternative, latent forms of racial group consciousness circulating in immigrant minority populations. Researchers are likely to miss these new or emergent forms of racial consciousness, however, if they continue to rely on measures that are too narrow, dated, or biased toward those who have had exposure to a particular set of beliefs.

To advance research on group identity, political scientists need to catalog less familiar forms of racial consciousness, devise items for survey instruments to capture them, and explore whether they have any impact on political behavior. Interviews can play a critical role in furthering this agenda. Their flexible, open-ended format makes them an ideal research tool for discovering, probing, and cataloging new forms of group identity among both African Americans and the country's growing foreign-born minority populations. The racialized transnational consciousness uncovered and documented in my interviews with Afro-Caribbean immigrants is just one example. The deep, detailed questioning that interviews facilitate not only enables researchers to identify these unfamiliar or burgeoning forms of group identity and race consciousness; it also can help scholars to develop a fully informed understanding of the political significance of these group identities. With interviews, researchers can pose to respondents direct questions about why, how, and when these identities matter politically.

Even in the case of the more familiar forms of group identity and consciousness captured by conventional survey items, interviews can shed light on why they may be less meaningful for foreign-born minority groups. Researchers can use interviews in conjunction with surveys to generate explanations for opaque results. For instance, if there are questions about whether respondents fully understand the items that appear on a survey instrument, researchers can turn to interviews with a panel of respondents to probe the issues more deeply. Finally, interviews can be used to chart the dynamic consciousness-raising processes in minority populations that ultimately might lead to new or alternative forms of group identity. All in all, the distinctive methodological strengths of interviews make them a vital tool for establishing a new conceptual road map for studying the politics of group identity in minority populations.

Appendix: Sample Materials for Interview Research

The contributors to this volume have used interviews in a variety of ways, and they have conducted interviews with a wide range of populations. This appendix collects some of the materials used by the contributors in their interview studies; these range from protocols or instructions to consent forms and questionnaires. While we do not expect that these will be useful verbatim, we hope that they will help readers to address many of the practical issues involved with interview research. These documents are ordered by chapter.

CHAPTER 2 (SARAH M. BROOKS)

Consent Template for Behavioral and Social Research
[Requirements for this template may vary slightly across institutions and IRBs]

Consent to Participate in Research

Study Title:

Researcher:

Sponsor:

This is a consent form for research participation. It contains important information about this study and what to expect if you decide to participate.

Your participation is voluntary.
Please consider the information carefully. Feel free to ask questions before making your decision whether or not to participate. If you decide to participate, you will be asked to sign this form and will receive a copy of the form.

Purpose:

Procedures/Tasks:

Duration:

You may leave the study at any time. If you decide to stop participating in the study, there will be no penalty to you, and you will not lose any benefits to which you are otherwise entitled. Your decision will not affect your future relationship with [University name].

Risks and Benefits:

Confidentiality:

Efforts will be made to keep your study-related information confidential. However, there may be circumstances where this information must be released. For example, personal information regarding your participation in this study may be disclosed if required by state law. Also, your records may be reviewed by the following groups (as applicable to the research):

- Office for Human Research Protections or other federal, state, or international regulatory agencies;
- [University name] Institutional Review Board or Office of Responsible Research Practices;
- The sponsor, if any, or agency (including the Food and Drug Administration for FDA-regulated research) supporting the study.

Incentives:

Participant Rights:

You may refuse to participate in this study without penalty or loss of benefits to which you are otherwise entitled. If you are a student or employee at [University name], your decision will not affect your grades or employment status.

If you choose to participate in the study, you may discontinue participation at any time without penalty or loss of benefits. By signing this form, you do not give up any personal legal rights you may have as a participant in this study.

An Institutional Review Board responsible for human subjects research at [University name] reviewed this research project and found it to be acceptable, according to applicable state and federal regulations and University policies designed to protect the rights and welfare of participants in research.

Contacts and Questions:
For questions, concerns, or complaints about the study, you may contact

_____.

For questions about your rights as a participant in this study or to discuss other study-related concerns or complaints with someone who is not part of the research team, you may contact [Institutional contact name].

If you are injured as a result of participating in this study or for questions about a study-related injury, you may contact _____.

Signing the Consent Form:

I have read (or someone has read to me) this form, and I am aware that I am being asked to participate in a research study. I have had the opportunity to ask questions and have had them answered to my satisfaction. I voluntarily agree to participate in this study.

I am not giving up any legal rights by signing this form. I will be given a copy of this form.

_____	_____
Printed name of subject	**Signature of subject**
	_____ AM/PM
	Date and Time
_____	_____
Printed name of person authorized to consent for subject (when applicable)	**Signature of person authorized to consent for subject (when applicable)**
	_____ AM/PM
_____	**Date and Time**
Relationship to the subject	

Investigator / Research Staff

I have explained the research to the participant or his/her representative before requesting the signature(s) above. There are no blanks in this document. A copy of this form has been given to the participant or his/her representative.

_____	_____
Printed name of person obtaining consent	**Signature of person obtaining consent**
	_____ AM/PM
	Date and Time

CHAPTER 5 (CATHIE JO MARTIN)

Questionnaire for Semi-structured Interviews, Danish Employers

Company name:
Person interviewed:
Address:
Telephone number:
E-mail address:
Date:

DEPENDENT VARIABLES

Does the firm participate in any programs for protected workers: those with reduced working capacities, those on early retirement with reduced working capacities, job training for the long-term unemployed, collective bargaining–specified jobs, informal protected jobs, and regular apprenticeships?

How many are in each group?
What are the characteristics of the people in each group—skill levels, etc.?
Were the people hired into these positions already employees of the firm, or were they new hires?

PROCESS QUESTIONS

<u>Information and Deliberation</u>

How did the firm find out about these programs?

Did anyone from the local municipality contact the firm to ask it to participate?

Did anyone from the local or regional labor offices ask the firm to participate?

How were the hires made? Was the firm given choices in the hires?

Were the applicants sent from the municipality/local labor office, and if so, was the firm given choices in personnel/discretion in deciding to make the hire?

Was there any conflict over whether to participate?

If the company has branch offices, was this a top-down or bottom-up decision, or both?

Did different divisions within the firm have different views of these programs?

Was there a split between the directors and the floor level?

What is the general structure of decision making in the firm?

Did any other firms play a major role in bringing the firm to participate?

What position did the work councils take? How have their concerns been represented?

Incentives

What were the firm's motives for participating in the program?

How important was the availability of subsidies to the firm's decision to hire special-needs workers?

Might the firm have hired ordinary workers in these positions if the subsidies were not available, or are these slots that would not otherwise have been filled?

If the firm has not participated in the programs, why not? What are the biggest concerns?

Has the firm hired workers with reduced working capacities in the past in any kind of position?

Experience

What has been the firm's experience with these workers? Could you locate your experience on a 5-point scale, from very positive to very negative?

What have been the problems?

Has the *kommune* or AF been responsive in dealing with these problems?

Do you think that the social and labor market reforms of the nineties are asking employers to get involved with public policy in a new way?

If not, what earlier experiments were similar to the present one, and how did this company get involved?

<u>Workers' Reactions</u>

What has been the reaction of the other workers?

Have the unions expressed concerns that normal jobs are being made into special jobs at subminimum wages?

Are workers paid according to their output in this company?

Have workers raised questions about the impact of special workers on general productivity?

INSTITUTIONAL INDEPENDENT VARIABLES

To which groups and networks does the firm belong? (*number of groups*)

1. Peak employer associations
2. Sector associations
3. Task forces on ALMP within the peak or sector associations (if these exist)
4. Regional business networks—formal or informal
5. Local networks with a policy focus—formal or informal
6. *Kommune* business advisory groups
7. *Amtskommune* business advisory groups (Erhvervsråd)
8. Members of Arbejdsformidling Rådet
9. Human resource manager groups
10. Advisory groups to ministries, etc., at national level
11. Membership in the Lions Club or Rotary Club
12. Other important groups or clubs

Which of these groups has been most important in shaping the firm's thinking on this subject?

What roles do each of these groups play in providing companies with information about the policies and the politics of active labor market policy?

Do you get information about best practices through regional business networks?

Does your firm have a personnel or human resource department?

How many employees are placed in this department?

Is there an explicit policy within the personnel department about hiring special-needs persons?

Who within the firm decides to make these hires?

To what extent was the CEO involved in the decision, and to what extent was the decision made at the personnel level?

Does the firm use the services of management consultants or any other type of consultants?

How much does the company spend on training its own workers?

Do you know about the "Det angår os alle" campaign?

Do you know about the Udvikling Center?

ECONOMIC INDEPENDENT VARIABLES

How large is the firm in terms of total sales? (*size in sales*)
    Moody's International Manual under "turnover" category

What is the total number of employees?
    Firm info. plus Moody's

What is the average job duration or tenure for employees?
    Firm data

What are the total staff costs?
    Firm info. plus Moody's staff costs

What is the firm's average worker wage? (*average worker wage*)
> Moody's—"staff costs" divided by number of employees

What are the firm's net profits? (*net profits*)
> Moody's—"net income" divided by "turnover" or net income as a percentage of sales

What is the average skill level of the firm? (*average skill level*)
> Get firm data on occupational composition of the workforce.
> Get sector-level data on labor inputs (e.g., production versus non-production workers) provided in special labor market studies on occupation and education published by the OECD and International Labour Organization *Yearbooks*.

How capital-intensive is the firm? (*capital intensity*)
> Capital-output ratios of firms: pretax profits divided by total sales (from Moody's, calculate "net income" divided by sales)

Is the firm in an exposed sector or protected sector? (*exposed sector*)
> At firm level: percentage of total sales derived from exports (data from the firm).
> At sector level: import penetration in the firm's sector (data from the United Nations, Department of Economics and Social Affairs, *International Trade Statistics Yearbook*).

Are workers at the firm unionized? Are unionized workers members of principal sectoral and national associations?

Are workers subject to collective bargaining agreements by peak associations?

Have protected jobs been negotiated as part of collective bargaining in this sector?

How does the company raise investment capital? Through long-term relations with banks? Through equity markets?

CHAPTER 6 (MELANI CAMMETT)

ACCESS TO SOCIAL SERVICES IN LEBANON
Interview Schedule

I. INTERVIEW INFORMATION AND EVALUATION
(TO BE FILLED OUT BEFORE AND AFTER INTERVIEW.)

INFORMATION ON INTERVIEWEE:

1. Code: _____

2. Name of village/town/neighborhood in city where interview was conducted:
_____

3. Describe community in which interview was conducted:
    1 = A big city
    2 = The suburbs or outskirts of a big city
    3 = A town or small city
    4 = A country village
    5 = A farm or home in the countryside
    6 = Other _____

4. Interview site: _____
(i.e., place where interview was conducted. For example, reception room of respondent's house.)

5. Gender of interviewee:
F _____
M _____

6. Religious/confessional identification of interviewee: _____

INFORMATION ON INTERVIEWER:

7. Interviewer name: _____

8. Interviewer gender:

9. (Perceived) Religious/confessional identification of interviewer:

10. Mode of access to interviewee:
(i.e., how made initial contact with interviewee and/or relationship with interviewee.)

_____

11. Language used in interview: _____

12. Date of interview: _____

13. Time of interview start: _____

14. Time of finish: _____

II. OVERALL INTERVIEW QUALITY (CHECK AS MANY AS APPLY)

_____ 1. No major problems, respondent cooperative.

_____ 2. Respondent at first reluctant, but satisfactory interview and all responses obtained.

_____ 3. All responses obtained, but respondent seemed insincere in his/her answers.

_____ 4. Respondent reluctant, and several responses not obtained.

_____ 5. Respondent encountered difficulty with questions due to personal physical problems or problems of recall.

_____ 6. Interviewer did not cover one or more topics.

_____ 7. Interview interrupted or other persons were present.

If so, who was this? (CHECK ALL THAT APPLY)

_____ 1 = Husband/wife/partner

_____ 2 = Son/daughter (inc. step, adopted, foster, child of partner)

_____ 3 = Parent/parent-in-law/stepparent/partner's parent

_____ 4 = Other relative

_____ 5 = Other non-relative

_____ 6 = Don't know

8. Were there any particular parts of the interview for which you doubted the respondent's sincerity?

9. Note any other impressions of interview:

III. GREETINGS AND INTRODUCTION OF PROJECT, INCLUDING VERBAL INFORMED CONSENT

Thank you very much for agreeing to share your experiences with me about your access to social services in Lebanon. This project is part of a study by a researcher affiliated with the Faculty of Health Sciences at the American University of Beirut. I am a researcher/graduate student at _____ and can be contacted at _____.

We want to learn more about how people in Lebanon gain access to basic health care, schooling on the primary and secondary levels, and short-term assistance. We would like to learn from you and others about what types of social services are available in your community.

Your answers will be kept confidential. They will be put together with those of over 100 other people we are talking to in order to get an overall picture, as well as with responses from a larger national study of about 2,000 families in Lebanon. It will be impossible to pick you out from what you say.

Please be as candid as possible. There are no right or wrong answers. Just tell us what you think. If we should come to a topic you do not want to discuss, just let me know and we can go on to another topic. Your participation in this research is completely voluntary. You are free to refuse to participate without causing any problems to me or anyone else, including to yourself. If you do participate, we will not use your name in any reports, unless you want your name to be used.

While there is no immediate benefit for participating, the results will provide a better picture of social and economic conditions in your community. We intend to share the results of the study with others so that they can better understand the challenge of social service provision in Lebanon, and hopefully conditions will improve over the long term.

The interview should take about one hour. If you have any questions about the research, feel free to ask them while we are here, or contact me later.

Do you have any questions that you would like to ask? [PAUSE]
[IF SO, WRITE DOWN QUESTIONS.]

Can you participate in the project?

Yes _____   No _____

Can I record this interview? Keep in mind that we will not share the recording with anyone.

Yes _____   No _____

IV. QUESTIONNAIRE

A: ACCESS TO HEALTH CARE

Let's start by talking about health facilities in your area.

CLINICS

1. What health clinics (*mustawssafat*) are located in this area?

2. What clinic do you go to if you or a family member gets sick or if you just need a checkup?
[IT MAY BE APPROPRIATE TO INCLUDE A COMMENT TO THE EFFECT OF "GOD WILLING, YOU AND YOUR FAMILY WILL NOT BECOME SICK."]

3. How did you learn about this clinic?

4. What are the fees? Does the clinic provide financial assistance? Are there other sources of financial assistance available? If so, what are they?

5. Which organization runs the clinic that you use?

6. How long have you been going to this clinic?

7. Why did you choose this clinic?

HOSPITALS

1. What hospitals are located in this area?

2. What hospital do you go to if you or a family member gets sick or needs medical attention?

[IT MAY BE APPROPRIATE TO INCLUDE A COMMENT TO THE EFFECT OF "GOD WILLING, YOU AND YOUR FAMILY WILL NOT BECOME SICK."]

3. How did you learn about this hospital?

4. What are the fees? Does the hospital provide financial assistance? Are there other sources of financial assistance available? If so, what are they?

5. Which organization runs the hospital that you use?

6. How long have you been going to this hospital?

7. Why did you choose this hospital?

PHARMACIES

1. What pharmacies are located in this area?

2. What pharmacy do you go to if you or a family member gets sick or needs medical attention?

3. How did you learn about this pharmacy?

4. What are the fees? Does the pharmacy provide financial assistance? Are there other sources of financial assistance available for medicines?

5. Which organization runs the pharmacy that you use?

6. How long have you been going to this pharmacy?

7. Why did you choose this pharmacy?

B: ACCESS TO SOCIAL SERVICES: EDUCATION

Next, let's talk about schooling in your community.

1. What kinds of schools are there in your community? Are there public schools? Private, nonsubsidized schools? Private, subsidized schools?

2. Do you have children?

[IF SO, GO TO FOLLOWING QUESTIONS.]

[IF NO CHILDREN, ASK:]
If you had children, where *would* you send your children to school? Why this school?

3. Are any of your children currently in primary or secondary school, or were they in school recently?
[PROMPT INTERVIEWEE TO TELL MORE ABOUT HIS/HER CHILDREN—E.G., AGE, GRADE]

4. What kind of school does your child attend? Is it public or private? If private, is it subsidized or nonsubsidized?
[REPEAT FOR EACH CHILD.]

5. Does the school provide financial assistance to help cover the costs of school fees and expenses? Are other sources of financial assistance available to families?

6. What is the name of the school that your child attends?

7. Are you involved in the school? Do you attend school meetings? Are you a member of the school board or any other school-related committee?

C: ACCESS TO SHORT-TERM FINANCIAL/MATERIAL ASSISTANCE

1. Are there institutions that provide short-term loans in your community? These might be credit associations, voluntary organizations, religious organizations, or political groups.

2. Are there any institutions that provide food, household supplies, building materials, or other types of material assistance in your community?

3. How do you know about these institutions? Where did you hear about them?

4. Have you ever benefited from any financial or material assistance from these institutions?
[IT MAY BE APPROPRIATE TO INCLUDE A COMMENT TO THE EFFECT OF "GOD WILLING, YOU AND YOUR FAMILY WILL NOT FACE HARD TIMES."]

    [IF YES, GO TO FOLLOWING QUESTIONS.]

    [IF NOT, ASK:]
    Where *would* you go if you needed short-term financial or material assistance?

5. What did you receive?

6. Which organization runs the association that helped you or that you would turn to for help? What is the name of the association?

7. Why did you turn to this organization for assistance?

D: CIVIC PARTICIPATION

Now let's talk about the organizations that people join in your community.

1. Have you contacted local government officials or other types of community representatives about an issue facing your family or community? If so, whom did you contact and what did it concern?

2. Are you a member of any kinds of civic, social, religious, or political clubs or organizations?

3. How active are you in this organization? In what ways do you participate in the organization? Do you attend meetings? If so, how often?

4. Why did you decide to join this organization?

[REPEAT ABOVE QUESTIONS 3 AND 4 FOR ALL CLUBS OR ORGANIZATIONS.]

E: POLITICAL PARTICIPATION

Now let's talk about political organizations in Lebanon.

1. Are you a member of a political party?

2. How long have you been a member of this party?

3. Why did you join this party?

4. If you are not a member of a political party, do you support a particular party?

5. How long have you been a supporter of this party?

6. Why do you support this party?

7. How active are you in this party? In what ways do you participate in the party? Do you attend meetings? If so, how often?

8. Did you vote in the 2005 National Assembly elections?

9. If so, where did you vote? In which district?

10. If you voted, how did you get to the polling station?

11. Whom did you vote for (i.e., individuals, a list, or a mix)?

12. Why did you vote for this individual, list, or combination?

F: RELIGIOSITY

Now let's talk about the role of religion in your life.

1. How important is religion in your life? Do you pray a lot? Do you attend religious services?
2. Are you involved in any committees or organizations in your religious community?

V. BASIC PERSONAL AND SOCIAL INFORMATION

And finally, could you tell me more about you and the other members of your household?

1. How long have you lived here?

2. Are you originally from here? If not, where are you from originally?

3. How many people—including children—live here regularly as members of this household?

4. What is the last grade or class that you completed in school? What degree do you hold? What degrees do others in your family hold?

5. Do you work? If so, what do you do? Do the other adult members of your household work? If so, what do they do?

6. How long have you been working? How long have your family members been working?

7. How would you describe your financial situation?

8. Do you:
   Own or rent a house?
   Have plumbing and electricity?
   Save money for the future?
   Own other consumer goods such as a TV, satellite dish, telephone, cell phone, stereo, refrigerator, car, moped?

9. What is your annual income?

[OBSERVE THINGS IN THE HOME—NUMBER OF ROOMS, APPLI-ANCES AND OTHER CONSUMER GOODS IN THE HOME SUCH AS TV, SATELLITE DISH, TELEPHONE, CELL PHONE, STEREO, RE-FRIGERATOR, CAR, MOPED.]

VI. END OF INTERVIEW

Thank you very much for your time and effort. Your participation is really valuable for this research and will promote a better understanding of how people cope with economic pressures and how social service provision works in your community and in Lebanon overall.

Please feel free to ask any questions you may have about me or this research. If you would like to contact me at a later time, here is my contact information. [PRO-VIDE CONTACT INFORMATION.]

CHAPTER 10 (MATTHEW N. BECKMANN AND RICHARD L. HALL)

Sample Letter

[UC Irvine Letterhead]

Re: Interview Confidentiality Policy

Dear Respondent:

This letter is just meant to confirm what I told you at the outset of our interview.

First, this interview is part of an academic research project. Anything we discuss will be used solely for academic purposes; nothing will appear in any popular or journalistic outlet.

Second, our discussion is totally "off the record." I will neither use your name nor identify you in any way. I will not associate your remarks with your position or any other affiliations you might have. Moreover, I will not convey your comments to any other people I might interview.

Third, my commitment of confidentiality extends to any research assistant or collaborator who might work with me as part of this project. Before having access to any notes or recordings, s/he will sign a confidentiality commitment, which I will keep on file. Again, their access and use would be solely for academic research.

Finally, if you permit me to record our interview, it will be for my own note-taking purposes only. It will not be released, distributed, or used by anyone not directly involved with this project. As with everything else, your anonymity will be strictly preserved.

If you have any questions about respondents' rights in academic research, please contact UC Irvine's Human Research Protections Program, 4199 Campus Drive, Suite 300, Irvine, CA 92697-7600. The phone number is (949) 824-4768.

Thank you for your help with this project.

Sincerely,

Matthew N. Beckmann
Associate Professor of Political Science

Sample Form
WHITE HOUSE ADVOCATES   TAX CUTS (HR 1836)

Please check off the category that best reflects the number of conversations—face to face or on the phone—that your senator and his/her staff had with the following people regarding *President Bush's tax cut legislation.*

	NONE 0	A COUPLE TIMES 1–3	SEVERAL TIMES 4–8	MANY TIMES 9–15	REPEATEDLY >15
President George Bush	___	___	___	___	___
Vice president Richard Cheney and VP staff	___	___	___	___	___
Chief of staff Andrew Card	___	___	___	___	___
Deputy chief of staff for policy Joshua Bolten	___	___	___	___	___
Office of Legislative Affairs Nicholas Calio and staff	___	___	___	___	___
Office of Management and Budget Mitchell Daniels and staff	___	___	___	___	___
Faith-Based and Community Initiatives John Dilulio and staff	___	___	___	___	___
Domestic Policy Council Margaret La Montagne and staff	___	___	___	___	___
National Economic Council Lawrence Lindsey and staff	___	___	___	___	___
Council of Economic Advisers R. Glenn Hubbard and staff	___	___	___	___	___
Office of Strategic Initiatives Karl Rove and staff	___	___	___	___	___
Office of Political Affairs Kenneth Mehlman and staff	___	___	___	___	___
Office of Communications Karen Hughes and staff	___	___	___	___	___

	NONE 0	A COUPLE TIMES 1–3	SEVERAL TIMES 4–8	MANY TIMES 9–15	REPEATEDLY >15
Agriculture Ann Veneman and staff	____	____	____	____	____
Commerce Donald Evans and staff	____	____	____	____	____
Health and Human Services Tommy Thompson and staff	____	____	____	____	____
Labor Elaine Chao and staff	____	____	____	____	____
Treasury Paul O'Neill and staff	____	____	____	____	____

CHAPTER 11 (BETH L. LEECH, FRANK R. BAUMGARTNER, JEFFREY M. BERRY, MARIE HOJNACKI, AND DAVID C. KIMBALL)

Interview Protocol for Issue Identification Interviews, "Lobbying and Policy Change" Project

(1)   Could you take the **most recent** issue you've been spending time on and describe what you're trying to accomplish on this issue and what type of action you are taking to make that happen?

The issue we talk about doesn't have to be associated with a particular bill, rule, or regulation, and it doesn't have to be an issue that has been receiving coverage by the media—whatever issue you've most recently spent a significant amount of time on is fine, so long as it involves the federal government.

[*If the interviewee seems uncomfortable picking an issue or expresses concern about boredom, etc.*] How about if we talk about whatever issue most recently came across your desk?

- *Probe about lobbying activities, lobbying targets.*

(2)   *Recap what they're doing and what they're trying to accomplish.* So who else is involved in this issue both inside and outside of government?

- *Probe about coalition partners (formal or informal).*
- *Probe about whom they are speaking with about this issue.*

(3)   So you're talking to these various people [*be specific if it's relevant*] about why it's necessary to move forward on this issue [or, if relevant, why it's necessary to prevent something from happening, etc.]. What's the fundamental argument you use to try to convince people to do this?

- *Probe about different arguments for different targets.*
- *Probe for secondary arguments.*
- *Probe for partisan differences in terms of how people respond to this issue.*

(4)   What impediments do you face in achieving your objectives on this issue—in other words, who or what is standing in your way? What arguments do they make?

- *Probe for the arguments of opponents and others.*

(5)   I was wondering if you could tell me a bit about whether and how your organization uses research when you communicate with other organizations and people in government. From talking to people in organizations like yours I've noticed that some emphasize research and try to supply their representatives with a steady stream of original research and data to be used in presentations with government officials, their aides, and others. Others say that if research or data are needed, they can be gotten from think tanks, universities, research organizations, or consultants. And then there are others who don't spend a lot of time gathering issue-related research at all.

Where along this continuum would you place this organization? Do you rely a lot on research when you talk to people in government/other groups? If so, do you do much research in-house?

- *Probe for examples about the type of research they do in-house, whether and how often they gather it from outside sources, and what types of outside sources they rely on.*

(6)   Now I'd like to ask you a couple of general questions about your organization. How are you organized here in terms of people and units that are involved in public affairs and advocacy?

- *Probe for the different units within the organization that play a role.*
- *Probe for the number of people in these units.*

(7)   Before we finish up, could you tell me about yourself and how you came to work at this organization?

Those are all the questions I have for you, but I do have a favor to ask. I wonder if I could call you in about six months or so to follow up with you on this issue. I'll be back in [city], so it would be over the phone. I'd just like to see how things have progressed—since I have all this background, the follow-up should only take about fifteen minutes.

Also, could I get a copy of [whatever they mention that I want a copy of]?

Leave them a card.

Advocate Summary Form

Issue:
Advocate #:
Interviewee:
Organization:
Date of Interview:

Basic Background:

Prior Activity on the Issue:

Advocacy Activities Undertaken:

Future Advocacy Activities Planned:

Key Congressional Contacts/Champions:

Targets of Direct Lobbying:

Targets of Grassroots Lobbying:

Coalition Partners (Names/Participants):

Other Participants in the Issue Debate:

Ubiquitous Arguments and Evidence:

Secondary Arguments and Evidence:

Targeted Arguments, Targets, and Evidence:

Nature of the Opposition:

Ubiquitous Arguments and Evidence of the Opposition:

Secondary Arguments and Evidence of the Opposition:

Targeted Arguments, Targets, and Evidence of the Opposition:

Described as a Partisan Issue:

Venues of Activity:

Action Pending or Taken by Relevant Decision Makers:

Policy Objectives and Support for / Opposition to the Status Quo:

Advocate's Experience: Tenure in Current Job / Previous Experience:

Reliance on Research: In-House/External:

Number of Individuals Involved in Advocacy:

Units in Organization Involved in Public Affairs/Policy:

Advocate's Outstanding Skills/Assets:

Type of Membership (None, Institution, Individuals, Both):

Membership Size:

Organizational Age:

Miscellaneous:

Notes

INTRODUCTION

1. Recent symposiums on fieldwork generally and on interviews specifically begin to address some of the "nuts and bolts" of interview methods (see Leech 2002b; Ortbals and Rincker 2009a; and Kapiszewski, MacLean, and Read forthcoming), but they are only a start. The 2002 symposium, for instance, focuses exclusively on elite interviewing, and most of its contributors have worked in the context of the United States. Contributors to the 2009 symposium come exclusively from the subfield of comparative politics, and they are particularly concerned with the effects of the researcher's race, gender, religion, and class on the fieldwork process.

2. Note that, throughout this volume, we use a variety of terms to refer to individuals who are interviewed by researchers. I expand on this point below.

3. Since the mid-1990s, the International Monetary Fund and other intergovernmental institutions have encouraged governments to provide information regarding how their various statistical indicators are calculated and collected. The hope is that these metadata will increase scholars' confidence in the reliability and comparability of these data. See Mosley (2003b).

4. Rogers (chapter 12) does discuss his use, along with one-on-one interviews, of focus groups.

5. Note that the interpretivist argument that data are mediated by the context in which they are generated and collected is one that applies to all types of evidence. That is, interpretivists also would worry about the difference that exists in quantitative data sets between "reality" and "representation" (Weeden 2010).

6. For further discussion of interview research that is self-consciously interpretivist in its orientation, see the symposium edited by Ortbals and Rincker (2009a).

7. Just as there is diversity among more positivist scholars, debates also exist among those on the interpretivist side of the continuum. For instance, views differ on whether the object of inquiry is causal explanation or causal understanding. See Wedeen 2010.

8. This is not a statement about the relative merits of interpretivism or positivism; rather, it is an empirical observation about political science as a discipline.

9. For example, see Clifford and Marcus 1986; Geertz 1977; Spradley 1979; van Maanen 1988; Westbrook 2008; and Schatz 2009a.

10. For example, Brady and Collier 2010; Gerring 2007; Mahoney 2009; King, Keohane and Verba 1994.

11. Some scholars also use the term "reflexivity" to label this phenomenon.

12. The "do no harm" standard for research is codified, in the United States, in the 1979 Belmont Report. See chapter 2 for a summary.

13. This type of question wording is often used in studies that seek to measure vote buying or corruption (e.g., Jensen, Li, and Rahman 2010). Another strategy for such settings is the list experiment, in which a respondent reports how many from a list of behaviors he (or "people like him") have engaged in. By splitting the sample into two groups, one whose list includes the behavior of interest (e.g., vote buying) and one that does not, and then comparing the mean number of items offered across the groups, one can gain a sense of the prevalence of the behavior (e.g., Gonzales-Ocantos et al. 2010).

14. Political science is not the only discipline to confront this particular issue. In seeking information about sexual behaviors, for instance, public health scholars, instead of relying on face-to-face interviews, have begun to use other methods, which can provide more-accurate information. See Jaya and Ahmed (2008).

15. Note that the U.S. Department of Health and Human Services has slated the Common Rule, which governs human subjects research, for revision in the near future. Some proposed changes might make it easier for social scientists to receive expedited review for interview-based work, while other changes could increase the restrictions on the use of secondary (i.e., survey) data.

16. Beckmann and Hall maintain, however, that scholars should not use any information gathered in confidential interviews for public advocacy—for instance, writing an op-ed piece on immigration reform.

17. See Wood (2006) for a description of the procedures she used to protect her data and informants while conducting fieldwork in El Salvador.

18. Leech et al. (chapter 11) point out that their strategy—coding information quantitatively from interviews with Washington lobbyists, and using this along with indicators gathered from other sources—precludes the release of some aspects of their quantitative dataset. Because they guaranteed confidentiality to informants, and because other indicators in the database could be used to deduce the identity of informants, many variables had to be dropped from the data they released to the public.

19. This raises another point: social scientists often need personnel management skills, something rarely taught in PhD programs.

20. Thompson (2009) goes further, arguing that scholars can couple their objective research efforts with "transformative activism" at, or on behalf of, the local research site.

21. Scholars using an experimental research design worry less about random sampling of participants; rather, their focus is on random assignment: theoretically relevant qualities of the participants should not affect their propensity to be assigned to the treatment or control groups. See Dunning 2008; Morton and Williams 2010.

22. Beck (2009) questions the extent to which causal process observation (CPO) improves scholars' inferential capacity and, indeed, the extent to which CPO is a useful concept. He maintains that researchers should always possess contextual knowledge about the general phenomenon of interest (for instance, what leads voters to stay home or go to the polls, or what motivates leaders to undertake economic reform), and it is this knowledge that allows for a theoretically accurate interpretation of findings based on data set observations.

23. Likewise, Cammett (chapter 6) reports difficulty gaining access to supporters of Hezbollah, because of the group's hostile relations with the U.S. government.

24. Note, however, that some contributors (Lynch, and Beckmann and Hall) report that they had less difficulty gaining access to elites than they had initially expected. Also see Aldrich 2009 and Wood 2006.

25. There is debate among scholars regarding the extent to which bias in the selection of cases is a threat to inference. See Geddes 1990, 2003; and Collier et al. 2004.

26. If, however, interviewer effects are sufficiently strong, this form of replication is unlikely to produce similar findings. Wedeen (2010) argues, from an interpretivist perspective, that replication is possible despite positionality: if one defines "replication" as "discovering meaning," then a scholar may go to a given field location, engage in ethnography with the same or different individuals, and gain the same sense of (socially constructed) meanings.

27. This concern fits with one of the ways in which MacLean (chapter 3) describes the operation of power in political science research—the power to interpret the findings, usually exercised independently from the group or community under study.

28. Many of the International Monetary Fund's documents, however, are released only after a long delay. Comparing government archives with interview accounts may be more useful when exploring issues that are more distant chronologically.

29. For instance, there was a vigorous debate regarding Moravcsik's (1998) use of primary sources. See Lieshout, Segers, and van der Vleuten (2004).

30. Using an interpreter also can increase the validity of interview findings, as it does not constrain one's sample to only those who speak English (or French or Spanish).

31. In my case, this second round of field research also involved sampling a new population. Hence, the cost of conducting reinterviews was minimal, given that I already was planning to be in London for the new set of interviews.

32. Of course, either as a result of prior training or of individual cultural and ethnic ties, some researchers enter graduate school with a range of linguistic skills. These skills may increase the practical appeal of interview research in a given country.

33. Also see the Symposium on Field Research in the newsletter of the Qualitative Methods Organized Section of APSA, in 2004, edited by Evan Lieberman, Marc Morje Howard, and Julia Lynch. This symposium focuses on more-general issues related to conducting fieldwork abroad, including how best to structure one's time in the field. Available at http://www.maxwell.syr.edu/moynihan/programs/cqrm/newsletters/News letter2.1.pdf.

34. Barrett and Cason 2010 and Goldstein 2002 also offer "how to" advice. For an even briefer "how to," see Aldrich's contribution to the Ortbals and Rincker (2009b) symposium.

1. ALIGNING SAMPLING STRATEGIES WITH ANALYTIC GOALS

1. Deciding how to interview is also an important consideration. Lane, Fenno, and Hochschild also all use semi-structured, in-depth, one-on-one in-person interviews; but equally useful data can come from focus groups, participant observation, incidental conversations, or even over the phone. In this chapter, the main concern is matching decisions about whom to interview with the role that interviews play in the overall research agenda. I leave questions about how to interview to the other chapters in this book.

2. On sampling concerns related to various contemporary types of surveys, see Yeager et al. (2011).

3. For an overview of exemplary work in a historical institutionalist vein, much of which uses interview data to establish causal processes, see Fioretos et al. (forthcoming).

4. What is a sufficient number? In statistics, the central limit theorem implies that random samples of more than thirty or so are generally sufficient to generate estimates of population parameters that would on average, in repeated measurement, fall close to the true value. The variance of estimates derived from such small samples is, however, likely to be large, and hence decreases the certainty of the parameter estimates. When statistical analysis is not used to make inferences, the ideal sample size is less clear. Also see Bleich and Pekkanen (this volume).

5. A number of social science methodology textbooks provide guidance on how to construct simple and stratified random samples, as well as the non-random forms of sampling described below. For an overview, see Bernard (2002). Daniel (2012) provides more in-depth treatment of sampling methods.

6. Seminal works on purposive sampling include Allen (1971), Seidler (1974), Godambe (1982), and Zelditch (1962).

7. Useful guidance on snowball sampling may be found in Biernacki and Waldorf (1981), Heckathorn (1997), Salganick and Heckathorn (2004), and Heckathorn (2002).

2. THE ETHICAL TREATMENT OF HUMAN SUBJECTS AND THE INSTITUTIONAL REVIEW BOARD PROCESS

1. I use the term "subjects" in this chapter to refer to the participants in social science research who are interviewed as part of the research, i.e., the interviewees. The term is conventional usage for institutional review boards.

2. The World Medical Association's Declaration of Helsinki: Ethical Principles for Medical Research Involving Human Subjects was adopted by the Eighteenth WMA General Assembly, Helsinki, Finland, June 1964, and amended six times, including most recently in Tokyo in 2001.

3. The OHRP web page provides useful information and guidelines for researchers engaging in interview research, especially when such research involves international fieldwork or the engagement of collaborators other than the principal investigator. See http://www.hhs.gov/ohrp/.

4. Expedited review entails review of proposed research by the IRB chair or a designated voting member or group of members, rather than the full IRB panel.

5. The Office for Human Research Protections (OHRP) has compiled a list of international human subjects research protection regulations to facilitate this task. The 2010 document lists approximately 1,100 laws, regulations, and guidelines governing human subjects research in ninety-six countries. See http://www.hhs.gov/ohrp/international/.

6. This may be the case in particular where researchers are obliged to provide phone or e-mail contact information to research subjects who lack any means, such as telephone or Internet access, to make use of this information.

3. THE POWER OF THE INTERVIEWER

1. Many other political scientists both inside and outside the "mainstream" of the discipline have already asserted that objectivity is impossible. See, for example, Weber (1949, 10); Easton (1969); Wolin (1969); Lindblom (1998); R. Smith (1998); Steinmetz (2005); Norton (2004a); Schram and Caterino (2004); and Schwartz-Shea (2004).

2. Spivak, in his classic article (1988), highlights the politics involved in speaking for others. Other scholars also talk about this issue of distance in data collection—for example, Pollner and Emerson (1983).

3. Anne Norton (2004a, 76) also argues that when political scientists pretend that objectivity is possible, they "are not acting ethically but acting the ethical: performing a fictional character."

4. On Nazi experimentation, see Annas and Grodin (1992). The Nazis were not alone in conducting unethical experiments with humans. The Japanese during World War II conducted experiments to test the results of biological warfare. And in the United States in the early 1940s, prisoners in Chicago were infected with malaria, and servicemen were exposed to mustard gas.

5. Reutter (2005) talks about "partnerships." See also Chataway (2001).

6. I am grateful to Julia Lynch for making this point.

7. Agrawal and Gibson (1999) argue that policymakers need to investigate the institutions and multiple interests that shape politics and decision-making *within* communities. Cornwall (2003) highlights how community participation can actually exclude the least powerful voices in gendered ways.

8. I thank an anonymous reviewer for stimulating this example.

9. Cornwall and Jewkes (1995) elaborate on Biggs's four modes of participation in their discussion of participatory research approaches.

10. See also Bolak (1996) and Medicine (2001).

11. Lisa Wedeen (2010) argues that political science abandoned anthropology at the earlier moment of individualist "navel-gazing" and has subsequently missed the value of the later positionality debates.

12. McCorkel and Myers (2003) actually take a similar position but persist in striving for a notion of objectivity, whereas Rose (1997) and Wasserfall (1993) give up on the idea of objectivity altogether.

13. See Schafer (2004) for a report of a recent problem and how it was handled.

14. Haney (1996) urges caution, however, in sharing texts with the individuals and communities being studied. In an appendix to an article, she discusses her decision not to share her writing because of the possible harm it might cause on an interpersonal level for her respondents.

15. Schram (2004, 20) borrows the term of "critical connectedness" from Lemert (2001).

4. HOW TO REPORT INTERVIEW DATA

1. See Bennett and Elman (2006) and Mahoney (2010) for overviews of this literature.

2. See especially Tansey (2007).

3. Other chapters in this volume provide added grist for this view of compatibility, albeit sometimes as an early stage in the research process, which we feel is not a necessary qualification. Reuel Rogers (chapter 12) discusses the problems of using "old" survey instruments with "new" (immigrant, minority) populations, and how interviews can identify some of these questions. Mary Gallagher (chapter 9) similarly discusses the use of interviews as a stage prior to formulating survey questions.

4. Interviews may form the primary source of information for some research projects, but they are more often used in a process of multi-method triangulation that seeks information from a variety of sources.

5. See also Beckmann and Hall's discussion (chapter 10) of interviews that are much more like surveys than like open-ended interviews.

6. Snowball sampling is also discussed in this volume by Lynch (chapter 1) and Martin (chapter 5).

7. This is a good place to point out that other approaches (e.g., interpretive or ethnographic) to interviews are not necessarily at odds with the positivist approach we advocate here, but neither do they converge. An interpretivist, for example, might spend time considering the reluctance of an interviewee to concede "facts" in this situation. Evasions and silences are also worth investigating, perhaps as separate research questions (also see Fujii, chapter 7).

8. Reporting such statements would raise serious ethical questions, not to mention likely run afoul of IRB processes (see Brooks, chapter 2). We return to the ethical and IRB issues of reporting below.

9. Lee Ann Fujii (chapter 7) argues that such deficiencies can be mitigated by working with interpreters, and provides guidelines on how to successfully research using interpreters.

10. Tansey (2007) makes this point with respect to process-tracing methodologies, but it also can be true of other types of research projects.

11. Graduate students (and others) may want a simple answer to the question "How many interviews do I need to do?" We seek in this chapter to progress beyond "It depends," to "Construct your sample frame, and that will tell you." For those categories within a sample frame, researchers may still want to know when they have done "enough" interviews; the question can often be reframed as one of saturation. When new interviews cease to provide additional information, saturation has been achieved (at least for that

type of interviewee) and no more interviews are necessary (because no new information is expected to be gained—again for that type of interviewee—although interviews with other interviewee types might continue to be valuable). Interviewing need not continue once saturation is achieved across all interview types or across other variables hypothesized to influence the results. The same guidelines on saturation apply to those operating—despite our advice—without a sample frame.

12. For especially interesting and insightful takes on the process of interviewing, see Aberbach and Rockman (2002), Berry (2002), and Beckmann and Hall (chapter 10).

13. Researchers can state their rationale for not posting interview transcripts in cases where resources or ethical considerations constrain them from doing so. No scholar would try to publish an article that relied only on two anonymous sources. But scholars very commonly cite newspaper articles that rely on precisely such evidence. We do not condemn this practice. Citing newspaper articles is perfectly acceptable. It is commonly accepted because the entire newspaper article is a matter of public record and can be examined by other scholars. Were such standards common for interview data gathered by political scientists, we would see the data more widely employed and accepted.

14. This is more the norm in American politics than in many other fields (Aberbach and Rockman 2002; Berry 2002; Kingdon 1995). See also the discussion by Beckmann and Hall (chapter 10).

15. Note also the parallels to quantitative research, which deals with uncertainty through explicit reporting.

16. For an entertaining example of an activist exaggerating his role in the decision-making process, see Berry (2002). Note, though, that some organizations—perhaps pharmaceutical lobbyists—may have an interest in understating their role in the policy-making process.

17. Researchers who conduct interviews in languages other than those in which they are publishing the results should also indicate that language of the interview. If all interviews are conducted in the same language, a simple note in the text, or (better) at the bottom of the Interview Methods Table, will suffice. If multiple languages were employed, a new column in the Interview Methods Table should be created to specifying the language of the interview. In cases where an interpreter was used, this should also be indicated in the same way.

18. These concerns are common among researchers who use quantitative methods (Albright and Lyle 2010).

6. USING PROXY INTERVIEWING TO ADDRESS SENSITIVE TOPICS

1. Hezbollah is a Shia Muslim political party, social movement, and militia based in Lebanon and is the self-proclaimed "resistance" against Israel in the region. The United States and some EU countries label the organization or some of its subcomponents "terrorist" for their connections to various acts of violence, particularly in the 1980s.

2. In plural societies—as opposed to societies with diverse cultural communities—ethnicity, religion, or other types of identity-based cleavages are politically salient, and communities are politically organized (Rabuska and Shepsle 2009, 62).

3. Some short pieces, many of which are based on reflections from fieldwork experiences, highlight the relevance of positionality for political science research (Cammett 2006; Clark 2006; Henderson 2009; Reinhardt 2009; Schwedler 2006). See MacLean's contribution in this volume for a brief overview of anthropological discussions of positionality and related issues from the perspective of a political scientist.

4. This, too, can be interpreted as a positivist argument in that it may presume that insiders are more equipped to arrive at "true" interpretations of their findings (Herod 1999, 314).

5. See Chavez (2008, 476–479) for a brief review of the merits and drawbacks of insider status.

6. I found this to be true when interviewing top government officials and members of the business elite in Morocco and Tunisia. Whereas many Moroccan and Tunisian faculty and graduate student colleagues were unable to gain access to these informants, it was relatively easy for me to set up appointments with them, thanks to referrals from U.S. contacts. Also, many were intrigued that a Western researcher would devote time and resources to carry out overseas research. In conducting research elsewhere in the Middle East, Schwedler (2006) claims that being Western and female provides advantages in gaining access to informants, including Islamists—a claim that accords with my own experiences and those of other Western researchers in the region.

7. Chavez (2008) also emphasizes the importance of thorough training for insider researchers.

8. One month prior to the training session, I sent the team members selections from Hochschild (1981) and Soss (2000), which make exemplary use of data derived from in-depth interviews, as well as from Rubin and Rubin (2005), which provides basic information on how to establish rapport and conduct interviews. I also sent them a relevant chapter from my own book (Cammett 2007a), to familiarize them with how I collected, analyzed, and used interview data in a prior research project.

9. I discuss sampling in more detail below.

10. This part of the training session was greatly enhanced by the participation of Scheherezade Faramarzi, a thirty-year veteran Associated Press reporter with a stellar reputation for thorough, on-the-ground reporting from multiple conflict zones, including Lebanon. Ms. Faramarzi shared insights based on her experiences interviewing ordinary people in difficult circumstances and answered questions about useful techniques for establishing rapport.

11. For a description of the CITI program, see https://www.citiprogram.org/aboutus .asp?language=english.

12. To establish fair compensation rates, I followed official guidelines for graduate research assistants issued by the human resources office of the American University of Beirut in Lebanon.

13. See Gallagher's and Rogers's contributions to this volume, on the complementarities between interviewing and survey research.

14. In my earlier research on business responses to trade reform in North Africa, I selected firms that varied according to national location (i.e., Morocco versus Tunisia), subnational geographic location, and industry subsectors, because each of these factors enabled me to test the implications of distinct explanations for business collective action. In my research in Lebanon, the team of interviewers selected non-elite respondents with distinct religious affiliations, demographic characteristics, and partisan preferences and behavior, among other characteristics, in order to provide an additional source of evidence for the welfare targeting strategies of sectarian providers.

15. A recent symposium published in *Qualitative Methods*, however, highlights the limitations of multi-methods research ("Symposium" 2009).

16. Although it has received less overt attention, class also may be an important factor for matching interviewers and interviewees for some projects.

17. One exception is Scacco (2009), who matched interviewers by religion (Christian and Muslim) for both a mass survey and in-depth interviews in Nigeria.

7. WORKING WITH INTERPRETERS

1. I thank Stephanie McNulty for this point.

2. Translating transcripts from one language to another raises additional questions about representation (Nikander 2008).

3. In highly emotional interviews, "neutrality" may not always be desirable or appropriate. See Cole's superb discussion of the use of interpreters during the hearings of the Truth and Reconciliation Commission in South Africa and, especially, how different interpreters dealt with "interpreting" highly charged testimonies (Cole 2010, chap. 3).

4. The institutional review board, or IRB, is the university-level committee that is charged with approving research protocols. In Canada, the committee is called the research ethics board. There are similar boards in other countries. On obtaining IRB approval, see chapter 2. On research ethics more broadly, see Fujii (2012).

5. On positionality and power, see chapters 3 and 6, this volume.

6. *Interahamwe* is often translated as "those who work together." It can refer to militia that were specially recruited and trained in Kigali or to local people who participated in the genocide (who were not part of any formal militia). *Igitero* refers to the attack groups (often composed of twenty or more people) that were responsible for the violence during the genocide.

8. THE PROBLEM OF EXTRATERRITORIAL LEGALITY

1. The International Crisis Group was organized in 1995 after the failures of the international community to respond to tragedies in Somalia, Rwanda, and Bosnia. Its founders include the president of the Carnegie Endowment for Peace (later head of the UN Development Programme), the UN deputy-secretary, and a U.S. senator.

2. The U.S. list is at http://www.state.gov/j/ct/rls/other/des/123085.htm (accessed March 27, 2012).

3. The UK list is available at http://www.homeoffice.gov.uk/publications/counter-terrorism/proscribed-terror-groups/proscribed-groups?view=Binary (accessed March 26, 2012).

9. CAPTURING MEANING AND CONFRONTING MEASUREMENT

1. For example, dissertation prospectuses that rely mainly on qualitative interviews often under-theorize the methodologies and strategies needed for effective interviews.

2. For more in-depth discussion of these issues, see Read (2010) and Chen (2010).

10. ELITE INTERVIEWING IN WASHINGTON, DC

1. We particularly recommend the elite interviewing symposium edited by Leech (2002b). Represented there are scholars who employ interviews for purposes both similar to and quite different from our own. The essays about Washington include Aberbach and Rockman (2002), Berry (2002), Goldstein (2002), and Leech (2002a).

2. Focusing on specific cases does not by itself anchor responses in the way that King and Wand (2007) recommend, however. In Richard Hall's study of participation in Congress (1996), for instance, he asked each legislative assistant to rate the importance of specific issues to the district her boss represents, but he structured the answers with categories ("major," "moderate," etc.) that were not anchored, leaving open the possibility that different respondents might interpret the same category differently.

3. To illustrate, consider how legislators might go about summarizing their overall voting behavior. Every year each member casts hundreds of votes, not all of which he can mentally revisit. So does the member somehow sample from that population? If so, what

implicit sampling design might he be using? And given whatever sample he draws, how then does he summarize its distribution? Is the respondent weighting some cases more heavily than others (the most recent, the most difficult, the *least* typical)? And, equally pressing, what is the summary statistic that underlies the verbal characterization: the mean, the median, or the mode? Absent additional information, the answer to each of these questions is, ominously, "Don't know."

4. This is important because although one may occasionally need the high-profile principal, more often than not, the study's goals will be better served by interviewing lower-profile staffers. The reason is that staffers not only know what they did, but they also know what their boss was doing. The converse is not true.

5. One noteworthy pitfall is that respondents will often ask if the interviewer has already met with particular people. To preserve confidentiality, it is important to neither confirm nor deny specific contacts. We deal with this by simply telling the respondent, "Because I assure everyone confidentiality, I cannot say whom else I met. But as you know, I am trying to talk with everyone, so it is nice even if you just confirm names I have already heard."

6. Also noteworthy, persistence pays off. Do not call once and then wait for respondents to call back. Our general rule of thumb was to call back every other day, but sometimes it was even more frequent than that.

7. Practitioners are loath to schedule interviews more than a couple of days beforehand. So rather than use the e-mail to set up an interview, it is better to view it as little more than an introduction—a way to facilitate a subsequent contact down the road.

8. Our answer was that the interview included a few figures, so a face-to-face meeting would be a lot easier and go a lot quicker. If needed, we would also assert it was important for the research that all interviews followed the same procedure.

9. Importantly, one cannot begin interviews until his or her home campus's institutional review board (IRB) has approved of the study. Confidentiality agreements are an important part of this, and we hope our template proves helpful. We hasten to warn, however, because IRB expectations vary, amendments may be required. Also see Brooks, chapter 2.

10. Of course, other cases may play differently from the ones we studied. If not, we very much recommend researchers record their interviews.

11. It is fairly common for interviews to end shortly after an assistant enters the room and declares, "Your next appointment is here." So a researcher ought not to be lulled into a lackadaisical pace merely because an interview is "going great." Bad rapport may shorten one's allotted interview time, but good rapport will not necessarily extend it.

12. Had Hall paid closer attention to the question wording in Wright's pathbreaking study, he would have avoided the term "lobbying." See Wright (1989, 1990) and Caldiera and Wright (1988), as well as Hojnacki and Kimball (1998) and Leech (2002a).

13. Once a respondent begins the first form, she is likely to continue through the last. So while we certainly remain courteous and appreciative, we will diligently attempt to press through initial reluctance, at least until we reach the first form.

11. LESSONS FROM THE "LOBBYING AND POLICY CHANGE" PROJECT

1. Summaries of each of our issues, as well as copies of all secondary source materials on these issues—including the texts of laws, bills, hearing testimonies, news articles, and interest group press releases—are available on our website, http://lobby.la.psu.edu.

2. Our approach for the most part did not treat these case studies as "causal process observations" (Brady and Collier 2010) in that we tried to avoid drawing conclusions from our cases that were not supported by our quantitative data analyses. Still, the qualitative aspects of these interviews helped suggest additional hypotheses to test and were used to help us interpret the quantitative output.

3. We ended up with ninety-eight case studies, not one hundred, because two of the identified issues turned out to be two sides of the same issue; also, interviews were not completed on the final issue.

4. The issue was identified as part of the first question posed to our ninety-eight randomly selected interest groups. The issue to talk about thus was determined ahead of time for all the 217 subsequent interviews, and we started by asking specifically about that issue.

5. If the researcher does that many interviews per day, audio recording becomes more important, since there will not be time to type up notes immediately after the interview; it is easy for interview responses to begin to run together in an imperfect memory.

12. USING INTERVIEWS TO UNDERSTAND RACIAL GROUP IDENTITY AND POLITICAL BEHAVIOR

1. Source: 1993 National Black Politics Survey.

2. Researchers who study African American public opinion during the formative years leading up to the civil rights movement cannot rely on surveys from that period because most did not feature questions about racial attitudes or include significant samples of African Americans. They therefore often turn to other methods, such as analyzing letters, excavating organizational archives, and interviewing elites to map black political views during the years preceding the civil rights movement (e.g., Lee 2002).

References

Abbott, Andrew. 1992. "From Causes to Events: Notes on Narrative Positivism." *Sociological Methods & Research* 20(4): 428–455.

Aberbach, Joel D., James D. Chesney, and Bert A. Rockman. 1975. "Exploring Elite Political Attitudes: Some Methodological Lessons." *Political Methodology* 2:1–27.

Aberbach, Joel D., Robert D. Putnam, and Bert A. Rockman. 1981. *Bureaucrats and Politicians in Western Europe*. Cambridge, MA: Harvard University Press.

Aberbach, Joel D., and Bert A. Rockman. 2002. "Conducting and Coding Elite Interviews." *PS: Political Science & Politics* 35(4): 673–676.

Abu-Lughod, L. 1991. "Writing against Culture." In *Recapturing Anthropology*, ed. R. Fox, 137–162. Santa Fe: School of American Research Press.

———. 1993. Introduction to *Writing Women's Worlds: Bedouin Stories*. Berkeley and Los Angeles: University of California Press, 1–44.

Acker, J., I. Barry, and U. Esseveld. 1999. "Objectivity and Truth: Problems in Doing Feminist Research." In *Beyond Methodology: Feminist Scholarship as Lived Research*, ed. M. M. Fonow and J. A. Cook, 133–153. Bloomington: Indiana University Press.

Adler, P., and P. Adler. 1987. *Membership Roles in Field Research*. Beverly Hills, CA: Sage.

Agrawal, Arun, and Clark Gibson. 1999. "Enchantment and Disenchantment: The Role of Community in Natural Resource Conservation." *World Development* 27:629–649.

Ahmed, Amel, and Rudra Sil. 2009. "Is Multi-Method Research Really Better?" *Newsletter of the APSA Organized Section in Qualitative & Multi-Method Research*. Fall.

Albright, Jeremy J., and Jared A. Lyle. 2010. "Data Preservation through Data Archives." *PS: Political Science & Politics* 43(1): 17–21.

Aldrich, Daniel P. 2009. "The 800-Pound *Gaijin* in the Room: Strategies and Tactics for Conducting Fieldwork in Japan and Abroad." *PS: Political Science & Politics* 42(2): 299–303.

Allen, Harold B. 1971. "Principles of Informant Selection." *American Speech* 46(1–2): 47–51.

Allina-Pisano, Jessica. 2009. "How to Tell an Axe Murderer: An Essay on Ethnography, Truth, and Lies," in Edward Schatz (ed.), *Political Ethnography: What Immersion Contributes to the Study of Power*. Chicago, IL: University of Chicago Press, 53–73.

American Indian Law Center Inc. 1999. *Model Tribal Research Code: With Materials for Tribal Regulation for Research and Checklist for Indian Health Boards*. 3rd ed. Albuquerque, NM: American Indian Law Center Inc.

Annas, George J., and Michael A. Grodin, eds. 1992. *The Nazi Doctors and the Nuremberg Code: Human Rights in Human Experimentation*. New York: Oxford University Press.

Anderson, Paul V. 1996. "Ethics, institutional review boards, and the involvement of human participants in composition research." In Peter Mortensen and Gesa E. Kirsch (eds.) *Ethics and Representation in Qualitative Studies of Literacy*. Urbana: National Council of Teachers of English.

Anonymous. 2009. "TRC's Economic Criminals." *New Democrat* [Monrovia], July 6, p. 1.

Arendell, T. 1997. "Reflections on the Researcher-Researched Relationship: A Woman Interviewing Men." *Qualitative Sociology* 20:341–368.

Atkinson, Rowland, and John Flint. 2001. "Accessing Hidden and Hard-to-Reach Populations: Snowball Research Strategies." *Social Research Update*. Surrey, UK: Dept. of Sociology, University of Surrey, 1–4.

Australian Institute of Aboriginal and Torres Strait Islander Studies (AIATSIS). 2000. *Guidelines for Ethical Research in Indigenous Studies*. Canberra: AIATSIS.

Axelrod, Robert. 1976. *Structure of Decision: The Cognitive Maps of Political Elites*. Upper Saddle River, NJ: Prentice-Hall.

Baker, Ross K. 1995. *House and Senate*. 2nd ed. New York: Norton.

Barbaro, Michael, and Tom Zeller Jr. 2006. "A Face Is Exposed for AOL Searcher No. 4417749." *New York Times*, August 9.

Barbour, Rosaline. 2008. *Introducing Qualitative Research*. Thousand Oaks, CA: Sage.

Barrett, Christopher B., and Jeffrey W. Cason. 2010. *Overseas Research: A Practical Guide*. 2nd ed. New York: Routledge.

Bartunek, Jean M., and Meryl Reis Louis. 1996. *Insider/Outsider Team Research*. Thousand Oaks, CA: Sage.

Barz, Gregory. 1997. "Confronting the Field (Note) in and out of the Field: Music, Voices, Texts and Experiences in Dialogue." In *Doing and Undoing Fieldwork*, ed. Gregory F. Barz and Timothy J. Cooley, 45–62. New York: Oxford University Press.

Bassett, Elizabeth, and Kate O'Riordan. 2002. "Ethics of Internet Research: Contesting the Human Subjects Research Model." *Ethics and Information Technology* 4(3): 233–247.

Bates, Robert H., Avner Greif, Margaret Levi, Jean-Laurent Rosenthal, and Barry Weingast. 1998. *Analytic Narratives*. Princeton, NJ: Princeton University Press.

Bauer, Raymond, Ithiel de Sola Pool, and Lewis Anthony Dexter. 1963. *American Business and Public Policy: The Politics of Foreign Trade*. New York: Atherton Press.

Baumgartner, Frank R., Jeffrey M. Berry, Marie Hojnacki, David Kimball, and Beth L. Leech. 2009. *Lobbying and Policy Change: Who Wins, Who Loses, and Why*. Chicago: University of Chicago Press.

Beck, Nathaniel. 2009. "Is Causal-Process Observation an Oxymoron?" *Political Analysis* 14(3): 347–352.

Becker, Heike, Emile Boonzaier, and Joy Owen. 2005. "Fieldwork in Shared Spaces: Positionality, Power and Ethics of Citizen Anthropologists in Southern Africa." *Anthropology Southern Africa* 28(3, 4): 123–132.

Becker-Blease, Kathryn A., and Jennifer J. Freyd. 2006. "Research Participants Telling the Truth about Their Lives: The Ethics of Asking and Not Asking about Abuse." *American Psychologist* 61:218–226.

Beckmann, Matthew N. 2010. *Pushing the Agenda: Presidential Leadership in U.S. Lawmaking, 1953–2004*. New York: Cambridge University Press.

Beecher, A. 2003. "A Tale of Two Betrayals." *Standard Times* [Freetown], May 27, p. 3.

Bennett, Andrew, and Colin Elman. 2006. "Qualitative Research: Recent Developments in Case Study Methods." *Annual Review of Political Science* 9(1): 455–476.

Bernard, H. Russell. 2002. *Research Methods in Anthropology: Qualitative and Quantitative Methods*. 3rd ed. Walnut Creek, CA: AltaMira Press.

Berry, Jeffrey M. 2002. "Validity and Reliability Issues in Elite Interviewing." *PS: Political Science & Politics* 35(4): 679–682.

Biernacki, Patrick, and Dan Waldorf. 1981. "Snowball Sampling: Problems and Techniques of Chain Referral Sampling." *Sociological Methods and Research* 10(2): 141–163.

Bolak, Hale C. 1996. "Studying One's Own in the Middle East: Negotiating Gender and Self-Other Dynamics in the Field." *Qualitative Sociology* 19(1): 107–131.

Borchgrevink, Axel. 2003. "Silencing Language: Of Anthropologists and Interpreters." *Ethnography* 4(1): 95–121.

Bosk, Charles, and Raymond G. De Vries. 2004. "Bureaucracies of Mass Deception: Institutional Review Boards and the Ethics of Ethnographic Research." *Annals of the American Academy of Political and Social Science* 595:249–263.

Brady, Henry E., and David C. Collier. eds. 2004. *Rethinking Social Inquiry: Diverse Tools, Shared Standards*. 1st ed. Lanham, MD: Rowman & Littlefield.

Brady, Henry, and David Collier, eds. 2010. *Rethinking Social Inquiry: Diverse Tools, Shared Standards*. 2nd ed. Lanham, MD: Rowman & Littlefield.

Brehm, John. 1993. *The Phantom Respondents: Opinion Surveys and Political Representation*. Ann Arbor: University of Michigan Press.

Brunner, Borgna. 2010. The Tuskegee syphilis experiment. Retrieved January, 2010, from http://www1.cbsd.org/sites/teachers/hs/pwheeles/apstatistics/Shared%20Documents /Ch%2013/Tuskegee%20Experiment.pdf.

Brydon-Miller, Mary. 1997. "Participatory Action Research: Psychology and Social Change." *Journal of Social Issues* 53:657–666.

Caldeira, Gregory A., and John R. Wright. 1988. "Organized Interests and Agenda-Setting in the U.S. Supreme Court." *American Political Science Review* 82(4): 1109–1128.

Caldwell, Joyce Y., Jamie D. Davis, Barbara Du Bois, Holly Echo-Hawk, Jill Shephard Erickson, R. Turner Goins, Calvin Hill, et al. 2005. "Culturally Competent Research with American Indians and Alaska Natives: Findings and Recommendations of the First Symposium of the Work Group on American Indian Research and Program Evaluation Methodology." *American Indian and Alaska Native Mental Health Research* 12(1): 1–21.

Cammett, Melani. 2006. "Political Ethnography in Deeply Divided Societies." *Qualitative Methods: Newsletter of the American Political Science Association Organized Section on Qualitative Methods* 4(2): 15–18.

———. 2007a. *Globalization and Business Politics in Arab North Africa: A Comparative Perspective*. Cambridge: Cambridge University Press.

———. 2007b. "The War on Terror: Implications for Research and Data Collection in the Middle East." *APSA-CP* 18(1): 16–19.

Campbell, Andrea Louise. 2003. *How Policies Make Citizens: Senior Citizen Activism and the American Welfare State*. Princeton, NJ: Princeton University Press.

Campbell, Donald T. 1975. "Degrees of Freedom and the Case Study." *Comparative Political Studies* 8(2): 178–193.

Carpenter, Daniel. 2000. "Commentary: What Is the Marginal Value of 'Analytic Narratives'?" *Social Science History* 24(4): 653–667.

———. 2010. *Reputation and Power: Organizational Image and Pharmaceutical Regulation at the FDA*. Princeton, NJ: Princeton University Press.

Catania, Joseph A., Diane Binson, Jesse Canchola, Lance M. Pollack, and Walter Hauck. 1996. "Effects of Interviewer Gender, Interviewer Choice, and Item Wording on Responses to Questions Concerning Sexual Behavior." *Public Opinion Quarterly* 60(3): 345–375.

Chacko, Elizabeth. 2004. "Positionality and Praxis: Fieldwork Experiences in Rural India." *Singapore Journal of Tropical Geography* 25:51–63.

Chandra, Kanchan. 2007. *Why Ethnic Parties Succeed: Patronage and Ethnic Head Counts in India*. Cambridge: Cambridge University Press.

Charmaz, Kathy, and Richard G. Mitchell Jr. 1997. "The Myth of Silent Authorship: Self, Substance and Style in Ethnographic Writing." In *Reflexivity and Voice*, ed. Rosanna Hertz, 193–215. Thousand Oaks, CA: Sage.

Chataway, C. J. 2001. "Negotiating the Observer-Observed Relationship: Participatory Action Research." In *From Subjects to Subjectivities: A Handbook of Interpretive and Participatory Methods*, ed. D. Tolman and M. Brydon-Miller, 239–258. New York: NYU Press.

Chavez, Christina. 2008. "Conceptualizing from the Inside: Advantages, Complications, and Demands on Insider Positionality." *Qualitative Report* 13(3): 474–494.

Chen, Calvin. 2010. "The Worm's-Eye View: Using Ethnography to Illuminate Labor Politics and Institutional Change in Contemporary China." In *Contemporary Chinese Politics: New Sources, Methods, and Field Strategies*, ed. Allen Carlson, Mary Gallagher, Kenneth Lieberthal, and Melanie Manion, 129–144. New York: Cambridge University Press.

Chikwanha, Annie, Tulani Sithole, and M. Bratton. 2004. "The Power of Propaganda: Public Opinion in Zimbabwe, 2004." *Afrobarometer Working Papers*. Legon-Accra, Ghana: Afrobarometer.

Chong, Dennis, and Reuel Rogers. 2005. "The Influence of Racial Solidarity on Political Participation." *Political Behavior* 27:347–374.

Chwieroth, Jeffrey. 2009. *Capital Ideas: The IMF and the Rise of Financial Liberalization*. Princeton, NJ: Princeton University Press.

Clark, Janine A. 2006. "Field Research Methods in the Middle East." *PS: Political Science & Politics* 39(3): 417–424.

Clifford, James, and George E. Marcus. 1986. "Introduction: Partial Truths." In *Writing Culture: The Poetics and Politics of Ethnography*, ed. James Clifford and George E. Marcus. Berkeley and Los Angeles: University of California Press, 1–26.

Cohen, Cathy. 2010. *Democracy Remixed: Black Youth and the Future of American Politics*. Oxford: Oxford University Press.

Cole, Catherine M. 2010. *Performing South Africa's truth commission: Stages of transition*. Bloomington: Indiana University Press.

Collier, David, and James Mahoney. 1996. "Insights and Pitfalls: Selection Bias in Qualitative Research." *World Politics* 49(1): 56–91.

Collier, David, James Mahoney, and Jason Seawright. 2004. "Claiming Too Much: Warnings about Selection Bias." In *Rethinking Social Inquiry: Diverse Tools, Shared Standards*, ed. Henry Brady and David Collier, 85–102. Lanham, MD: Rowman & Littlefield.

Collier, Paul. 2000. "Rebellion as a Quasi-criminal Activity." *Journal of Conflict Resolution* 44(6): 839–853.

Commonwealth Human Rights Initiative. 2002. *In Pursuit of Justice: A Report on the Judiciary in Sierra Leone*. Freetown: CHRI.

Conibere, Richard, Jana Asher, Kristen Cibelli, Jana Dudukovich, Rafe Kaplan, Patrick Ball, 2004. Statistical Appendix to the Report of the Truth and Reconciliation Commission of Sierra Leone. Palo Alto, CA: Benetech.

Coppedge, Michael J. 1999. "Thickening Thin Concepts and Theories: Combining Large N and Small N in Comparative Politics." *Comparative Politics* 31(4): 465–476.

———. 2005. "Explaining Democratic Deterioration in Venezuela through Nested Inference." In *The Third Wave of Democratization in Latin America*, ed. Frances Hagopian and Scott Mainwaring, 289–316. Cambridge: Cambridge University Press.

Corbin, Juliet, and Janice Morse. 2003. "The Unstructured Interactive Interview: Issues of Reciprocity and Risks When Dealing with Sensitive Topics." *Qualitative Inquiry* 9(3): 335–354.

Cornwall, A. 2003. "Whose Voices? Whose Choices? Reflections on Gender and Participatory Development." *World Development* 31:1325–1342.

Cornwall, A., and R. Jewkes. 1995. "What Is Participatory Research?" *Social Science and Medicine* 41:1667–1676.

Corstange, Daniel. 2009. "Sensitive Questions, Truthful Answers? Modeling the List Experiment Multivariately with Listit." *Political Analysis* 17(1): 45–63.

Cumming, J. F., A. R. Sahni, and G. R. McClelland. 2006. "The Importance of the Subject in Informed Consent." *Applied Clinical Trials* (March): 64–70.

Dahl, Robert A. 1957. "The Concept of Power." *Behavioral Science* 2:201–215.

Daniel, Johnnie. 2012. *Sampling Essentials: Practical Guidelines for Making Sampling Choices*. Thousand Oaks, CA: Sage.

Davis, S., and R. Reid. 1999. "Practicing Participatory Research in American Indian Communities." *American Journal of Clinical Nutrition* 69(4): 755s–759s.

Dawson, Michael. 1994a. *Behind the Mule: Race and Class in African-American Politics*. Princeton, NJ: Princeton University Press.

———. 1994b. "A Black Counterpublic? Economic Earthquakes, Racial Agenda(s), and Black Politics." *Public Culture* 7:195–223.

———. 2011. *Not in Our Lifetimes: The Future of Black Politics*. Chicago: University of Chicago Press.

Denzin, N. K. 1994. "The Art and Politics of Interpretation." In *The Handbook of Qualitative Research*, ed. N. K. Denzin and Y. S. Lincoln, 500–515. Thousand Oaks, CA: Sage.

Des Forges, Alison. 1999. "Leave none to tell the story." New York: Human Rights Watch & Fédération internationale des ligues des droits de l'homme.

Deutsch, Nancy. 2004. "Positionality and the Pen: Reflections on the Process of Becoming a Feminist Researcher and Writer." *Qualitative Inquiry* 10:885–901.

Devereux, Stephen. 1993. "'Observers are worried': Learning the Language and Counting the People in Northeast Ghana." In *Fieldwork in Developing Countries*, ed. Stephen Devereux and John Hoddinott, 43–56. Boulder, CO: Lynne Rienner.

Dexter, Louis Anthony. 1970. *Elite and Specialized Interviewing*. Evanston, IL: Northwestern University Press.

Dobbin, Frank. 1992. "The Origins of Private Social Insurance: Public Policy and Fringe Benefits in America, 1920–1950." *American Journal of Sociology* 97 (5):1416–1450.

Dowling, Robyn. 2000. "Power, Subjectivity and Ethics in Qualitative Research." In *Qualitative Research Methods in Human Geography* 19–29, ed. I. Hay. Melbourne: Oxford University Press.

Dreze, J. 2002. "On Research and Action." *Economic and Political Weekly* 37 (March 2, 2002): 817.

Druckman, James M., and Michael F. Thies. 2002. "The Importance of Concurrence: Impact of Bicameralism on Government Formation and Duration." *American Journal of Political Science* 46:760–771.

Dunning. Thad. 2008. "Improving Causal Inference: Strengths and Limitations of Natural Experiments." *Political Research Quarterly* 61 (2): 282–293.

Easterby-Smith, Mark, and Danusia Malina. 1999. "Cross-Cultural Collaborative Research: Toward Reflexivity." *Academy of Management Journal* 42(1): 76–86.

Easton, David. 1969. "The New Revolution in Political Science." *American Political Science Review* 63:1051–1061.

Eckstein, Harry. 1975. "*Case Study and Theory in Political Science*." In *Handbook of Political Science*, ed. Fred Greenstein and Nelson Polsby, 94–137. Reading, MA: Addison-Wesley.

Egan, Paul. 2007. "Feds Tie Dearborn Charity to Terror." *Detroit News*, July 25. Available at http://detnews.com/article/20070725/METRO/707250395.

Elman, Colin, Diana Kapiszewski, and Lorena Vinuela. 2010. "Qualitative Data Archiving: Rewards and Challenges." *PS: Political Science & Politics* 43(1): 23–27.

Emerson, Robert, Rachel Fretz, and Linda Shaw. 1995. *Writing Ethnographic Fieldnotes.* Chicago: University of Chicago Press.

Engel, David M., and Barbara Yngvesson. 1984. "Mapping the Terrain: 'Legal Culture,' 'Legal Consciousness,' and Other Hazards for the Intrepid Explorer." *Law and Policy* 6:299–307.

England, Kim V. L. 1994. "Getting Personal: Reflexivity, Positionality, and Feminist Research." *Professional Geographer* 46:80–89.

Ewick, Patricia, and Susan Silbey. 1998. *The Common Place of Law: Stories from Everyday Life.* Chicago: University of Chicago Press.

Falleti, Tulia G. 2010. *Decentralization and Subnational Politics in Latin America.* New York: Cambridge University Press.

Fals-Borda, O. 1997. "Participatory Action Research in Colombia: Some Personal Feelings." In *Participatory Action Research: International Contexts and Consequences,* ed. R. McTaggart, 107–112. Albany, NY: SUNY Press.

Fals-Borda, O., T. Koch, P. Selim, and D. Kralik. 2002. "Enhancing Lives through the Development of a Community-Based Participatory Action Research Program." *Journal of Clinical Nursing* 11:109–117.

Fenno, Richard F., Jr. 1966. *The Power of the Purse.* Boston: Little, Brown.

———. 1973. *Congressmen in Committees.* Boston: Little, Brown.

———. 1978. *Home Style: House Members in Their Districts.* Boston: Little, Brown.

Fioretos, Orfeo, Tulia Falleti, and Adam Sheingate, eds. Forthcoming [2014]. *Oxford Handbook of Historical Institutionalism.* New York: Oxford University Press.

Fowler, Floyd J., Jr. 1993. *Survey Research Methods.* 2nd ed. Newbury Park, CA: Sage.

Francis, Elizabeth. 1993. "Qualitative Research: Collecting Life Histories." In *Fieldwork in Developing Countries,* ed. Stephen Devereux and John Hoddinott, 86–101. Boulder, CO: Lynne Rienner.

Freire, Paulo. 1970. *Pedagogy of the Oppressed.* New York: Continuum.

———. 1982. "Creating Alternative Research Methods: Learning to Do by Doing It." In *Creating Knowledge: A Monopoly? Participatory Research in Development,* ed. B. Hall, A. Gillette, and R. Tandon, 29–37. New Delhi: Society for Participatory Research in Asia.

Frey, James H., and Sabine Mertens Oishi. 1995. *How to Conduct Interviews by Telephone and in Person.* Thousand Oaks, CA: Sage.

Friedman, Jeffrey, ed. 1996. *The Rational Choice Controversy: Economic Models of Politics Reconsidered.* New Haven: Yale University Press.

Fritz, Katherine. 2008. "Ethical Issues in Qualitative Research." Unpublished presentation, Johns Hopkins School of Public Health, Department of International Health, Johns Hopkins University.

Fujii, Lee Ann. 2009. *Killing Neighbors: Webs of Violence in Rwanda.* Ithaca: Cornell University Press.

Fujii, Lee Ann. 2010. "Shades of Truth and Lies: Interpreting Testimonies of War and Violence." *Journal of Peace Research* 47(2): 231–241.

Fujii, Lee Ann. 2012. "Research ethics 101: Dilemmas and responsibilities." *PS: Political Science and Politics* 45 (4): 717–23.

Gallagher, Mary E. 2006. "Mobilizing the Law in China: 'Informed Disenchantment' and the Development of Legal Consciousness." *Law and Society Review* 40(4): 783–816.

Gay, Claudine. 2004. "Putting Race in Context: Identifying the Environmental Determinants of Black Racial Attitudes." *American Political Science Review* 98:547–562.

Geddes, Barbara. 1990. "How the Cases You Choose Affect the Answers You Get: Selection Bias in Comparative Politics." *Political Analysis* 2:131–152.

Geddes, Barbara. 2003. *Paradigms and Sand Castles: Theory Building and Research Design in Comparative Politics.* Ann Arbor: University of Michigan Press.

Geertz, Clifford. 1977. *The Interpretation of Cultures.* New York: Basic Books.

George, Alexander, and Andrew Bennett. 2005. *Case Studies and Theory Development in the Social Sciences.* Cambridge, MA: The MIT Press.

Gerber, Alan, and Neil Malhotra. 2008. "Do Statistical Reporting Standards Affect What Is Published? Publication Bias in Two Leading Political Science Journals." *Quarterly Journal of Political Science* 3(3): 313–326.

Gerring, John. 1999. "What Makes a Concept Good? A Criterial Framework for Understanding Concept Formation in the Social Sciences." *Polity* 31:357–393.

———. 2004. "What Is a Case Study and What Is It Good For?" *American Political Science Review* 98(2): 341–354.

———. 2007. *Case Study Research: Principles and Practices.* Cambridge: Cambridge University Press.

———. 2012. *Social Science Methodology: A Unified Framework.* 2nd ed. Cambridge: Cambridge University Press.

Gilkes, P. 1989. "Somalia: Conflicts within and against the Military Regime." *Review of African Political Economy* 16:53–58.

Godambe, Vidyadhar P. 1982. "Estimation in Survey Sampling: Robustness and Optimality." *Journal of the American Statistical Association* 77(378): 393–403.

Goemans, Hein E. 2007. "Qualitative Methods as an Essential Component to Quantitative Methods." *Qualitative Methods Newsletter* 5(1): 11–12.

Goertz, Gary. 2006. *Social Science Concepts: A User's Guide.* Princeton, NJ: Princeton University Press.

Gold, Lorna. 2002. "Positionality, Worldview and Geographical Research: A Personal Account of a Research Journey." *Ethics, Place and Environment* 5:223–237.

Golden, Miriam. 1995. "Replication and Non-Quantitative Research." *PS: Political Science & Politics* 28:481–483.

Goldstein, Kenneth. 2002. "Getting in the Door: Sampling and Completing Elite Interviews." *PS: Political Science & Politics* 35:669–672.

Gonzales-Ocantos, Ezequiel, Chad Kiewiet de Jonge, Carlos Meléndez, Javier Osorio, and David W. Nickerson. 2010. "Vote Buying and Social Desirability Bias: Experimental Evidence from Nicaragua." Working paper, University of Notre Dame.

Gordon, Elisa. 2003. "Trials and Tribulations of Navigating IRBs: Anthropological and Biomedical Perspectives of 'Risk' in Conducting Human Subjects Research." *Anthropological Quarterly* 76(2): 299–320.

Goss, Kristin A. 2006. *Disarmed: The Missing Movement for Gun Control in America.* Princeton, NJ: Princeton University Press.

Gottlieb, Alma, and Philip Graham. 1994. *Parallel Worlds: A Writer and an Anthropologist Encounter Africa.* Chicago: University of Chicago Press.

Gray, Bradford H. 1979. "Human Subjects Review Committees and Social Research." In *Federal Regulations: Ethical Issues and Social Research.* Murray L. Wax and Joan Cassell, eds. 43–59. Boulder, CO: Westview.

Green, Donald, and Ian Shapiro. 1996. *Pathologies of Rational Choice Theory: A Critique of Applications in Political Science.* New Haven, CT: Yale University Press.

Gubrium, Jaber F., and James A. Holstein. 2002. *Handbook of Interview Research: Context and Method.* Thousand Oaks, CA: Sage.

Guest, Greg, Arwen Bunce, and Laura Johnson. 2006. "How Many Interviews Are Enough? An Experiment with Data Saturation and Variability." *Field Methods* 18(1): 59–82.

Gunsalus, C. K., Edward M. Bruner, Nicholas C. Burbules, Leon Dash, Matthew Finkin, Joseph P. Goldberg, William T. Greenough, et al. 2007. "The Illinois White Paper: Improving the System for Protecting Human Subjects: Counteracting IRB 'Mission Creep.'" *Qualitative Inquiry* 13:617–649.

Hajnal, Zoltan, and Taeku Lee. 2011. *Why Americans Don't Join the Party: Race, Immigration and the Failure (of Political Parties) to Engage the Electorate.* Princeton, NJ: Princeton University Press.

Hall, Bud. 1981. "Participatory Research, Popular Knowledge and Power: A Personal Reflection." *Convergence* 14:6–17.

Hall, Peter A. and David Soskice, eds. 2001. *Varieties of Capitalism: The Institutional Foundations of Comparative Advantage.* New York: Oxford University Press.

Hall, Richard L. 1996. *Participation in Congress.* New Haven, CT: Yale University Press.

Haney, L. 1996. "Homeboys, Babies, Men in Suits: The State and the Reproduction of Male Dominance." *American Sociological Review* 61:759–778.

Haraway, D. J. 1991. *Simians, Cyborgs, and Women: The Reinvention of Nature.* London: Free Association Books.

Harding, Sandra. 1986. *The Science Question in Feminism.* Ithaca, NY: Cornell University Press.

———. 1991. *Whose Science? Whose Knowledge? Thinking from Women's Lives.* Ithaca, NY: Cornell University Press, 1991.

Harris-Lacewell, Melissa. 2004. *Bibles, Barbershops, and BET: Everyday Talk and Black Political Thought.* Princeton: Princeton University Press.

Hatchett, Shirley, and Howard Schuman. 1975. "White Respondents and Race-of-Interviewer Effects." *Public Opinion Quarterly* 39(4): 523–528.

Hatzfeld, Jean. 2003. *Une saison de machetes.* Paris: Seuil.

Hauck, Robert J-P. 2008. "Protecting Human Research Participants, IRBs, and Political Science Redux: Editor's Introduction." *PS: Political Science & Politics* 41(3): 475–476.

Heckathorn, Douglas D. 1997. "Respondent-Driven Sampling: A New Approach to the Study of Hidden Populations." *Social Problems* 44(2): 174–199.

———. 2002. "Respondent-Driven Sampling II: Deriving Valid Estimates from Chain-Referral Samples of Hidden Populations." *Social Problems* 49(1): 11–34.

Henderson, Frances B. 2009. "'We Thought You Would Be White': Race and Gender in Fieldwork." *PS: Political Science & Politics* 42(2): 291–294.

Herod, Andrew. 1999. "Reflections on Interviewing Foreign Elites: Praxis, Positionality, Validity, and the Cult of the Insider." *Geoforum* 30:313–327.

Hertel, Shareen, Matthew M. Singer, and Donna Lee Van Cott. 2009. "Field Research in Developing Countries: Hitting the Ground Running." *PS: Political Science & Politics* 42(2): 305–310.

Hochhauser, Mark. 2005. "Memory Overload: The Impossibility of Informed Consent." *Applied Clinical Trials* (November): 70.

Hochschild, Jennifer. 1981. *What's Fair? American Beliefs about Distributive Justice.* Cambridge, MA: Harvard University Press.

Hojnacki, Marie and David C. Kimball. 1998. "Organized Interests and the Decision of Whom to Lobby in Congress." *American Political Science Review* 92(4): 775–90.

Horowitz, R. 1986. "Remaining an Outsider: Membership as a Threat to Research Rapport." *Urban Life* 14:409–430.

Hudson, James, and Amy Bruckman. 2004. "'Go Away': Participant Objections to Being Studied and the Ethics of Chatroom Research." *Information Society* 20:127–139.

International Commission of Jurists. 1977. *Uganda and Human Rights: Reports to the UN Commission on Human Rights.* Geneva: International Commission of Jurists.

International Commission on Intervention and State Sovereignty. 2001. *The Responsibility to Protect: Report of the International Commission on Intervention and State Sovereignty*. Ottawa: Canada: International Development Research Centre.

International Court of Justice. 2002. Case concerning the Arrest Warrant of 11 April 2000, Judgment of 14 February 2002. Viewed March 31, 2010, http://www.icj-cij .org/docket/files/121/8126.pdf.

International Crisis Group. 2003. *Sierra Leone: The State of Security and Governance*. Freetown: ICG.

International Telecommunications Union. 2011. Viewed August 27, 2011. http://www.itu .int/ITU-D/ict/statistics.

Jaya, Hindin M. J., and S. Ahmed. 2008. "Difference in Young People's Reports of Sexual Behaviors according to Interview Methodology: A Randomized Trial in India." *American Journal of Public Health* 98(1): 169–174.

Jensen, Nathan M., Quan Li, and Aminur Rahman. 2010. "Understanding Corruption and Firm Responses in Cross-National Firm-Level Surveys." *Journal of International Business Studies* 41(9): 1481–1504.

Johnson, Janet Elise. 2009. "Unwilling Participant Observation among Russian *Siloviki* and the Good-Enough Field Researcher." *PS: Political Science & Politics* 42(2): 321–324.

Jones-Correa, Michael, and David L. Leal. 1996. "Becoming 'Hispanic': Secondary Panethnic Identification among Latin American–Origin Populations in the United States." *Hispanic Journal of Behavioral Sciences* 18:214–253.

Junn, Jane, and Natalie Masuoka. 2008. "Identities in Context: Politicized Racial Group Consciousness among Asian American and Latino Youth." *Applied Developmental Science* 12:93–101.

Kaldor, Mary. 2001. *New and Old Wars: Organized Violence in a Global Era*. Palo Alto, CA: Stanford University Press.

Kalton, Graham, and Dallas W. Anderson. 1986. "Sampling Rare Populations." *Journal of the Royal Statistical Society*. Series A (General) 149(1): 65–82.

Kapiszewski, Diana, Lauren M. MacLean, and Benjamin L. Read. Forthcoming. *Field Research in Political Science*. New York: Cambridge University Press.

Kaplan, Robert. 1994. "The Coming Anarchy." *Atlantic Monthly* 273(2): 44–76.

Kasinitz, Philip. 1992. *Caribbean New York: Black Immigrants and the Politics of Race*. Ithaca, NY: Cornell University Press.

Kaufman, Herbert. 1960. *The Forest Ranger: A Study in Administrative Behavior*. Baltimore: Johns Hopkins University Press.

Kelly, Patricia J. 2005. "Practical Suggestions for Community Interventions Using Participatory Action Research." *Public Health Nursing* 22:65–73.

Kemmis, S., and R. McTaggart. 2008. "Action Research: Communicative Action and the Public Sphere." In *Strategies of Qualitative Research*, 3rd ed., ed. N. Denzin and Y. Lincoln, 271–330. Thousand Oaks, CA: Sage.

Khan, Shahnaz. 2005. "Reconfiguring the Native Informant: Positionality in the Global Age." *Journal of Women in Culture and Society* 30(4): 2017–2035.

Kidd, Sean A., and Michael J. Kral. 2005. "Practicing Participatory Action Research." *Journal of Counseling Psychology* 52:187–195.

Kilkullen, D. 2009. *The Accidental Guerrilla: Fighting Small Wars in the Midst of a Big One*. New York: Oxford University Press.

King, Gary. 1995. "Replication, Replication." *PS: Political Science & Politics* 28:444–452.

King, Gary, Robert O. Keohane, and Sidney Verba. 1994. *Designing Social Inquiry: Scientific Inference in Qualitative Research*. Princeton, NJ: Princeton University Press.

King, Gary, and Jonathan Wand. 2007. "Comparing Incomparable Survey Responses Evaluating and Selecting Anchoring Vignettes." *Political Analysis* 15:46–66.

Kingdon, John W. 1981. *Congressmen's Voting Decisions.* 2nd ed. New York: Harper & Row.

Kingdon, John W. 1989. *Congressmen's Voting Decisions,* 3rd ed. Ann Arbor, MI: University of Michigan Press.

———. 1995. *Agendas, Alternatives, and Public Policies.* 2nd ed. New York: Harper-Collins.

Kish, Leslie. 1962. "Studies of Interviewer Variance for Attitudinal Variables." *Journal of the American Statistical Association* 57(297): 92–115.

Kreiger, S. 1985. "Beyond Subjectivity: The Use of Self in Social Science." *Qualitative Sociology* 8:309–324.

Krippendorff, Klaus H. 2003. *Content Analysis: An Introduction to Its Methodology.* Thousand Oaks, CA: Sage.

Kritzer, Herbert, and John Voelker. 1998. "Familiarity Breeds Respect: How Wisconsin Citizens View Their Courts." *Judicature* 82(2): 59–64.

Kuhn, Thomas S. 1970. *The Structure of Scientific Revolutions.* 2nd ed. Chicago: University of Chicago Press.

Kvale, Steinar, and Svend Brinkmann. 2009. *InterViews: Learning the Craft of Qualitative Research Interviewing.* Thousand Oaks, CA: Sage.

Labaki, Boutros. 1984. "Min Al-'Aila Al-Imtidadiyya Ila at-Taifa Fi Lubnan" (From the Extended Family to the Sect in Lebanon). *Al-Waq'ia* (7).

Labaree, Robert V. 2002. "The Risk of 'Going Observationalist': Negotiating the Dilemmas of Being an Insider Participant Observer." *Qualitative Methods* 2(1): 97–122.

Labott, Susan M., and Timothy P. Johnson. 2004. "Psychological and Social Risks of Behavioral Research." *IRB: Ethics and Human Research* 26(3): 11–15.

Laitin, David. 1986. *Hegemony and Culture: Politics and Change among the Yoruba.* Chicago: University of Chicago Press.

———. 1998. *Identity in Formation: The Russian-Speaking Populations in the Near Abroad.* Ithaca, NY: Cornell University Press.

———. 2003. "The Perestroikan Challenge to Social Science." *Political Sociology* 31(1): 163–184.

Lake, David A. 2010. "Who's on First? Listing Authors by Relative Contribution Trumps the Alphabet." *PS: Political Science & Politics* 43(1): 43–47.

Lane, Robert. 1962. *Political Ideology: Why the American Common Man Believes What He Does.* Oxford: Free Press of Glencoe.

Lawless, Jennifer, and Richard L. Fox. 2005. *It Takes a Candidate: Why Women Don't Run for Office.* New York: Cambridge University Press.

———. 2010. *It Still Takes a Candidate: Why Women Don't Run for Office.* New York: Cambridge University Press.

Lazarsfeld, Paul. 1966. "Concept Formation and Measurement in the Behavioral Sciences: Some Historical Observations." In *Concepts, Theory, and Explanation in the Behavioral Sciences,* ed. Gordon DiRenzo, 144–204. New York: Random House.

LeCompte, Margaret D., and Jean J. Schensul. 1999. *Designing and Conducting Ethnographic Research: Ethnographer's Toolkit.* Walnut Creek, CA: AltaMira Press.

Lederman, Rena. 2006. "The Perils of Working at Home: IRB 'Mission Creep' as Context and Content for an Ethnography of Disciplinary Knowledges." *American Ethnologist* 33:482–491.

Lee, Taeku. 2002. *Mobilizing Public Opinion: Black Insurgency and Racial Attitudes in the Civil Rights Era.* Chicago: University of Chicago Press.

———. 2007. "From Shared Demographic Categories to Common Political Destinies? Immigration and the Link from Racial Identity to Group Politics." *Du Bois Review* 4:433–456.

Lee, Taeku, and Nicole Willcoxon. 2011. "Race, Public Opinion, and the Media." In *The Oxford Handbook of American Public Opinion and the Media*, ed. Robert Shapiro and Lawrence Jacobs. 605–621. Oxford: Oxford University Press.

Leech, Beth L. 2002a. "Asking Questions: Techniques for Semistructured Interviews." *PS: Political Science & Politics* 35(4): 665–667.

———. ed. 2002b. "Symposium: Interview Methods in Political Science." *PS: Political Science & Politics* 35(4): 663–688.

Leighley, Jan E., and Arnold Vedlitz. 1999. "Race, Ethnicity, and Political Participation: Competing Models and Contrasting Explanations." *Journal of Politics* 61:1092–1114.

Lemert, Charles. 2001. *Social Things.* Lanham, MD: Rowman & Littlefield.

Lieberman, Evan S. 2005. "Nested Analysis as a Mixed-Method Strategy for Comparative Research." *American Political Science Review* 99(3): 435–452.

———. 2010. "Bridging the Qualitative-Quantitative Divide: Best Practices in the Development of Historically Oriented Replication Databases." *Annual Reviews of Political Science* 13:37–59.

Lien, Pei-te. 1994. "Ethnicity and Political Participation: A Comparison between Asians and Mexican Americans." *Political Behavior* 19:237–264.

Lien, Pei-te, Margaret Conway, and Janelle Wong. 2004. *The Politics of Asian Americans: Diversity and Community.* New York: Routledge.

Lieshout, Robert H., Mathieu L. L. Segers, and Anna M. van der Vleuten. 2004. "De Gaulle, Moravcsik, and *The Choice for Europe*: Soft Sources, Weak Evidence." *Journal of Cold War Studies* 6(4): 89–139.

Lindblom, Charles. 1998. "Political Science in the 1940s and 1950s." In *American Academic Culture in Transformation*, ed. Thomas Bender and Carl Schorske. 243–270 Princeton, NJ: Princeton University Press.

Loftus, Elizabeth F. 1979. *Eyewitness Testimony.* Cambridge, MA: Harvard University Press.

Lust-Okar, Ellen, Lisa Anderson, Steven Heydemann and Mark Tessler. 2007. "Comparative Politics of the Middle East and Academic Freedom." *APSA-CP* 18(1): 12–15.

Lynch, Julia. 2006. *Age in the Welfare State: The Origins of Social Spending on Pensioners, Workers and Children.* Cambridge: Cambridge University Press.

Maass, Peter. 1996. *Love Thy Neighbor: A Story of War.* New York: Vintage Books.

Macauley, A. C., T. Delormier, A. M. McComber, E. J. Cross, L. P. Potvin, G. Paradis, R. L. Kirby, C. Saad-Haddad, and S. Desrosiers. 1998. "Participatory Research with Native Community of Kahnawake Creates Innovative Code of Research Ethics." *Canadian Journal of Public Health* 89:105–108.

MacLean, Lauren Morris. 2010. *Informal Institutions and Citizenship in Rural Africa: Risk and Reciprocity in Ghana and Côte d'Ivoire.* New York: Cambridge University Press.

———. (n.d.) "Constructing Democracy in America: Tribal-State Consultation in Indian Health Policy, 1970 to the Present" (unpublished).

Mahoney, Christine. 2008. *Brussels vs. the Beltway: Advocacy in the United States and the European Union.* Washington, DC: Georgetown University Press.

Mahoney, James. 2010. "After KKV: The New Methodology of Qualitative Research." *World Politics* 62(1): 120–47.

Mahoney, James, and Gary Goertz. 2004. "The Possibility Principle: Choosing Negative Cases in Comparative Research." *American Political Science Review* 98:653–670.

Manley, John F. 1970. *The Politics of Finance.* Boston: Little, Brown.

Marschall, Melissa. 2001. "Does the Shoe Fit? Testing Models of Participation for African-American and Latino Involvement in Local Politics." *Urban Affairs Review* 37:227–248.

Marshall, Patricia. 2003. "Human Subjects Protections, Institutional Review Boards, and Cultural Anthropological Research." *Anthropological Quarterly* 76(2): 269–285.

Martin, Cathie Jo. 1995. "Nature or Nurture? Sources of Firm Preference for National Health Reform." *American Political Science Review* 89(4): 898–913.

———. 2000. *Stuck in Neutral: Business and the Politics of Human Capital Investment Policy.* Princeton, NJ: Princeton University Press.

———. 2004. "Reinventing Welfare Regimes." *World Politics* 57(1): 39–69.

———. 2005. "Corporatism from the Firm Perspective." *British Journal of Political Science* 35(1): 127–148.

Martin, Cathie Jo, and Duane Swank. 2004. "Does the Organization of Capital Matter? Employers and Active Labor Market Policy at the National and Firm Levels." *American Political Science Review* 98(4): 593–611.

———. 2012. *The Political Construction of Corporate Interests: Cooperation and the Evolution of the Good Society.* New York: Cambridge University Press.

Matthews, Donald R. 1960. *U.S. Senators and Their World.* New York: Vintage Books.

McAdam, Doug. 1982. *Political Process and the Development of Black Insurgency, 1930–1970.* Chicago: University of Chicago Press.

McCorkel, Jill, and Kristen Myers. 2003. "What Difference Does Difference Make? Position and Privilege in the Field." *Qualitative Sociology* 26:199–231.

McCracken, Grant. 1988. *The Long Interview.* Newbury Park, CA: Sage.

McDermott, Rose, and Peter K. Hatemi. 2010. "Emerging Models of Collaboration in Political Science: Changes, Benefits and Challenges." *PS: Political Science & Politics* 43(1): 49–58.

McDowell, Linda. 1997. *Capital Culture: Gender at Work in the City.* Oxford: Blackwell.

Medicine, B. 2001. "Learning to Be an Anthropologist and Remaining 'Native.'" In *Learning to Be an Anthropologist and Remaining "Native": Selected Writings*, ed. S. E. Jacobs and B. Medicine, 3–17. Chicago: University of Illinois Press.

Merriam, Sharan B., Juanita Johnson-Bailey, Ming-Yeh Lee, Youngwha Kee, Gabo Ntseane, and Mazanah Muhamad. 2001. "Power and Positionality: Negotiating Insider/Outsider Status within and across Cultures." *International Journal of Lifelong Education* 20(5): 405–416.

Merry, Sally Engle. 1990. *Getting Justice and Getting Even: Legal Consciousness among Working-Class Americans.* Chicago: University of Chicago Press.

Mihesuah, Devon. 1993. "Suggested Guidelines for Institutions with Scholars Who Conduct Research on American Indians." *American Indian Culture and Research Journal* 17(3): 131–139.

Milgram, Stanley. 1963. "Behavioral Study of Obedience." *The Journal of Abnormal and Social Psychology* 67(4): 371–378.

Miller, Arthur, Patricia Gurin, Gerald Gurin, and Oksana Malanchuk. 1981. "Group Consciousness and Political Participation." *American Journal of Political Science* 25: 494–511.

Moravcsik A. 1998. *The Choice for Europe: Social Purpose and State Power from Messina to Maastricht.* Ithaca, NY: Cornell University Press.

———. 2010. "Active Citation: A Precondition for Replicable Qualitative Research." *PS: Political Science & Politics* 43(1): 29–35.

Morris, Aldon. 1984. *The Origins of the Civil Rights Movement: Black Communities Organizing for Change.* New York: Free Press.

Morton, Rebecca B., and Kenneth Williams. 2010. *From Nature to the Lab: Experimental Political Science and the Nature of Causality.* Cambridge: Cambridge University Press.

Mosley, Layna. 2003a. *Global Capital and National Governments.* New York: Cambridge University Press.

Mosley, Layna. 2003b. "Attempting Global Standards? National Governments, International Finance, and the IMF's Data Regime." *Review of International Political Economy* 10(2): 332–363.

Mosley, Layna, and David A. Singer. 2009. "The Global Financial Crisis: Lessons and Opportunities for International Political Economy." *International Interactions* 35(4): 420–429.

Murphy, Michael D., and Agneta Johannsen. 1990. "Ethical Obligations and Federal Regulations in Ethnographic Research and Anthropological Education." *Human Organization* 49(2): 127–134.

Nader, Laura. 1969. "Up the Anthropologist: Perspectives Gained from Studying Up." In *Reinventing Anthropology*, ed. Dell Hymes, 284–311. New York: Vintage Press.

Nagar, Richa, with Farah Ali and the Sangatin Women's Collective. 2003. "Collaboration across Borders: Moving beyond Positionality." *Singapore Journal of Tropical Geography* 24(3): 356–372.

Nasr, Salim. 1993. "New Social Realities and Post-War Lebanon: Issues for Reconstruction." In *Recovering Beirut: Urban Design and Post-War Reconstruction*, ed. Samir Khalaf and Philip S. Khoury, 63–80. London: E. J. Brill.

National Commission for the Protection of Human Subjects of Biomedical and Behavioral Research. 1979. *The Belmont Report: Ethical Principles and Guidelines for the Protection of Human Subjects of Research*. Washington, DC: Government Printing Office.

Neuendorf, Kimberly A. 2001. *The Content Analysis Guidebook*. Thousand Oaks, CA: Sage.

Neustadt, Richard E. 1960. *Presidential Power*. New York: Wiley.

Nikander, Pirjo. 2008. "Working with Transcripts and Translated Data." *Qualitative Research in Psychology* 5:225–31.

Nisbett, Richard E., and Timothy Wilson. 1977. "Telling More Than We Can Know: Verbal Reports on Mental Processes." *Psychological Review* 84(3): 231–259.

Nissenbaum, Helen. 1998. "Protecting Privacy in an Information Age: The Problem of Privacy in Public." *Law and Philosophy* 17(5/6): 559–596.

Norton, Anne. 2004a. *Ninety-five Theses on Politics, Culture, and Method*. New Haven, CT: Yale University Press.

———. 2004b. "Political Science as Vocation." In *Problems and Methods in the Study of Politics*, ed. Ian Shaprio, Rogers Smith, and Tarek Masoud 67–82. New York: Cambridge University Press.

Oakes, J. Michael. 2002. "Risks and Wrongs in Social Science Research: An Evaluator's Guide to the IRB." *Evaluation Review* 26(5): 443–479.

O'Connor, Patricia. 2004. "The Conditionality of Status: Experience-Based Reflections on the Insider/Outsider Issue." *Australian Geographer* 35(2): 169–176.

Office of Human Research Protections (OHRP). 1993. *Institutional Review Board Guidebook: Protecting Research Subjects*. Office of Human Research Protections, Department of Health and Human Services. Assembled March 2003, Ohio State University; available at http://ohrp.osophs.dhhs.gov/irb/irb_guidebook.htm.

Ortbals, Candice D., and Meg E. Rincker. 2009a. "Embodied Researchers: Gendered Bodies, Research Activity and Pregnancy in the Field." *PS: Political Science & Politics* 42(2): 315–319.

———, eds. 2009b. "Symposium: Fieldwork, Identities and Intersectionality: Negotiating Gender, Race, Class, Religion, Nationality and Age in the Research Field Abroad." *PS: Political Science & Politics* 42(2): 287–328.

Padgett, Deborah K. 1998. *Qualitative Methods in Social Work Research: Challenges and Rewards*. Sage Sourcebooks for the Human Services, 36. Thousand Oaks, CA: Sage.

Park, P. 1992. "The Discovery of Participatory Research as a New Scientific Paradigm: Personal and Intellectual Accountability." *American Sociologist* 23:29–42.

Parry, Mark. 2011. "Harvard Researchers Accused of Breaching Students' Privacy." *Chronicle of Higher Education*, July 10. Available at http://chronicle.com/article /Harvards-Privacy-Meltdown/128166/.

Parry, Odette, and Natasha S. Mauthner. 2004. "Whose Data Are They Anyway?" *Sociology* 38(1): 132–152.

Pollner, Melvin, and Robert M. Emerson. 1983. "The Dynamics of Inclusion and Distance in Fieldwork Relations." In *Contemporary Field Research: A Collection of Readings*, ed. Robert M. Emerson, 235–252. Boston: Little Brown.

Price, David E. 1972. *Who Makes the Laws?* Cambridge, MA: Schenkman.

Price, M. D. 2001. "The Kindness of Strangers." *Geographical Review* 91:143–150.

Putnam, Robert D. 1993. *Making Democracy Work: Civic Traditions in Modern Italy*. Princeton, NJ: Princeton University Press.

Rabushka, Alvin, and Kenneth A. Shepsle. 2009 [1972]. *Politics in Plural Societies: A Theory of Democratic Instability*. New York: Pearson Longman.

Radcliffe, S. A. 1994. "(Representing) Post-colonial Women: Authority, Difference and Feminisms." *Area* 26(1): 25–32.

Ragin, Charles. 2008. *Redesigning Social Inquiry: Fuzzy Sets and Beyond*. Chicago: University of Chicago Press.

Read, Benjamin. 2010. "More Than an Interview, Less Than Sedaka: Studying Subtle and Hidden Politics with Site-Intensive Methods." In *Contemporary Chinese Politics: New Sources, Methods, and Field Strategies*, ed. Allen Carlson, Mary Gallagher, Kenneth Lieberthal, and Melanie Manion, 145–161. New York: Cambridge University Press.

Reason, P., and H. Bradbury. 2001. "Introduction: Inquiry and Participation in Search of a World Worthy of Human Aspiration." In *Handbook of Action Research: Participative Inquiry and Practice*, ed. P. Reason and H. Bradbury, 1–14. Thousand Oaks, CA: Sage.

Reed, Adolph. 1999. *Stirring in the Jug: Black Politics in the Post-Segregation Era*. Minneapolis: University of Minnesota Press.

Reeher, Grant. 2006. *First Person Political: Legislative Life and the Meaning of Public Service*. New York: NYU Press.

Reinhardt, Gina Yannitell. 2009. "I Don't Know Monica Lewinsky, and I'm Not in the CIA. Now How About That Interview?" *PS: Political Science & Politics* 42(2): 295–298.

Republic of Liberia. 2009a. *Volume II: Consolidated Final Report*. Monrovia: Truth and Reconciliation Commission.

———.2009b *Volume II, Title III: Economic Crimes and the Conflict, Exploitation and Abuse*. Monrovia: Truth and Reconciliation Commission.

Reutter, Linda. 2005. "Partnerships and Participation in Conducting Poverty-Related Health Research." *Primary Health Care Research and Development* 6:356–366.

Rich, Motoko. 2003. "What Else Was Lost in Translation." *New York Times*, September 21.

Rivera, Sharon Werning, Polina M. Kozyreva, and Eduard G. Sarovskii. 2002. "Interviewing Political Elites: Lessons from Russia." *PS: Political Science & Politics* 35(4): 683–688.

Rogers, Reuel. 2006. *Afro-Caribbean Immigrants and the Politics of Incorporation: Ethnicity, Exception, or Exit*. New York: Cambridge University Press.

Rose, Gillian. 1997. "Situating Knowledges: Positionality, Reflexivity, and Other Tactics." *Progress in Human Geography* 21:305–320.

Rubin, Herbert, and Irene Rubin. 2005. *Qualitative Interviewing: The Art of Hearing Data*. 2nd ed. Thousand Oaks, CA: Sage.

Said, Edward. 1978. *Orientalism*. New York: Vintage Books.

Salganik, Matthew J., and Douglas D. Heckathorn. 2004. "Sampling and Estimation in Hidden Populations Using Respondent-Driven Sampling." *Sociological Methodology* 34(1): 193–239.

Scacco, Alexandra. 2009. "Who Riots? Explaining Participation in Ethnic Violence in Nigeria." PhD dissertation, Columbia University.

Schafer, M. 2004. "Havasupai Blood Samples Misued." *Indian Country Today*. Posted March 9, 2004. http://indiancountry.com.

Schaffer, Frederic Charles. 2006. "Ordinary Language Interviewing." In *Interpretation and Method: Empirical Research Methods and the Interpretive Turn*, pp. 150–160. Dvora Yanow and Peregine Schwartz-Shea, eds. Armonk, NY: M.E. Sharpe.

Schatz, Edward. 2009a. "Ethnographic Immersion and the Study of Politics." In *Political Ethnography: What Immersion Contributes to the Study of Power*, ed. Edward Schatz, 1–22. Chicago: University of Chicago Press.

———, ed. 2009b. *Political Ethnography: What Immersion Contributes to the Study of Power*. Chicago: University of Chicago Press.

Schram, Sanford. 2004. "Post-Paradigmatic Political Science." In Schram, Sanford, and Brian Caterino. 2004. *Making Political Science Matter: Debating Knowledge, Research and Method*. New York: NYU Press.

Schram, Sanford, and Brian Caterino. 2004. *Making Political Science Matter: Debating Knowledge, Research and Method*. New York: NYU Press.

Schwartzman, Helen. 1993. *Ethnography in Organizations*. Qualitative Research Methods. Vol. 27. Newbury Park, CA: Sage.

Schwartz-Shea, Peregrine. 2004. "Conundrums in the Practice of Pluralism." In *Making Political Science Matter: Debating Knowledge, Research and Method*, ed. Sanford Schram and Brian Caterino 209–221. New York: NYU Press.

Schwedler, Jillian. 2006. "The Third Gender: Western Female Researchers in the Middle East." *PS: Political Science & Politics* 39(3): 425–428.

Seawright, Jason. 2002. "Testing for Necessary and/or Sufficient Causation: Which Cases are Relevant?" *Political Analysis* 10(4): 178–193.

Seidler, John. 1974. "On Using Informants: A Technique for Collecting Quantitative Data and Controlling Measurement Error in Organization Analysis." *American Sociological Review* 39(6): 816–831.

Seiler, Lauren H., and James M. Murtha. 1980. "Federal Regulation of Social Research Using 'Human Subjects:' A Critical Assessment." *The American Sociologist* 15 (3): 146–157.

Seligson, Mitchell. 2008. "Human Subjects Protection and Large-N Research: When Exempt Is Non-Exempt and Research Is Non-Research." *PS: Political Science & Politics* 41:477–482.

Shea, Christopher. 2000. "Don't Talk to the Humans: The Crackdown on Social Science Research." *Lingua Franca* 10(6).

Shepsle, Kenneth, and Barry Weingast. 1987. "The Institutional Foundations of Committee Power." *American Political Science Review* 81:85–104.

Smith, Mark A. 2000. *American Business and Political Power: Public Opinion, Elections, and Democracy*. Chicago: University of Chicago Press.

Smith, Rogers. 1998. "Still Blowing in the Wind: The American Quest for a Democratic, Scientific Political Science." In *American Academic Culture in Transformation*, ed. Thomas Bender and Carl Schorske, 271–307. Princeton, NJ: Princeton University Press.

Snyder, Jack, and Robert Jervis. 1999. "Civil War and the Security Dilemma." In *Civil Wars, Insurgencies, and Intervention*, ed. Barbara Walter and Jack Snyder, 15–37. New York: Columbia University Press.

Solinger, Dorothy. 2006. "Interviewing Chinese People: From High-Level Officials to the Unemployed." In *Doing Fieldwork in China*, ed. Maria Heimer and Stig Thøgersen, 153–167. Honolulu: University of Hawai'i Press.

Soss, Joe. 2000. *Unwanted Claims: The Politics of Participation in the U.S. Welfare System.* Ann Arbor: University of Michigan Press.

Special Court for Sierra Leone. 2006. The Prosecutor against Charles Ghankay Taylor, Case No. SCSL-2003-01-I (amended indictment), March 16, p. 10. Freetown: Special Court for Sierra Leone.

Special Court Task Force. 2002. Briefing Paper on the Relationship between the Special Court and the Truth and Reconciliation Commission. Freetown: Office of the Attorney General.

Spivak, G. 1988. "Can the Subaltern Speak?" In *Marxism and the Interpretation of Culture*, ed. C. Nelson and L. Grossberg, 271–313. Urbana: University of Illinois Press.

Spradley, James P. 1979. *The Ethnographic Interview*. New York: Holt, Rinehart and Winston.

Steinmetz, George. 2005. "Positivism and Its Others in the Social Sciences." In *The Politics of Method in the Human Sciences*, ed. G. Steinmetz, 1–56. Durham, NC: Duke University Press.

Stockmann, Daniela, and Mary E. Gallagher. 2011. "Remote Control: How the Media Sustains Authoritarianism in China." *Comparative Political Studies* 44(4): 436–467.

Stone, Randall. 2002. *Lending Credibility: The IMF and the Post-Communist Transition.* Princeton, NJ: Princeton University Press.

"Symposium: Cautionary Perspectives on Multi-Method Research." 2009. *Qualitative and Multi-Method Research: Newsletter of the American Political Science Association Organized Section for Qualitative and Multi-Method Research* 7(2): 2–22.

Tajfel, Henri. 1978. "Social Categorization, Social Identity, and Social Comparison." In *Differentiation between Social Groups: Studies in the Social Psychology of Intergroup Relations*, ed. Henri Tajfel, 2–28. New York: Academic Press.

———. 1981. *Human Groups and Social Categories.* Cambridge: Cambridge University Press.

Tamale, S. R. 1996. "The Outsider Looks In: Constructing Knowledge about American Collegiate Racism." *Qualitative Sociology* 19:471–495.

Tansey, Oisín. 2007. "Process Tracing and Elite Interviewing: A Case for Non-probability Sampling." *PS: Political Science & Politics* 40(4): 765–772.

Tate, Katherine. 1993. *From Protest to Politics: The New Black Voters in American Elections.* Cambridge, MA: Harvard University Press.

Temple, Bogusia. 2002. "Crossed Wires: Interpreters, Translators, and Bilingual Workers in Cross-Language Research." *Qualitative Health Research* 12 (6):844–54.

Thøgersen, Stig. 2006. "Beyond Official Chinese: Language Codes and Strategies." In *Doing Fieldwork in China*, ed. Maria Heimer and Stig Thøgersen, 110–126. Honolulu: University of Hawai'i Press.

Thompson, Marshall. 2009. "Research, Identities, and Praxis: The Tensions of Integrating Identity into the Field Experience." *PS: Political Science & Politics* 42 (2):325–328.

Thorne, Barrie. 1983. "Political Activist as Participant Observer." In *Contemporary Field Research*, ed. R. Emerson, 216–234. Boston: Little, Brown.

Tierney, William G., and Zoë Blumberg Corwin. 2007. "The Tensions between Academic Freedom and Institutional Review Boards." *Qualitative Inquiry* 13(3): 388–398.

Townsend-Bell, Erica. 2009. "Being True and Being You: Race, Gender, Class and the Fieldwork Experience." *PS: Political Science & Politics* 42(2): 311–314.

Trippi, Aili Mari. 2002. "Combining Intercontinental Parenting and Research: Dilemmas and Strategies for Women." *Signs* 27(3): 793–811.

Tsebelis, George, and Jeannette Money. 1997. *Bicameralism*. New York: Cambridge University Press.

United Nations Security Council. 2000a. *Fourth Report of the Secretary-General on the United Nations Mission in Sierra Leone*, May 19. New York: UN Security Council.

———. 2000b. *Report of the Panel of Experts Appointed Pursuant to UN Security Council Resolution 1306 (2000), Paragraph 19 in Relation to Sierra Leone*, December 20. New York: United Nations.

———. 2003. *List of Individuals Subject to the Measures Imposed by Paragraph 4 of Security Council Resolution 1521 (2003) concerning Liberia*. Viewed on March 31, 2010. http://www.un.org/sc/committees/1521/tblist.shtml.

U.S. Department of State. 2010. "Foreign Terrorist Organizations." Washington, DC: Office of the Coordinator for Counterterrorism. Available at http://www.state.gov/s/ct/rls/other/des/123085.htm.

U.S. National Archives and Records Administration. 2010. Code of Federal Regulations. Title 34. Education. Subtitle A: Office of the Secretary, Department of Education.

U.S. National Archives and Records Administration. 2010. Code of Federal Regulations. Title 45: Public Welfare. Part 46: Protection of Human Subjects. Subpart A: Basic HHS Policy for Protection of Human Research Subjects.

United States Code: Title 18 § 2339B. 2006. Viewed on March 31, 2010. http://www.law.cornell.edu/uscode/uscode18/usc_sec_18_00002339—B000-.html.

University of Illinois at Chicago (UIC). 2009. "Tip Sheet: IRB Review of Oral History and Other Social Science Projects." Office for the Protection of Research Subjects, Institutional Review Board. University of Illinois at Chicago.

Van Maanen, John. 1988. *Tales of the Field: On Writing Ethnography*. Chicago: University of Chicago Press, 1st edition.

Verba, Sidney, Kay Schlozman, and Henry Brady. 1995. *Voice and Equality: Civic Voluntarism in American Politics*. Cambridge, MA: Harvard University Press.

Vickerman, Milton. 1999. *Crosscurrents: West Indian Immigrants and Race*. New York: Oxford University Press.

Wasserfall, R. 1993. "Reflexivity, Feminism and Difference." *Qualitative Sociology* 16:23–41.

Waters, Mary. 2001. *West Indian Immigrant Dreams and American Realities*. Cambridge, MA: Harvard University Press.

Weber, Max. 1949. *The Methodology of the Social Sciences*. Trans. and ed. Edward Shils and Henry Finch. New York: Free Press.

Wedeen, Lisa. 2010. "Reflections on Ethnographic Work in Political Science." *Annual Reviews of Political Science* 13:255–272.

Wells, Gary L., and Elizabeth A. Olson. 2003. "Eyewitness Testimony." *Annual Review of Psychology* 54:277–295.

Werner, Oswald, and G. Mark Schoepfle. 1987. *Systematic Fieldwork: Foundations of Ethnography and Interviewing*. Vol. 1. Newbury Park, CA: Sage.

Westbrook, David. 2008. *Navigators of the Contemporary: Why Ethnography Matters*. Chicago: University of Chicago Press.

Wilson, Timothy D., and Elizabeth W. Dunn. 2004. "Self-Knowledge: Its Limits, Value, and Potential for Improvement." *Annual Review of Psychology* 55:493–518.

Winchatz, Michaela R. 2006. "Fieldworker or Foreigner? Ethnographic Interviewing in Nonnative Languages." *Field Methods* 18(1): 83–97.

Wolfe, Alan. 2001. *Moral Freedom: The Search for Virtue in a World of Choice*. New York: Norton.

Wolin, Sheldon. 1969. "Political Theory as Vocation." *American Political Science Review* 63:1062–1082.

Woliver, Laura R. 2002. "Ethical Dilemmas in Personal Interviewing." *PS: Political Science & Politics* 35(4): 677–678.

Wood, Elisabeth Jean. 2006. "The Ethical Challenges of Field Research in Conflict Zones." *Qualitative Sociology* 29:373–386.

———. 2007. "Field Methods." In *The Oxford Handbook of Comparative Politics*, ed. Carles Boix and Susan Stokes, 123–146. Oxford: Oxford University Press.

Wright, John R. 1989. "PAC Contributions, Lobbying, and Representation." *The Journal of Politics* 51(3): 713–729.

Wright, John R. 1990. "Contributions, Lobbying, and Committee Voting in the U.S. House of Representatives." *American Political Science Review* 84(2): 417–438.

Yanow, Dvora, and Peregrine Schwartz-Shea, eds. 2006. *Interpretation and Method: Empirical Research Methods and the Interpretive Turn.* Armonk, NY: M. E. Sharpe.

———. 2008. "Reforming Institutional Review Board Policy: Issues in Implementation and Field Research." *PS: Political Science & Politics* 41(3): 483–494.

Yeager, D.S., J. Krosnick, L-C Chang, H. Javitz, M. Levendusky, A. Simpser, and R. Wang. 2011. "Comparing the accuracy of RDD telephone surveys and Internet surveys conducted with probability and non-probability samples." *Public Opinion Quarterly*, 75,709–747.

Zelditch, Morris, Jr. 1962. "Some Methodological Problems of Field Studies." *American Journal of Sociology* 67(5): 566–576.

Index